Business Basics
for Veterinarians

Business Basics for Veterinarians

Lowell Ackerman DVM DACVD MBA MPA

ASJA Press
New York Lincoln Shanghai

Business Basics for Veterinarians

ASJA Press
an imprint of iUniverse, Inc.

For information address:
iUniverse
2021 Pine Lake Road, Suite 100
Lincoln, NE 68512
www.iuniverse.com

The authors have made every effort to ensure the accuracy of the information herein. However, appropriate information sources and professionals should be consulted where appropriate. It is the responsibility of every veterinarian to evaluate the appropriateness of a particular opinion in the context of actual clinical and financial situations, and with due consideration to new developments and contrary viewpoints.

ISBN: 0-595-25087-4

Printed in the United States of America

To my wonderful wife Susan
and
my three adorable children—Nadia, Rebecca, and David

Contents

PREFACE

While many veterinarians choose to believe that expertise in medicine necessarily precludes having business sense, nothing could be further from the truth. In fact, business and medicine are both evidence-based disciplines with much in common. When a patient is sick, we use standard algorithms to determine the most likely causes, and run appropriate diagnostic tests. We do the same thing with a business that is in failing health. We might run an inventory audit instead of a radiograph, or look at financial statements rather than laboratory results, but the problem-solving approach is the same.

Once a medical problem is unearthed, we prescribe appropriate treatment. The same holds for businesses. A practice may not need an antibiotic injection, but an infusion of capital might be just what the doctor orders for an outdated facility. Finally, once the problem is corrected, we periodically monitor the patient with wellness exams, assuring continued health. Businesses are no different. We continue to take their vital signs, benchmark them against established "normals" and make sure that they continue on a healthful trend. What could possibly be a more natural extension of expertise than applying the same care to practice management as to patient management?

This book includes information on the basic skills important in business, from understanding the marketplace to operations management. While veterinary graduates may not need to apply specific details related to accounting, economics, or other such topics, understanding the basic premises of business disciplines is no different than the notion of learning physiology, anatomy, histology and embryology as a prelude to a better understanding of clinical veterinary medicine.

The chapters in this book were selected based on the applicability of material for all veterinary graduates, not just those in small animal practice. Thus, the principles involved in most chapters are relevant regardless of whether a veterinarian is employed by government, private practice, academia or industry. By the same token, some subjects such as human resources were not included in this book, although they do have relevance in all business settings. There is a wealth of books on practice management and so the specifics of operating a veterinary practice, including human resource issues, were not duplicated here.

The goal of this work is to provide veterinary graduates with a basic foundation in business skills. I would like to thank everyone who helped to make this book a reality, including the contributing authors and all of the individuals and organizations that have added to the body of knowledge encompassing business and veterinary medicine.

Lowell Ackerman DVM DACVD MBA MPA

ACKNOWLEDGEMENTS

I would like to thank Karen Felsted CPA MS DVM CVPM of Brakke Consulting, Kurt Oster MS SPHR of Veterinary Healthcare Consultants, Sarah Taylor DVM MBA of Novartis Animal Health, and Amy Thieling CPA of Thieling Co, CPA, for their chapter contributions to this book. I would also like to thank Leemore Dafny PhD (Economics) and Steve van der Veen MBA for their thoughtful reviews of specific chapters. Finally, I would like to acknowledge the contribution of those who allowed themselves to be photographed for inclusion in this book. In alphabetical order, this includes: Nadia Ackerman, Rebecca Ackerman, Janet Eckstrom, Holly Hughs, Linda Koutroubas, Deva Prather, and Sylvia Reiser.

LIST OF ABBREVIATIONS

AAHA	American Animal Hospital Association
AAVMC	Association of American Veterinary Medical Colleges
ACT	Average Client Transaction
APPMA	American Pet Products Manufacturers Association
ATC	Average Transaction Charge
AVMA	American Veterinary Medical Association
CBC	Complete Blood Count
CPA	Certified Public Accountant
Cr	Credit
CV	Curriculum vitae
DLH	Direct Labor Hours
Dr.	Debit
EOQ	Economic Order Quantity
GAAP	Generally Accepted Accounting Principles
GAO	General Accounting Office
GDP	Gross Domestic Product
FV	Future Value
MACRS	Modified Accelerated Cost Recovery System
MBA	Master in Business Administration
Megastudy	The Current and Future Market for Veterinarians and Veterinary Medical Services in the United States, 1999. KPMG LLP Economic Consulting Services
OCBOA	Other Comprehensive Basis of Accounting
PDCA	Plan, Do, Check, Act
PDP	Personal Development Plan
PPF	Production Possibilities Frontier

PV	Present Value
ROI	Return on Investment
SMART	Stretching, Measurable, Appropriate, Realistic, Time-limited
SWOT	Strengths, Weaknesses, Opportunities, Threats
TQM	Total Quality Management
VMDS	Veterinary Management Development School
VMI	Veterinary Management Institute
VTE	Veterinary Time Equivalents

LIST OF CONTRIBUTORS

Lowell J. Ackerman DVM DACVD MBA MPA
Karen Felsted CPA MS DVM CVPM
Kurt A. Oster MS SPHR
Sarah Taylor DVM MBA
Amy K. Thieling CPA

THE VETERINARY MARKETPLACE

Lowell Ackerman DVM DACVD MBA MPA

Dr. Lowell Ackerman is a Diplomate of the American College of Veterinary Dermatology and in addition holds an MBA from the University of Phoenix and an MPA from Harvard University. He is involved in clinical practice as a clinical assistant professor at Tufts University School of Veterinary Medicine as well as helping to develop the business skills curriculum there. In addition, Dr. Ackerman is affiliated with Veterinary Healthcare Consultants, primarily dealing with practice administration and management issues. Dr. Ackerman is the author/co-author of 74 books to date and numerous book chapters and articles. He lectures extensively, on an international basis.

If you are reading this book, you are likely involved, at least in some capacity, with veterinarians and/or veterinary medicine. Whether you are a practicing veterinarian, a student, or work for the government, academia, or a corporate entity, it is worth knowing something about the veterinary marketplace.

There was a time, presumably not that long ago, when veterinarians inferred, directly or indirectly, that business knowledge was anathema to the ethical practice of veterinary medicine. Have things ever changed! Thanks to some very nice economic-based research projects that has been done lately, it is now appreciated that veterinarians are in a very vulnerable position, especially if they don't get wise to the realities of the marketplace.

As strange as it may seem to those who cherish the purist image of the profession, veterinarians are not immune to the workings of the marketplace, to demand and supply, to inflation, to debt service obligations, to competition, and to the real costs of goods and services. Even if veterinarians are willing to forego a wage commensurate with their training, the same cannot be expected for others who work alongside them. Hence, unless veterinarians intend to do everything themselves, there is no escaping the realities of the marketplace, and therefore great incentive to learn from them.

Some cautions are warranted here. Since business is dynamic and not static, the information provided here reflects known events, and can therefore only be intuitively extrapolated to the future. It cannot be determined with any certainty what the situation will be even in a 12-month time span, be it a recession, depression, or a bull market. However, understanding the marketplace is not based on optimistic or pessimistic predictions, but on the realities that need to be applied across time. For instance, if you graduate with student debt that needs to be paid back over the next ten years, that is your reality, regardless of what people are spending on pet health care.

Veterinarians are a hard-working lot, and not very well paid for it. The 2000 AVMA Biennial Economic Survey provided 1999 data to support the conclusion that a workweek for most veterinarians is about 50 hours, with mean net income of only $29.85 per hour (about the same as a dental hygienist)! That reflected a mean hourly income for practice owners of $37.48 and only $24.13 for associates.

As for new graduates, the mean starting salary in 2001 was $39,120 for women and $40,052 for men, with the possibility of perhaps earning $5,000 or so in additional compensation. The 2001 Well-managed Practice Study found that the starting salaries for associates with 1-2 years of experience were $51,300, excluding benefits. Most new graduates receive at least some fringe benefits, but it is highly variable. While 75% of new graduates get some continuing education expense benefit, life insurance was only provided to 27.7% of graduates, and pension benefits to 24.3%. On the other hand, only about 15% of graduate veterinarians were without educational indebtedness. The mean debt among those with debt was $67,565 for men, and $67,929 for women.

So, what does the future hold for veterinarians and veterinary medicine? Despite some grave economic studies to the contrary, there are a lot of opportunities ahead, especially since veterinarians have practiced so inefficiently in the past. If veterinarians practice with the same business skills as evidenced in every other successful service model, the future is indeed rosy.

Here are some realities of the marketplace that need to be addressed:

- ❖ The pet population is not growing appreciably
- ❖ Small practices are inherently inefficient and prone to overcapacity
- ❖ Veterinarians are entitled to remuneration reflecting their knowledge and training
- ❖ Hiring qualified staff requires paying fair wages
- ❖ Practicing quality veterinary medicine has inherent high costs
- ❖ Pet care is a competitive business

The Pet Population is not Growing Appreciably

There is an old joke about veterinary practice in which a practice consultant informs a veterinarian that money is being lost on each procedure performed. "That's OK," says the veterinarian, "I intend to make it up on volume." Unfortunately, this is a little too close to being correct for comfort. However, the inaccuracy of this portrayal is that there really isn't a "volume" of clients waiting for our services; the "volume" of client transactions is actually holding or diminishing in most practices. There does not appear to be an endless steam of clients ready to line up for our services. This, in turn, reflects two other realities of the marketplace—that the pet population is not growing appreciably, and that veterinarians choose to cut up the pie finer and finer by competing with one another rather than working cooperatively. The former will be discussed here, the latter in the next section.

There is some variation in the numbers of pets claimed, and no official numbers to examine (pet ownership information is not solicited in the census), but about 39% of American households have dogs and 34% have cats (but more households have multiple cats), reflecting a rough estimate of over 60 million dogs and perhaps close to 70 million cats in the United States. The American Pet Products Manufacturers Association (APPMA), in their 2000 survey, reported that a total of 62% of households have pets. The relative shift in favor of cats over dogs is significant to veterinarians for many reasons, not the least of which is that owners spend less on medical care of cats, and are more price sensitive than dog owners.

There are about 60,000 veterinarians in the United States, perhaps 55% or so providing predominantly small animal practice (Table 1-1). While the number of veterinarians in the country has been growing at a pace of about 4% per year, this is expected to slow and the veterinary population should stabilize at about 75,000 within the next decade or so. The total veterinary population grew 45% between 1980 and 1995 and the nation's veterinary schools turn out about 2,200 graduates a year. Compare this with the realization that the pet-owning population actually dropped 2.3% between 1983 and 1996. There are not expectations that the rate of pet population growth will outpace veterinary growth in the foreseeable future. Accordingly, growth in veterinary practice incomes will likely not be a reflection of more pets needing services, but of increased services being provided to household pets.

Table 1-1: Types of Veterinary Practice

Type of Practice	Total Number	Percentage of Total
Small Animal*	32,963	54.5
Large Animal*	4,943	8.2
College or University	4,059	6.7
Mixed Animal	3,608	6.0
Equine	2,017	3.3
Private Practice, Other	1,584	2.6
Public & Corporate, Other	1,538	2.5
Industrial	1,496	2.5
Government	1,236	2.0
Uniformed Services	463	0.8
Other	6,583	10.9
Total	60,490	100

Abstracted from AVMA Veterinary Market Statistics, as of August 2001
* Implies exclusive or predominant practice

Small practices are inherently inefficient and prone to overcapacity

In the KPMG (Megastudy) report, the demand for veterinary services was hampered by the concept of overcapacity. Does that mean that there are too many veterinarians for the available job opportunities? Not really. The concept of overcapacity really relates to the fact that veterinarians in most situations could be seeing more cases and providing more services than they are currently. Essentially, in most practices, there are still openings in appointment slots and the ability to do surgeries and provide other services, just not clients calling up to fill those openings.

The problem with overcapacity is also one of inefficiency and underutilization. We have highly trained staff and expensive equipment but few opportunities to exploit them to their most profitable advantage. For example, physicians on the human side learned long ago that it was not profitable to maintain radiographic facilities in their offices. However, in veterinary offices, whether by legislation or choice, virtually every practice in the country owns or leases an x-ray machine. Let's say that we did an economic analysis and determined that it is most profitable to process 100 radiographic films a day, and the average veterinary practice processes six. This is an example of the overcapacity that is present in most veterinary hospitals today.

How does one deal with this type of overcapacity? The two most common and successful ways of dealing with the problem are consolidation and specialization, both still in their early evolutionary stages in veterinary medicine.

The future is not in 1- and 2-person (so-called "mom & pop") practices. Just ask the new graduate, or the small practice looking to hire an associate, or hoping to sell their practice. New graduates often come complete with sizable student debt, relative insecurities about their abilities to practice in an unsupervised environment, and a desire to not work excessive hours. While the veterinarians of old considered this "paying their dues," such is not the case with students graduating today. Accordingly, most want to practice in larger practices where there is better pay, benefits, mentoring and continuing education programs, and a fairly structured workweek.

The concept of consolidation is simple, but has been difficult to implement in a profession known for its staunch independence. The paradigm in the profession in the past has been for students to graduate, join a practice for a few years, and then set up their own practice, essentially in competition with existing practices rather than in new territories, and often in competition with the original practice that hired them. The notion has seemed to be that an associate could make only so much money, and if they wanted to make more (or be their own boss), they needed to establish their own practice. This essentially warranted that all veterinarians in the area were forced to bear the high fixed costs of maintaining a practice while the financial pie of the community (in terms of clients) was being cut in ever-smaller pieces. With the increased competition on the local front, raising prices was difficult (for fear of losing clients to the competition) and prices for veterinary services only inched up over the years. In fact, veterinary service prices have not risen as fast as general consumer prices since at least 1972. So, to maintain the same revenues, veterinarians have worked harder and not necessarily smarter.

Once again, on the human side, physicians long ago learned that there were advantages to group practice. In terms of benefits, client coverage, vacations and quality of life issues, it makes sense to share clients, office space, and relevant expenses. Amazingly enough, their profitability increased and their lifestyles improved—not a bad combination. On the veterinary side, there are too few good examples of group practices. Is the answer to join a corporate practice? Unfortunately, most of the corporate practices have not taken advantage of economies of scale or scope that should be available. Most are simply corporate owners of individual practices that are burdened by the same inefficiencies as most other practices.

There are great opportunities for the creation of group practices in the veterinary profession. The most logical approach is the consolidation of existing practices in an area to form regional powerhouse practices. By folding existing client bases into a single large practice and closing small individual practices in the area, there is the opportunity for cost savings in terms of facilities, equipment, supplies, management, and staff. After all, is there really a need to have a veterinary office on every corner? Would clients not be better served in a large group practice that likely has

24-hour coverage, diversified expertise, and available services that would not be profitable to offer on an individual practice basis? Now, rather than every practice in the area owning an x-ray machine that may be only marginally profitable, the consolidated practice may offer an imaging center, with state-of-the-art radiography and ultrasonography and client traffic to make imaging a true profit center in the facility. The increased client load also favors relative specialization, where individual veterinarians within the practice can concentrate somewhat on their main area of interest (e.g., surgery, dentistry, exotics, etc.). One of the other benefits of these powerhouse regional practices is that it discourages other small practices from establishing in an area. How could they effectively compete with a regional powerhouse practice? The only constraint to making these practices a reality is the ability of veterinarians to work cooperatively to create such facilities.

Specialization is another mechanism for dealing with inefficiency and overcapacity. The American Veterinary Medical Associated reports that, as of March 2001, there are 6,781 board-certified diplomates from the 36 specialty colleges and boards; this represents approximately 11% of veterinarians (Table 1-2). Specialists serve the needs of general practitioners rather than competing with them. By focusing on a single discipline, the specialist need only provide a facility, staff, and equipment to deal with that discipline, with considerable cost savings. There is even more room for economies of scale and scope when specialists practice together in a single facility, building out their own requirements and sharing others. For example, the dermatologist primarily works out of examination and treatment rooms, but occasionally there is need for access to a surgical suite, imaging facility, and cages. However, there is not enough use of surgery, imaging and cage space to make this cost-effective without other specialists around to better utilize them. Add an internist and a surgeon to the equation, and utilization rates are much more appropriate. Just as with general practitioners, specialty group practices are a much more cost-effective way to go.

Table 1-2: Numbers of Some Clinical Veterinary Specialists (from the AVMA Market Statistics, as of March 2001)

Behavior	26
Cardiology	100
Dentistry	54
Dermatology	130
Emergency and Critical Care	89
Internal Medicine	940
Neurology	100
Oncology	107
Nutrition	43
Ophthalmology	213
Radiology	223
Surgery	823

Veterinarians are entitled to remuneration reflecting their knowledge and training

There has been a pervasive myth that there may be some feelings of inadequacy within the profession and a hesitancy to charge clients appropriately so that veterinarians in turn can be compensated fairly. More realistically, veterinarians probably charged what they thought the market would bear, and compensation was a reflection of revenues collected relative to expenses.

Whether or not veterinarians believe they deserve to be compensated as medical professionals, it is a necessity if veterinary medicine is to remain a viable profession. It is also necessary if veterinary medicine wants to recruit the best and brightest candidates for veterinary school. If we are going to ask potential veterinary candidates to invest their time, energy and money (or student loans) to enter our profession, we must be able to deliver a reasonable return on that investment.

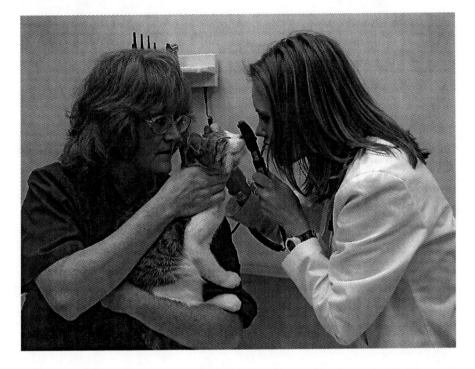

While it is not necessary that veterinary medicine be the most highly compensated medical profession, remuneration must reflect the time, training, and expense needed to become a veterinary professional (Table 1-3).

Table 1-3. Salaries of Some Medical Professionals

Profession	Annual Salary
Surgeon	$137,400
Pediatrician	$117,020
Dentist	$112,820
Physician, General Practice	$107,780
Podiatrist	$101,070
Optometrist	$84,980
Chiropractor	$74,790
Veterinarian	$68,620

*From the Bureau of Labor Statistics, based on year 2000 data

Student debt also necessitates that starting wages for veterinarians be reasonable. The Association of American Veterinary Medical Colleges (AAVMC) reports that veterinary graduates spend about 10% of their monthly income paying off student debt, and the Megastudy shows a troubling trend in which there is an increase in the ratio of debt to income. That means that student debt is climbing faster than starting salaries, so that it is getting progressively harder for new graduates to be able to afford paying off their debts with the salaries they will be making as veterinarians. It is not reasonable to assume that candidates will accept the enormous debt obligations associated with veterinary education if they are not able to adequately service that debt after graduation. Stagnant real income is a definite problem within the profession. While the incomes of other health care professionals have experienced considerable growth, real incomes (corrected for inflation) of veterinarians have actually fallen over the years.

While veterinary students don't rank income as a very important criterion for entering veterinary school, it is obvious that salary becomes more critical as students approach graduation and need to deal with student loans. Veterinarians have more difficulty dealing with their student debts than their MD and dentist counterparts because veterinary incomes don't keep adequate pace with their debt burdens. Make no mistake about it—the problem is an income issue, not a debt issue.

Hiring qualified staff requires paying fair wages

Unfortunately, when veterinary practices don't make enough money to fairly compensate veterinary personnel, there tends to be a trickle-down effect on the paraprofessionals in the practice, and even to the front-office staff. While veterinarians can argue amongst themselves as to why their real incomes are decreasing, veterinary technicians, technologists, and assistants needn't be burdened with the same excuses. They are entitled to be paid a reasonable wage for their skills (including benefits) and if they don't get it in general practice, they have the training to find it elsewhere (academic or corporate situations, laboratories, pharmaceutical companies, etc.).

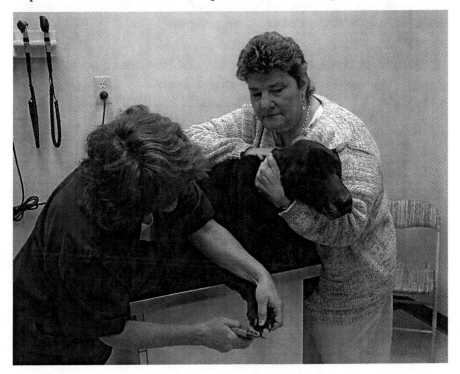

In fact, veterinary technicians have been so poorly paid in general practice that there is a real market shortage for those practices that can afford to pay them decently (Table 1-4). Once again, why would potential candidates want to enter the field when their two- or three-year training nets them little more than they could make working at a fast-food restaurant, and often without decent benefits? The AVMA Economic Report on Veterinarians and Veterinary Practices (2001) reported that technicians were making an average of $8.18 per hour, licensed technicians made slightly more at $9.94 per hour, and receptionists made an average of $8.32 per hour. By the same token, according to the 1999 Brakke Management and Behavior Study, practice owners who promoted employee longevity (which includes paying them appropriately) earned more than their colleagues that did not. If veterinarians want to practice high-quality medicine, and almost all do want this, then they need to invest in their paraprofessional staffs, and they need operate clinics on a profitable basis so that they can afford to do so.

Table 1-4: Salaries of Some Medical Paraprofessionals

Profession	Annual Salary
Physician Assistant	$60,680
Physical Therapist	$57,450
Dental Hygienist	$51,980
Registered Nurse	$46,410
Medical Lab Technologist	$41,260
Athletic Trainers	$33,650
Veterinary Technicians	$22,730

*From the Bureau of Labor Statistics, based on year 2000 data

The same principle holds true for front-office staff. The receptionist holds a vital role in the perception of value in the practice. They represent the "front line" in dealings with clients and delivering customer service. In fact, in many ways, the receptionist influences client perceptions even more than the veterinarian. Regardless of how well you perform a surgery, it is the receptionist's handling of the client at discharge that will likely dictate their satisfaction with the practice.

Table 1-5: Salaries of Some Service-Related Personnel

Profession	Annual Salary
Customer Service Rep	$26,530
Receptionist	$20,780

*From the Bureau of Labor Statistics, based on year 2000 data

Basically, when a client has spent what they consider to be a lot of money on pet care, they don't want to deal with a receptionist that may have been asking "do you want fries with that?" the week before. While the receptionist needn't be able to answer medical questions for clients, they must project a professional image to the public. A receptionist who acts in a professional manner, can address clients by name, and understands the concepts of value and customer service, is a true asset to any practice. Turnover in this position within a practice can have devastating effects on profitability, and the right individual must be fairly compensated from the start, and motivated to remain with the practice (Table 1-5).

Practicing quality veterinary medicine has inherent high costs

Staffing a veterinary hospital is a major expense, but the practice of high-quality medicine itself is also costly. From infusion pumps, ultrasonography and endoscopy units, which are likely affordable to most practices, to magnetic resonance imaging units which are only affordable to very large or specialized practices, offering the best in care can rarely be done cheaply.

Even without specialized equipment, offering the services that are routine at most hospitals may still be done in a substandard fashion, possibly reflecting cost awareness, and possibly not. Ovariohysterectomy and castration surgeries are routine, but what should not be considered routine is leaving animals overnight post-surgically without any supervision. Is it acceptable to leave an animal that has just had surgery, or one on intravenous therapy, or any number of other situations, without direct supervision? I think that most would agree that this is not an acceptable level of care, although it occurs commonly. In fact, most would argue that direct supervision is probably more important to animals in our care than most high-tech gadgetry that we might purchase.

Overhead is also expensive. Everyone wants to practice in a bright new building with large examination rooms, state-of-the-art treatment areas, and lots of room for offices, meeting areas, and cage space. Whether buying or renting, every square foot of space comes with a cost, and this cost must be covered by the revenue-generating activities in the facility.

How do we reconcile the high cost of client service with the desire to practice and deliver high-quality medicine? In short, there must be cost recovery from everything done in the practice. The time may soon be coming when veterinarians will divide the entire practice into profit centers and each will need to pay its own way to survive.

Do all veterinary practices need to perform surgeries? Do all need to have radiographic units? Do all need to provide overnight hospitalization? Certainly large group practices will want to provide these services, but does each and every veterinary practice in the country need to provide all of its own hospital services? By trying to do so, most practices end up being only marginally profitable. On the human side, physicians learned long ago that the bread and butter of their practice was the office visit. If a patient needs a radiograph, they are sent to an imaging center. If they need surgery or hospitalization, they are sent to a hospital. In fact, even if some basic laboratory testing is needed, most physicians send the patient to the laboratory for blood collection. Aren't they just sending money out the door? It may appear that way, but diversification in medicine doesn't always lead to increased profits. This will become more apparent in the economics chapter, but is worth visiting here as well. If you make most of your money in the examination room, every time you leave that profit center to perform a surgery, you cut into profits. That's why consolidation and specialization are so important to the evolution of veterinary practice.

Consolidation and specialization are also important because one medical model the profession does not want to emulate is the pharmacist. There, corporate consolidation wrested control of the profession away from the pharmacist, relegating the pharmacist to a glorified employee pill counter and customer service representative. Pharmacy is one of the few medical professionals paid less than the veterinarian, and the entire discipline has been commoditized, with medical expertise being a value add-on, rather than the core of the business.

Pet Care is a Competitive Business

Veterinarians have reason to worry about profitability, and if they don't take better care of certain aspects of practice, those revenue sources will be lost forever. It wasn't that long ago that veterinarians had to change practice philosophies when vaccination revenues were at risk. Prior to over-the-counter vaccine sales and low-cost vaccination options, veterinarians marketed the annual physical examination as a vaccination visit. When clients realized that they could get a vaccination for a few dollars at an alternate site, danger flags went up in the veterinary community. Some veterinarians fought to limit the availability of vaccines, but most just re-packaged their services and changed the emphasis from vaccina-tion to examination, and provided the vaccines at a reasonable markup. That turned out to be a good strategy, because one of the next crises that veterinarians will face is a change in vaccination schedules, perhaps with vaccines needed only every three years or so. The challenge will be for veterinarians to get clients to still come in annually for their physical examination. In a recent Roper/ASW poll (2002), only 38% of adults believe that an annual checkup for a pet is extremely important. When vaccines are no longer perceived as an annual essential, will client traffic continue for well patient visits?

Pet care is a $25-billion marketplace and this attracts other entities with better business knowledge and capitalization than veterinarians and their relatively small corporate ventures. Companies also see the inefficiencies in the veterinary model and visualize profits for the brave souls who man-age to revolutionize the industry. While corporate practices attempt to buy up clinics and establish a "brand", others toy with truly consolidating the marketplace, while others attempt to steal market share from unwary veterinary practitioners.

An example of the attempt to steal market share is the Internet pharmacy, which arose because veterinarians priced pharmaceuticals as professional items, making this an attractive profit center for those outside the profes-sion. Veterinarians are vulnerable to this kind of attack because in recent years, retail and pharmaceutical sales have accounted for approximately 25% of revenues in many practices, with product markups higher than in other industries. When veterinarians double or triple costs to set their prices, it should not be surprising that others will covet this situation. For example, in pet stores, the average product markup is 67.5% with pet food only receiving a 23-25% markup (Pet Age 2001-2002 Retailer Report). Who wouldn't like to see a 200% markup?

Expect to see increased competition for retail sales in the future, not less. In most cases, this is not a thing to be feared, but a realization that veterinarians cannot and probably shouldn't, control all aspects of the profession. As pharmacies become more competitive for business, it is natural that they should want to carry veterinary pharmaceuticals as well. Veterinarians will want to stock products that they use regularly in hospital (and can mark up significantly for in-hospital use) and a limited number of products that are profitable to dispense. There are likely cost savings in writing prescriptions for the balance of pharmaceuticals that are either expensive to stock or used infrequently.

There will also likely be a time when there is a competitive challenge for our laboratory market. After all, the laboratory can make a profit on a profile for which they charge the veterinarian $35 and that the veterinarian may charge the client $100. The limiting factor has always tended to be blood collection. Now, several DNA tests are run requiring only a cheek swab and veterinarians have been left behind as owners have submitted samples directly to the laboratories performing the tests. Can veterinarians mark up tests two to three times when clients know the true cost of running the test? This discussion will be picked up in the money matters chapter, but start thinking about the answers now!

Recommended Reading:

American Animal Hospital Association. Financial & Productivity Pulsepoints, Second Edition. Vital Statistics for your Veterinary Practice. AAHAPress, 2002, 180pp.

American Pet Product Manufacturers Association. National Pet Owner Survey of U.S. Pet-owning households, 2000.

American Veterinary Medical Association. Veterinary Market Statistics. www.avma.org/cim/ Accessed August 2002.

American Veterinary Medical Association. 2001 Economic Report on Veterinarians and Veterinary Practices

American Veterinary Medical Association. U.S. Pet Ownership and Demographics Sourcebook, 1997

Brakke Consulting Inc.: Brakke Management and Behavior Study, 1998

Giniat, EJ; Libert, BD: Value Rx for Healthcare. Harper-Collins, New York, 1999, 2001, 243pp.

KPMG LLP Economic Consulting Services: The Current and Future Market for Veterinarians and Veterinary Medical Services in the United States, 1999 [Megastudy].

Smith, CA: Gender and work: what veterinarians can learn from research about women, men and work. J Am Vet Med Assoc, 2002; 220(9): 1304-1311.

State of the Industry Report: Veterinary Practice 2002. Veterinary Economics, August, 2002.

Wise, JK: Gonzalez, ML: Employment of male and female graduates of US veterinary medical colleges, 2001. J Am Vet Med Assoc, 2002; 220(5): 600-602.

Wise, JK; Gonzalez, ML: Veterinary Income per hour, 1999. J Am Vet Med Assoc, 2002; 220(8): 1157-1158.

Wutchiett Tumblin and Associates; Veterinary Economics: 2001 Well-Managed Practice Study, Thomson Veterinary Healthcare Communications, 2002.

Yankelovich Partners: "The State of the American Pet" Survey. Ralson-Purina, 2000

LEADERSHIP

Lowell Ackerman DVM DACVD MBA MPA

Dr. Lowell Ackerman is a Diplomate of the American College of Veterinary Dermatology and in addition holds an MBA from the University of Phoenix and an MPA from Harvard University. He is involved in clinical practice as a clinical assistant professor at Tufts University School of Veterinary Medicine as well as helping to develop the business skills curriculum there. In addition, Dr. Ackerman is affiliated with Veterinary Healthcare Consultants, primarily dealing with practice administration and management issues. Dr. Ackerman is the author/co-author of 74 books to date and numerous book chapters and articles. He lectures extensively, on an international basis.

Veterinarians, by the very nature of possessing the title "doctor", are expected to be leaders. While veterinary schools teach all the basics of medicine and surgery and turn out competent practitioners, where are veterinarians expected to develop their leadership skills? While some believe that leadership is an innate attribute that can't be taught, there is compelling evidence that given the right individual, leadership can in fact be taught, or at least enhanced.

Trying to understand leadership causes us to also explore the origins of power within an organization. As students at veterinary school, soon-to-be veterinarians would seem to be almost devoid of power. Virtually everything that they do is under someone else's authority. Interestingly, upon graduation, leadership is supposedly conferred upon individuals with some pomp and circumstance and a diploma. The peons of yesterday somehow miraculously evolve into leaders of the profession and join the ranks of their mentors as respected colleagues. The terrified student who prays for a passing grade in surgery is now the "seasoned" practitioner who will be operating on owners' animals with their full confidence. By the same token, after a few years of practice, the relative neophyte may elect to own a practice and become an administrator and manager. This time there is no ceremony and no diploma—just a bank loan and a desire to succeed. The ultimate success has a little to do with quality medicine and a lot to do with leadership and understanding the realities of power.

Power

One often assumes that people in leadership positions have power merely by virtue of their position. And so it is that veterinarians are assumed to be leaders, not by virtue of their proven success in mobilizing others towards goal attainment, but because they are doctors, and doctors are presumed to know what needs to be done and are capable of doing so.

In reality, power does not come with a title. Interns are doctors, but few would interpret their credentials to signify power. The new associate in a practice may take case responsibility and be accountable for the action of the paraprofessionals assigned, but true power in this instance is just situational. In reality, even with veterinarians, power comes from more hidden political processes. The title alone is insufficient to convey power and authority.

Understanding power is key to acquiring it, and Rosabeth Moss Kanter has done much to objectively study the subject. Power is not domination, supremacy, or control. Ultimately, power arises from many sources (Table 2-1) and is the ability to get things done and to effectively mobilize and utilize resources needed to meet goals. Interestingly, power is not diminished when it is shared. Empowering others to have control over their actions allows more to get done. The despot with complete control is ineffectual as a true leader. Having power over those who are powerless allows nothing meaningful to be accomplished.

Table 2-1. Bases of Social Power (Adapted from French and Raven)

Base	Description
Reward Power	Having power by virtue of controlling system rewards (e.g., promotions, bonuses, salary increases, etc.)
Coercive Power	Having power by virtue of controlling system punishments (e.g., demotion, warnings, dismissal, etc.)
Expert Power	Having power by controlling information (e.g., scheduling, resources, educational opportunities, logs, etc.).
Reference Power	Having power by virtue of the fact that an individual is attractive to others so they seek relationships (e.g., a charismatic individual)
Legitimate Power	Having power by virtue of possessing the appropriate title and credentials and having those accepted by others as appropriate (e.g., DVM).
Connectional Power	Having power based on whom one knows and the support they engender from others as a result (bandwagon effect).
Hierarchical Power	Having power based on ranking within the power structure of an organization (e.g., head technician, chief of staff).
Organizational Power	Having power associated with status of the organization itself (e.g., being chief of staff at a well-respected institution, graduating from a prestige school).

Power is the ability to do and the powerful are those who have access to the tools to get things done. This includes the support of empowered individuals who themselves can make things happen.

An associate veterinarian can have power over subordinates in a practice, but that is not really power at all. It is the influence outward and upward that signals power to subordinates, the ability to command a favorable share of resources, rewards, and opportunities. An associate without the authority to make needed changes in a practice is powerless, at least as far as subordinates are concerned. The associate who has the ability to effect positive change for the employees, to encourage teamwork, and to reward exceptional performance will be regarded as a leader. The individual who puts in a regular workday but doesn't strive to make the environment better for all under his/her direction may be a valuable worker in the practice, but not necessarily a leader. A leader must have willing followers, and employees only follow an individual who has visions of leading everyone to a better place, and the authority to work towards that vision. Nobody needs a leader to help stand still.

A practice owner has power by controlling the purse strings of the organization, but that is not the same as real leadership. Paying a fair wage entitles an owner to a fair work effort, but this doesn't necessarily motivate employees to work towards your vision or show loyalty to your cause.

An associate in this practice may actually demonstrate significantly more power by having influence on the owner as to how things might operate better in the hospital. Something as simple as re-arranging the schedule to better accommodate staff, empowering staff to make appropriate decisions in caring for patients in their charge, and recognizing the efforts of individuals to make the hospital a better place to work and a better place to care for animals may define the associate as a leader in the practice. Notice that the associate needn't have the authority to be able to fire an employee, or to change their salary or benefits. Leadership is about having willing followers, not domination of those followers. Taking responsibility for the care of your followers is what makes them happy and keeps them motivated.

Caring about the workplace + Power = High Morale

Showing leadership ability is good, but it is also important to be able to get things done. This has to do with competence in the assigned role. Keep in mind that competence is not all encompassing and is situational in nature. The technician who supervises radiology and keeps it running in an efficient manner is not necessarily the best candidate for the role of hospital manager. The surgeon who runs a tight ship in the operating room and has the technicians scheduled to move patients in and out efficiently is not necessarily the best choice for Chief of Staff.

Power can also be accumulated by association. People already presumed to have power and well placed in an organization's hierarchy may also be more influential and more effective at motivating people in their charge. An individual in a position of authority that has access to resources (scheduling priorities, equipment, budget increases, etc.), has the ear of decision-makers "higher up" in the organization, or appears to bring something valued from outside the organization, will likely be a more effective leader.

In the end, leaders are known for their ability to get things done. This requires not only having the appropriate titles of power, but also the competence to do the job effectively. This combination contributes to the credibility of an individual as leader. It is credibility across the system, not just to subordinates, that allows a leader to be effective.

Credibility = competence + power

As mentioned previously, empowering subordinates does not strip power from the leader, but is a valuable tool for getting things done in an organization. The more independently people can work to complete their tasks, the less "politics" are necessary within that organization. When individuals are dependent on others giving approval for every step in a process, these supervisors can be considered as roadblocks and hindrances rather than worthy teammates. As will be discussed in the chapter on operations management, this is inefficiency that must be managed if productivity is to be improved.

This roadblock phenomenon can be a significant impediment given the small size of most veterinary practices. Since there is relatively little upward mobility, people who can influence promotions, schedules, salary increases, and job descriptions are a real source of power, and this creates a feeling of dependence for many employees. After all, if you are an associate veterinarian, you are dependent on the actions of the practice owner; if you are a technician, you are dependent on the actions of the owner, the hospital administrator, and perhaps the head technician. There is little chance of advancement without the support of these individuals. Unfortunately, there is also little chance of advancement with the support of these individuals.

When there are not many options for promotion, there are additional challenges to using power to get things done. When a supervisor is in a position to be promoted, they are more likely to share information, delegate authority and train their subordinates to accept responsibility. After all, if a supervisor is too indispensable in the job being done, leaders will hesitate to promote that individual because there is nobody groomed to step into that position. Hence, all "promotable" individuals will spend time in succession planning, making sure that there are individuals qualified to step into their position, to allow advancement of all parties. In this scenario, the high tide does indeed lift all ships.

Gaining Power

Power can be accumulated as a result of performance (i.e., job-related activities), but just doing one's duty is not enough to earn power and leadership. To gain power from work activities, they must be evident, extraordinary and relevant. They must be evident, because leadership is not awarded to self-promoters. For example, standing up for a receptionist who is being abused by a client becomes much more effective when relayed by other staff members, rather than by the crusading doctor.

It isn't possible to plan to accumulate power through extraordinary activities. It is just important to be prepared to be extraordinary every day in what you do. This includes being respectful to everybody, including other doctors, staff, and clients. Gossip, rudeness, lack of control, and aloofness are hard qualities to reconcile with being a leader.

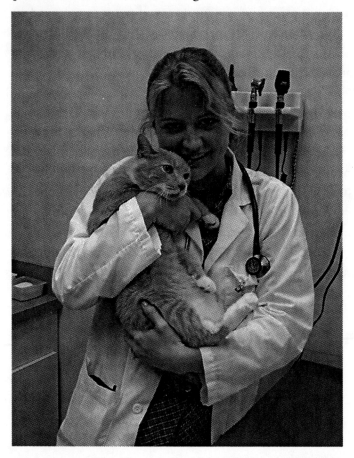

The easiest way to be recognized for extraordinary activities is to find a new way of doing something that makes a difference, making organizational changes, and by taking major risks and succeeding. Finding new ways of doing things should not be attempted solely to be recognized, but to improve the work environment for everyone. For example, converting an old storage room into a staff lounge may be an inexpensive way of demonstrating to staff that their contribution to the practice is truly appreciated. Making organizational changes is common in corporate America, and ensures leaders that their own teams are well placed politically, and gives the leader opportunities to provide rewards in the form of new job titles, responsibilities, and benefits; this in turn makes people dependent on the leader while they learn their new jobs and responsibilities. For example, an associate may organize a "critical care" team, responsible for very sick animals, those recovering from surgeries, etc. The team members are trained to triage, and provide emergency medical care and they get advanced continuing education opportunities, and commensurate monetary bonuses. Once again, for activities to enhance power they have to be visible and they also need to pass the test of relevance—that they could be identified with the solution to pressing organizational problems. If nobody utilizes the newly formed critical care team, it will quickly cease to be a source of empowerment for staff, and leadership for the veterinary associate.

Emotional Intelligence

Leaders come in all shapes and sizes and with extremely different personal attributes. Compare Bill Gates to Mahatma Gandhi. The effectiveness of their leadership is unquestioned, but their styles couldn't be more different. All leaders must have basic technical skills and intelligence to be competent, but leadership is not relegated to the person with the highest IQ, or the best surgical technique.

Interestingly enough, graduating from a top school is not enough to confer leadership. Neither are grades, inherent intellect, or originality of thought. While it may not be possible to divine precisely who would make a good leader, studies are demonstrating one important attribute that leads to leadership potential—emotional intelligence (Table 2-2). If these studies are any indication, individuals can improve their chances of attaining leadership by developing their emotional intelligence.

Table 2-2: Five components of Emotional Intelligence (Adapted from Goleman)

Attribute	Comment
Self-Awareness	Understanding your drives, emotions and behaviors and their effect on others
Self-Regulation	To think before acting
Motivation	To pursue goals with energy and persistence, for reasons that go beyond money or status
Empathy	Relating to the feelings and emotions of other people
Social Skills	Successfully managing relationships, networks, and building common ground for negotiations and relationships.

Knowing your strengths, your weaknesses, and your ambitions stands you in good stead to meeting your goals and impressing others with your candor. To refer a surgical case because you believe that others would be more qualified to offer the service is not a sign of weakness. Colleagues and staff will respect your good sense of judgment. Turning down a job that pays higher wages but requires you to spend more time away from home, when being at home is a priority, honestly conveys your values. Imagine what message would be sent if you accepted the high paying job, but were unhappy with the compromise and it showed in your work. The typical outcome is that neither party is well served. Self-aware individuals also know when to ask for help, are not threatened by constructive criticism, and can admit to failures without it affecting their self-esteem.

We are driven by our emotions, but self-regulation demonstrates that we can effectively manage them. Losing control is a leadership no-no. Things change. People make mistakes. By waiting until you have all the facts, you can respond calmly and thoughtfully, rather than impulsively. Do not underestimate the value of holding your tongue and thinking through the process before responding.

The classic hallmark of the leader, by most definitions, is the ability and desire to achieve beyond expectations. Not for glory or celebrity; not even for monetary rewards. True leaders love creative challenges, thrill to learn and grow, and take pride in a job well done. Not happy with the status quo, true leaders like to measure themselves against an imaginary performance bar, and want to continually stretch to move that bar to new heights. This is useful, because leaders still want to compete, even when the score is against them. It just makes them try harder and be more inventive in problem solving.

Empathy may seem misplaced in a discussion of business skills, especially regarding leadership qualities, but it has more application that its touchy-feely demeanor connotes. Empathy does not refer entirely to being dictated by others' feelings, but in thoughtfully considering others' feelings in the process of making intelligent decisions and making those decisions fairly and respectfully. In these days of consolidations, mergers, and bankruptcies, employees respect the leaders who keep them adequately informed, value their contributions to the organization, and understand they have their own needs to be satisfied.

Social skill is more than just having a good personality and being well liked. Social skills help leaders motivate others to follow the right path, develop common ground on which to interact, and influence teams to produce desired outcomes. Good leaders often interact with many divisions within an organization, and even with individuals outside the organization. This can produce unexpected and innovative solutions to problems.

Organizational Politics

Real information rarely moves through an organization as quickly as gossip. However, gossip does not travel randomly, coherently, or consistently within an organization, either. There are individuals with more of a vested interest in gossip and they are the main enablers of the grapevine. For example, politics are typically more important to those likely to be in the system the longest, and typically are more commonly played out by older employees. In these days of rightsizing, young people are typically on a 3-5 year plan and rarely assume that they will be in the same job position past that time. They therefore have little vested interest in the political arena within an organization, other than what meets their short-term needs.

This does point out that there are significant differences in motivation, rewards and leadership tactics to be appreciated across generational groups. Motivational guru Marilyn Moats Kennedy divides the workforce into five classes: Pre-boomers (1934-1945), Baby boomers (1946-1959), Cuspers (1960-1968), Busters (1969-1978), and Netsters (1979-1984+). Each generation has different motivations, lifestyle characteristics, social values and communication styles, and leaders must be capable of cross-generational motivation and integration. This is well illustrated by looking at perceptions of new graduates today compared with those immediately before, during and after the "baby boomers". Veterinary graduates of 30 years ago were prepared to work 60-80-hour weeks and give up significant lifestyle options to "pay their dues" within the profession. Few graduates at that time were ever mentored in the immediate post-graduate period. Stories abound within that generation of starting new at a practice only to learn that the practice owner was using this opportunity to take his first vacation in years, leaving the new graduate to handle all aspects of the practice. By contrast, today's veterinary graduate wants to work a regular workweek, be mentored closely and intellectually challenged, and be well compensated (complete with benefits) from the outset. Lifestyle issues are paramount. There is nothing wrong with the graduates of today or what and how they want to practice. It is just the reflection of a different generation, with different motivations, lifestyle expectations, social values, and communication styles. Vive la difference!

It may seem that it would be easier to just hire people who share the same motivation (e.g., money versus time off, for example), but diversity in the workplace is a good thing, and not something that can be avoided for long anyway. Sharing values and communication styles across generations is a trend to be encouraged, not avoided.

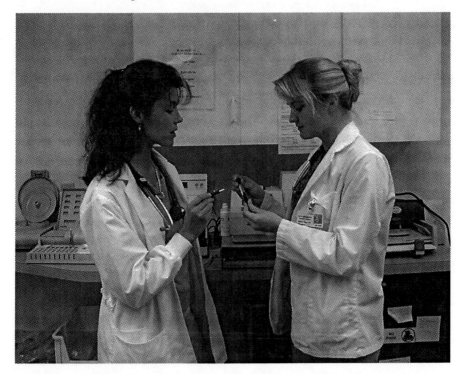

In dealing with organizational politics, it is imperative to play with a set of rules that can be universally applied (Table 2-3). Every industry has its own accepted rules of engagement, and veterinary medicine is no differ-ent. As a group of medical professionals, veterinarians should expect to be held to a high level of organizational discourse.

Table 2-3: Rules for Good Organizational Politics

❖ R-E-S-P-E-C-T
❖ Win-Win
❖ Praise in public, constructively criticize in private
❖ Quid Pro Quo
❖ Build bridges not walls
❖ Presentation is everything
❖ Prepare for Success
❖ Embrace Change

Regardless of cross-generational issues, there are some features important to all workers within an organization. Everyone deserves to be treated with respect, and therefore effective leaders should neither lie nor withhold important information. That does not mean that all company issues are open issues. If information is confidential, make this apparent in discus-sions. In being respectful to employees, associates and clients, provide rel-evant, honest information devoid of "spin", be forthright, avoid placing blame, avoid hearsay, gossip and innuendo, and take responsibility for your actions. In addition, treat civility as a virtue. Being polite demon-strates respect for others, and often challenges others to reciprocate.

In professional deliberations, it is best to work under the premise that nobody wins unless everybody wins. The notion that discussions must conclude with someone winning and someone losing are much past their prime. It is far better to strive for resolutions in which both parties bene-fit, even it means a parting of the ways, than to seek lopsided solutions in which one party feels disadvantaged.

Nobody likes to be chastised in public but most thrive on being praised within earshot of others. This is a basic human reaction, and one that is best kept in mind by leaders. When someone errs, it is important to maintain control and listen, before interjecting or reprimanding. Mistakes do happen and are part of the learning process. Assure that such occurrences are minimized by turning the event into a learning exercise rather than a punitive incident. Remember, too, to be quick with praise when something is done well. Just as in animal training, rewards are a better way to encourage appropriate actions than is punishment.

While many professionals deny it, there is a very strong human need for reciprocity, or *quid pro quo*. When we do a favor for someone, we anticipate that they will reciprocate. If they fail to do so when we believe it would be appropriate, we feel slighted. While we cannot control what other individuals do, relationships are strengthened in the vast majority of instances simply by doing favors for others. It is even more effective when these favors are not done in anticipation of immediate payback, because that need to reciprocate is often strong in individuals, and spans time as well as space.

In this same vein, it is important to remember that personal relationships are currency in professional life. All the talk about networks and networking is not hype. In this very small profession, it really is whom you know that helps shape your career options. People will naturally select others with which they have had good working relationships over those that are an unknown, even if there are differences in expertise between applicants.

Along the way up the organizational ladder, remember the people who helped make your journey an enjoyable one. Make sure they are recognized by their superiors for their contributions, ensure that they are aware of your gratitude, and be available if they should contact you for assistance at some time in the future. Never underestimate the significance of a simple thank you!

As you create new programs and activities, remember that coming up with a good idea is not nearly as important as successfully packaging a concept. Computer programmers can argue that Microsoft promotes programs inferior to others in the marketplace, but few can dispute that Microsoft sells products because they are attractively packaged for consumers. They work in most computers, they are relatively easy to use, they encompass the features that most people want, and they are widely available and universally supported. While coming up with the idea that a practice should be able to promote more retail sales for prescription diets is fine, creating an obesity management program with profit sharing between hospital and technicians and a budget that demonstrates increasing revenues by 12% over the next year goes a lot further and is more likely to be enthusiastically adopted by staff.

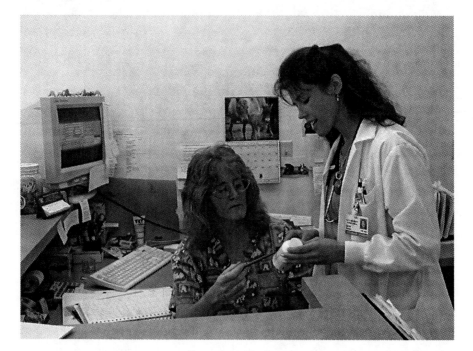

Being an effective leader means not only that you are successful, but that you are capable of dealing with success. With success and recognition comes opposition, sometimes from unexpected sources. For example, the hospital administrator who was enthusiastic about the obesity management program may feel threatened by your "power play". The older associates in the practice may feel that you are "overstepping your bounds". Even the practice owner, who is receiving an increased return on equity by you actions may be scared that the staff looks to you for leadership, rather than the owner. Others may worry that funds have been diverted from other worthwhile projects to fund your projects. High visibility within an organization is always a mixed blessing and comes with its own cautions.

Similarly, if you create successful projects, it is important to deal with success in terms of sustainability of the project. For example, suppose you advance the idea of a practice web site, help work with the web manager to create a dynamic site, and receive kudos from staff and colleagues for a job well done. In the creative process, did you plan for who would sustain, manage, update and improve the site after it was launched? Don't assume that in creating a worthwhile project that others will manage it on an ongoing basis.

It is also important to embrace change, because there are no ways to avoid it. There will always be new technological advances, new procedures, new expectations, and if you remain in the organization long enough, new generations of employees with their new values, communication styles and motivators. Just take a deep breath and "go with the flow". Not only is this the guiding message in the neo-classic "Who moved my cheese?" but a variety of "fish-isms" have sprung up in a new Fish! grassroots movement.

The Fish! movement is built around four axioms:

- ❖ Choose your attitude
- ❖ Make their day
- ❖ Be Present
- ❖ Play

It seems simple enough, but it conveys a powerful message. It is important to choose your attitude, because you have little control over the job you do. The Fish! movement was spawned from the happy work environment of Pike Place Fish, where fishmongers work in Seattle's famous open-air market. Being a fishmonger is not the most glamorous of professions, and yet these workers had fun at their jobs, regaled audiences with their antics (e.g., fish tossing), and did a brisk business in the process. While conventional business texts preach for workers to pursue careers that they love, the Fish! movement preaches that workers should love what they do, regardless of how mundane the job. Being a receptionist at a veterinary clinic is not necessarily someone's dream job and yet with the right attitude that worker could make all the difference in the world for a practice, and have fun in the process. It would be sad to think that all veterinary receptionists are just working there while waiting for a better offer to present itself. These workers can "make their day" for clients, doctors and staff, engaging these individuals rather than just doing their jobs to the minimum required. In the same vein, the "be present" axiom is meant to keep workers grounded in what they are doing, rather than daydreaming about what might have been. Finally, it is important for all workers to play and have fun. This doesn't mean unprofessional antics in the reception area, but creating an enjoyable work environment that fosters creativity, innovation, and collegiality.

Recommended Reading:

Badaracco Jr., JL: Leading quietly. Harvard Business School Press, 2002, 224pp.

Blanchard, K: The heart of a leader. Honor books, 1999, 157pp.

Buckingham, M; Coffman, C: First, Break All the Rules: What the World's Greatest Managers Do Differently. Simon & Schuster, 1999, 255 pp.

Covey, SR: The 7 habits of highly effective people. Simon & Schuster, 1990, 358pp.

French, JRP; Raven, B: Bases of Social Power. In, Studies in Social Power. Ed. Dorwin Cartwright. University of Michigan, Ann Arbor,1959

Goleman, D; McKee, A; Boyatzis, RE: Primal Leadership: Realizing the Power of Emotional Intelligence. Harvard Business School Press, 2002, 352pp.

Johnson, S; Blanchard, KH: Who Moved My Cheese? An Amazing Way to Deal with Change in Your Work and in Your Life. Putnam Publishing Group, 1998, 94pp.

Kanter, RM: Men and Women of the Corporation. NY: Basic Books 1993, 356pp.

Kennedy, Marilyn Moats; Mitchell, L: Office Politics for Dummies. Hungry Minds, Inc., 2002, 360pp.

Lundin, SC; Paul, H; Christensen, J: Fish! A Remarkable Way to Boost Morale and Improve Results. Hyperion, 2000, 115pp.

Warshaw, M: The Good guy's guide to Office politics. Fast Company, April/May 1998, 157-178.

Zigarmi, P; Zigarmi, D; Blanchard, KH: Leadership and the One Minute Manager: Increasing Effectiveness Through Situational Leadership. William Morrow & Co., 1985, 112pp.

PLANNING

Lowell Ackerman DVM DACVD MBA MPA

Dr. Lowell Ackerman is a Diplomate of the American College of Veterinary Dermatology and in addition holds an MBA from the University of Phoenix and an MPA from Harvard University. He is involved in clinical practice as a clinical assistant professor at Tufts University School of Veterinary Medicine as well as helping to develop the business skills curriculum there. In addition, Dr. Ackerman is affiliated with Veterinary Healthcare Consultants, primarily dealing with practice administration and management issues. Dr. Ackerman is the author/co-author of 74 books to date and numerous book chapters and articles. He lectures extensively, on an international basis.

As veterinarians, we are men and women of science, and science requires that we be prepared—prepared to consider options and alternatives—prepared to question age-old "truths",—and prepared to logically plan out "pathways" and objectively deal with the evidence involved. Whether it is strategizing to get into veterinary school, considering options for careers, or exploring the care pathways for a particular medical process, we should consider ourselves great planners. Yet, the evidence suggests that veterinarians might not be quite as good at planning as should reasonably be expected.

Career Planning

There are myriad ways of utilizing a veterinary degree to develop the career of your dreams. The most important component of making that happen is planning—identifying what you want, and how it can best be achieved.

While it may seem that the most critical business skills involve numbers (such as budgeting, financial management etc.), it is actually planning that has the most impact on what can, or cannot, become a possibility in your future. While most veterinarians plan their diagnostic approach and their therapeutic alternatives, it appears that many do not put the same effort into their career planning.

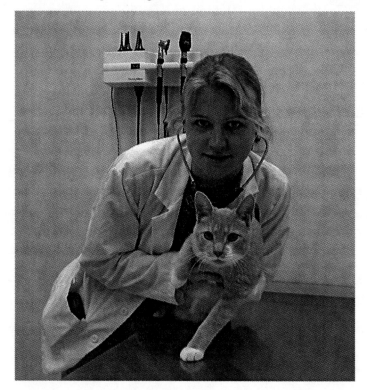

To be effective, planning should be instituted early, preferably before graduation, although it is never too late to take an active interest in your career options. However, some of the best tools to engineer your future are most accessible while still in veterinary school. The problem is that while students are still in veterinary school, they don't necessarily consider what will be best for them after graduation. After all, there's often a lot to contend with just attending classes and managing a burgeoning debt load.

Still, the earlier one determines what they would most like to do in their career, the easier it is to take steps to make it happen. Suppose that you wanted to be a board-certified veterinary surgeon in a private specialty practice. Researching the matter, you would have determined that it is not enough to have desire and good surgical skills. Getting into a surgical residency program is extremely competitive. You determine which programs would be your top choices, and set out to become the top candidate. You do this by interviewing the surgeons or program heads at these facilities to see what they are looking for in the ideal candidate, and then becoming that person (or alternatively deciding that you don't want to be that person after all). It probably involves working in those centers during externships, vacations, and/or clerkships, attending all surgery-related educational programs and workshops that you can accommodate, completing an internship program at a facility well respected for its surgeons and surgical training, and building relationships with surgeons who will later write letters of recommendation attesting to your abilities and suitability for a surgical residency program. While it may seem somewhat contrived (and is), what else do you think will distinguish you from the dozens of other qualified applicants—your ability to tie a perfect miller's knot?

Here's a different scenario. You've been in practice for ten years working as an associate in a high-quality practice and decide that you'd like to make the jump to industry. However, working as an associate, you've never even had exposure to clinic finances. Your research indicates that the industry position you covet requires budgeting and staff management skills. What could you do to make yourself a better candidate? Plan ahead. Take some courses in business or attend a program such as Veterinary Management Institute (VMI) or Veterinary Management Development School (VMDS). Volunteer within the practice you're already in to assume management responsibilities for the veterinary technicians, doing job appraisals, scheduling them, mentoring them and contributing to their continuing education. The practice owner may also allow you to manage the budget for the paraprofessional staff, providing you with that piece as well.

To thine own self be true

Before you start your planning in earnest, take a few moments (or longer) for some serious reflection. What is it that really appeals to you about being a board-certified veterinary surgeon? Does it seem glamorous to you? If so, take an opportunity to spend a week with a surgeon and see if it meets your expectations. Don't forget to research what remuneration surgeons get from the work they do. For a $2,000 surgery, how much does the surgeon actually get versus how much is required to pay for the expenses of these pricey procedures? If you think that this specialty will compensate for your inability to deal with clients in an examination room, better think again. Surgery isn't just about technique and you still need a good bedside manner to succeed in most circumstances.

Self-reflection is not easy for anyone, and may be extremely difficult for some veterinary professionals. However, it is the key to achieving happiness in work and at home. More and more companies are looking to determine an individual's "emotional intelligence" rather than rely on degrees and academic yardsticks. You should do the same since the stakes are much higher—after all, this is your life you're planning for.

It helps to be brutally honest with a self-assessment, and keep it private so that you don't worry what others may think of your priorities. Are you interested in a position that pays you the most money, even if it may place restrictions on your private life (travel, long hours, etc.)? Do you need to balance working with a prioritized private life (e.g., children, obligations elsewhere)? Do you need constant challenges to remain stimulated in a position? Do you prefer to spend time alone, or do you crave being around other people?

When you complete your self-assessment, understand your current motivation and how your motivation may change with time. This was first expounded by Abraham Maslow, and Maslow's Hierarchy of Needs (Figure 3-1) states that the needs of an individual grow progressively and that as a lower-level need is satisfied, the individual seeks fulfillment on the next level up. Those levels are:

- ❖ Physiological needs
- ❖ Emotional Safety
- ❖ Affection and belonging needs
- ❖ Esteem needs
- ❖ Self-actualization needs

Physiologic needs are those basic to survival and may include having enough money to buy groceries, afford rent, and pay off student debt. Emotional safety refers to feeling secure, without fear of reprisals or denigration. Affection and belonging is an important social aspect of affiliation and being accepted by others. Self-esteem comes from achievement and approval and recognition from others. Finally, self-actualization, finding self-fulfillment and reaching your own potential can only come when all of these other needs have been met.

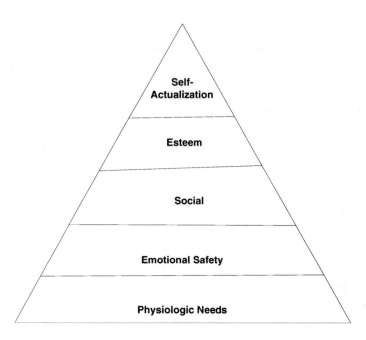

Figure 3-1. Maslow's Hierarchy of Needs

This implies that individuals only do their best when they feel respected and valued, are secure in their positions, and adequately compensated to meet their economic needs. So, keep in mind that it is possible that you are in the right career choice, but that your circumstances are such that your needs are not being met at your present position and location. Frederick Herzberg added some further insight into the needs situation, by identifying "hygiene factors" and "motivators" that influence people's needs. Hygiene factors are things like reasonable compensation, a safe work environment, suitable company policies, and decent working relationships. Motivators refer to the opportunity to advance in your position, responsibility on the job, recognition for your efforts, and the feeling of achievement for a job well done. Don't underestimate the value of these factors in feeling satisfaction with a position. Even if you believe otherwise, it's not all about the money.

So, once you have completed your self-assessment and are comfortable that you have correctly identified your personal skills, abilities, likes and dislikes, it is important to choose the right organization to work for. If you truly don't like working with people, escaping private practice isn't the answer. There are few veterinary companies that assign employees to work in solitary isolation in a little office or cubicle anymore. Companies are quick to appreciate team building and the value of cross-functional teams. Also, don't take a job for what it offers in the short term, such as an escape from your current situation. Plan for where you want to be in two years, or five years, and work towards that objective instead.

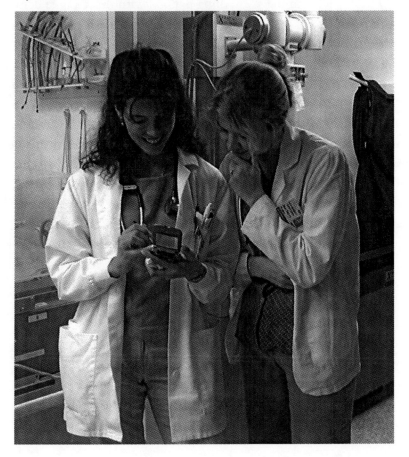

Personal Development Plan

A Personal Development Plan (PDP) is an attempt to answer the following questions

❖ What am I trying to do?
❖ How am I going to do it?
❖ What are the necessary steps in order to do it?

It is easy to set goals like "I want to be rich", or "I want to be happy in my career" but it is hard to make anything happen with those vague desires. If you want to achieve goals with any regularity, you need a plan. When you are presented with a patient with diabetes mellitus, you don't wish for the blood glucose levels to drop, you act in a very concerted effort to make it happen. The same is true with your personal development. If you want to have one million dollars available to you at retirement, you might be surprised to learn that this rarely involves winning a lottery. For most of us without an existing stash of cash, it involves a very prescribed manner of saving small amounts of cash on a regular basis and leaving that money to accumulate without disruption. Can you manage to contribute $100 weekly to your retirement fund, only $5,200 a year? You might need to bring a bag lunch for a while, or forego some non-essential purchases, but this is very attainable. If you can, and you invest in the stock market, which has an average return of 10.5% per year, in 30 years you will likely have amassed over 1.1 million dollars. All it takes is a well-thought-out plan.

So, the first lesson in creating a PDP is to be SMART:
Stretching and specific—Focus on one skill area
Measurable—Define targets and monitor your progress
Appropriate & Attainable—Can they reasonably be achieved?
Realistic—Are you really motivated to achieve this goal?
Time-limited—Set reasonable time schedules

Before you drop your current position and earnestly pursue your PDP, begin by thinking of maintaining and extending your existing professional knowledge and skills, enhancing this knowledge and skill base, and then consider whether there are certain requirements for professional development that need to be satisfied, how individuals have accomplished this in the past, and the preferred method of learning and studying.

Once you have analyzed the situation, break the requirements down into bite-sized digestible objectives and set out to accomplish them. For example, if you intend to make the leap to industry and your research suggests that you need finance, management, and networking skills, then these become objectives in your Personal Development Plan. To get finance training, you may sign up for a program like Veterinary Management Institute (VMI), the Veterinary Management Development School (VMDS), or business programs available at local Universities and Community Colleges. Remember that you don't necessarily need an MBA to succeed in industry, and in fact this degree may make you overqualified for some positions for which you may have interest. That's why you need to research your goals before proceeding with the implementation of your PDP. For management training, specifically learning about human resources, budgeting, etc., you might see if you can get that kind of experience in your current position. If not, consider all your possibilities, including providing these functions for local non-profits, such as a school committee, charity, religious group, etc. Experience is valuable, wherever you can achieve it. Regarding networking, you may elect to attend four major veterinary conferences over the next two years, not only for continuing education, but with the specific purpose of meeting people in industry and getting to learn more about the opportunities there. In this scenario, a reasonable time frame may be two years to make the successful transition. Just like saving a million dollars a few dollars at a time, the goal is not instant gratification, but to work towards a desirable goal at a reasonable pace.

Example of a Personal development Plan

Key Areas	Education & training needs	Possible activities	What I need to do to achieve this	Completed by (time scale)	How will I know I've succeeded	Has this been achieved
Financial Management	Budgeting, Human Resources, Finance, Accounting	VMI, local college courses	Enroll in VMI modules for 2003 & 2004; business skills program offered Spring 2004	Late 2004	VMI completion; college certificate completion	No
Management	Staff management, responsibility, training	Supervise/hire/fire paraprofessional staff in clinic including pay issues; teach at technician college	Get permission from practice owner; free up Wednesdays to teach at technician college	mid-2004	Teach at least 2 semesters; manage employees for at least 1 fiscal year and demonstrate improved efficiency	Still in discussion stage
Networking	Develop contact list; build relationships	Attend veterinary conferences to network; be more responsive to sales reps	Need to fund attendance at 4 major veterinary conferences and get time off work	February 2004	Have established contact with at least 10 senior individuals at my top four industry picks	Attended North American Veterinary Conference and met 3 good contacts so far

Résumé

A résumé is a brief document that provides useful information about you, your education, your job history, and your accomplishments in a fairly standardized form. While there is no absolutely correct or incorrect way to create a resume, it is generally accepted that it should be current, one to two pages, neat, and convey the most important aspects of your training and work experience. A well-written résumé tells a prospective employer what they need to know about you in synopsis form. Sections of a veterinary résumé should include the following:

Contact Information	Name, address, telephone number, fax, e-mail, web site
Date	Information current to date specified
Education	Academic institutions since high school, with name of school, location, date of graduation, and degree conferred.
Training	Non-degree certificates and programs (e.g., laser surgery, PennHip, ASIF, endoscopy course, etc.)
Licensure	States in which you are licensed and the appropriate license #
Present Job	Specify job title, organization, responsibilities, dates of employment, and supervisor
Previous Jobs	Specify information above for each job, starting with most recent
Skills	Include both veterinary and non-veterinary-specific
Languages	If you are conversant in another language, this can be an important business advantage

Following is an example of an acceptable résumé.

Dr. Fred Smith
24 Huron Avenue
Cambridge, MA 02138
(617) 555-1212
(617) 555-1213 (fax)
fsmith@vetlink.com
www.topvet.com

Current to February 15th, 2003

Objective	**To practice the highest level of small animal veterinary medicine in a private clinical setting**		
Education	1997-2001	UC Davis	Davis, CA
		Doctor of Veterinary Medicine	
	1994-1997	UC Davis	Davis, CA
		Bachelor of Science (Biology)	
		Graduated Summa Cum Laude	
Training	2001-2002	Tufts University Grafton, MA	
		Internship	
	2002	Tufts University Grafton, MA	
		Laser Surgery workshop certificate	
	2002	Purdue University	Lafayette, IN
		Veterinary Management Institute, Module I & II	
Experience	2002-2003	Littletown Pet Clinic	Anytown, MA
		Associate Veterinarian	
		Established client education program for weight management	
		Provided emergency services on a regular basis	
		Developed skills in orthopedic surgery	
Memberships		American Animal Hospital Association	
		American Veterinary Medical Association	
		Massachusetts Veterinary Medical Association	
Other Skills		Cornerstone software; Microsoft Word; Excel; Conversant in Spanish;	
Interests		Practice management, staff education, running, computers	

Curriculum Vitae (CV)

A Curriculum Vita (or curriculum vitae—there are arguments on which Latin form is more correct) is ongoing documentation of your professional life. You'll need one if you plan on doing any further postgraduate training, but a curriculum vita is a good thing to continually update, providing you with specifics on your professional life.

Writing curriculum vitae need not be a difficult task, but it is a very important component of your post-graduate evaluation. It is your CV that tells the specialty college credentials committees whether you have been practicing high-quality medicine; the fact that you attended veterinary school and have been in an internship program just won't do it. Whether you are applying for a position in general practice, a post-graduate degree program, a residency position, a faculty position or even a job in industry, placement is typically competitive. Your CV should document your competitive advantage.

There is no one accepted standard for a CV, but following is a 10-Step guide to creating one that will be accepted in most situations.

Step 1:   Contact Information

The first information to provide is the title, your name, and a time reference such as:

Curriculum Vita: John Smith, DVM
(Current to September 1, 2002)

You will then list all the particulars regarding contact information, such as home and office addresses, phone numbers, fax numbers, e-mail addresses, and web site URLs. You might also include your social security number.

Step 2:   Education

This is the place to list the academic institutions you have attended and the degrees, diplomas or certificates you have received. It is fine to include this information in table form with columns for college, date attended, degrees, and year of graduation. Make sure you include non-veterinary degrees and programs you may have started but didn't complete. For example, if you attended a university for undergraduate study but were accepted to veterinary school before you completed your undergraduate degree, list it anyway—just leave blank the year of graduation.

Institution	Program	Degree Awarded	Year of Graduation

Step 3:   Post-Graduate Training

This is the section where you will list your internship, residency, and any externship, clerkship or other recognized programs that you have successfully completed. Don't forget orthopedic programs (including ASIF and PennHip accreditation), laser training workshops, acupuncture certification, and business studies (e.g., VMI, VMDS). Any course or program that issues certification should be listed here.

Institution	Program	Certification	Year Awarded

Step 4:   **Publications**

You may include professional and non-professional publications here, including practice handouts if that is the only thing that you have written. Make sure you use proper referencing standards to cite your publications. If you have not done any publications, this section does not need to be included in your CV.

Step 5:   **Lectures**

While this topic is not a standard feature of the basic CV format, if you have done any public speaking, including to veterinary associations, regional meetings, or technician groups, this often helps bolster your acceptance as an expert and your ability to address groups of your peers.

Step 6:   **Continuing Education**

This is the place to really document your exposure to advanced training if you are a relatively recent graduate. In this section, you should list all of your CE training, including lectures, seminars, journal club, roundtables, workshops and wet labs. In time, you won't need to bulk up your CV with a CE section, but initially it helps document that you have far more exposure than would be suspected based on your time out of veterinary school.

Step 7:   **Memberships**

This is the spot to list your memberships in professional, scientific and honorary societies. Don't get into the civic or religious affiliations here. There's a very good probability that everyone belongs to six or more of these groups if you put your mind to it. Remember to include national groups such as the American Animal Hospital Association and the American Veterinary Medical Association.

Step 8:   Leadership roles in organizations & Community Activities

You don't need to go overboard here, but if you've ever held office in any professional organization, list it here. If you've never really been involved in any organization, you might still not have to leave the section blank. Don't forget organizations that you participated with in veterinary school. You can also document your civic-mindedness with everything from church committees and PTA/PTO, to the Boy Scouts. If you really have no leadership roles in organizations or community activities, leave this topic out of your CV.

Step 9:   Honors & Awards

Once again, be creative here, but don't lie. Perhaps you won some award while you were a student. Perhaps you won an Award of Appreciation for giving a talk at a school or breeder group. If you were awarded or honored in some way, by some group, list it here.

Step 10:   Employment

This is the big one, the place where you convince whatever credentials committee that you practice exceptional veterinary medicine, that you are an accomplished academician, that your research is world class, or that you are the pride of industry.

If you are in practice only a few years, you may list practices in which you worked while still a student, or even before you were accepted to veterinary school. You will start out by listing the following for each practice in which you have been involved, starting with the most current: Name and location of the practice; name of your supervisor (if applicable); dates you were there; approximate number of hours worked per week; and; a job description. The job description is critical, but should not exceed 150 words in length for each practice situation. Accordingly, you need to concentrate on those features of the position that are most appropriate to the review process. Examples might include that you had an opportunity to perform orthopedic surgeries in the practice, you developed skill in ultrasonography, you worked with and are comfortable with exotics, and that in your internship you had opportunities to interact extensively with specialists for excellent case management, etc. At the very least, you should have a good working relationship with specialists and take a very active role in cooperative case management.

When writing your job description, remember what the reviewers are looking for. Do you perform sophisticated surgical or dental procedures? Do you perform radiographic contrast studies, CSF taps, bone marrow aspirates, intradermal allergy tests, endoscopy, etc.? Do you feel confident handling emergency and critical care cases? Document them here. In any case, this is not the place to be modest or shy. The acceptance of your credentials depends on it.

If you are applying for a position that doesn't require clinical expertise, your emphasis will be slightly different, but you will still document all places at which you were employed, the responsibilities that came with each position, and a supervisor.

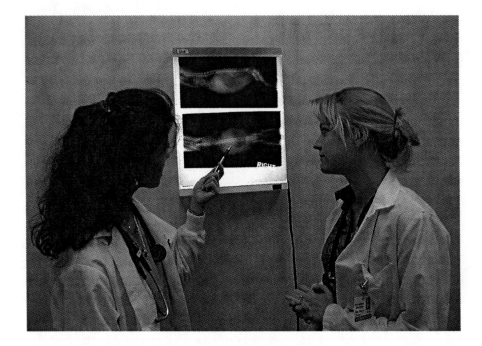

Planning & Decision-Making

Problem solving and decision-making are part of the veterinary profes-sional's everyday duties. Planning helps make a difficult situation infi-nitely more manageable. When first confronted with an issue, first decide if it is truly relevant to your work. While some veterinarians like to micro-manage situations, you should endeavor to limit yourself to situations that actually require your attention and action.

When faced with standard problems (e.g., the new x-ray machine is broken), your responses are almost automatic (get it repaired). When things are not as clear-cut (the old x-ray machine is broken—should we repair it or replace it), the best approach is to break the issue down into components, solicit advice from all involved, define the situation as a problem to be solved OR a decision to be made, and then review all the potential alternatives.

Sometimes it is even difficult to understand the problem itself. For instance, if you own your own practice and notice that revenues have fallen off lately, you might find it difficult to discern why. Is there a new competitor in town? Are your fees too high? Are the staff that are dealing with customers not providing them with exceptional service? Has the economy finally caught up with your client base? There is often a tendency to "trial fix" problems (e.g., lower prices, offer discounts), but this is often only marginally effective in terms of time or cost.

Interestingly, while veterinarians often focus on "cause", the answers may actually lie in "effect". Clearly identify what the problem is (are revenues down across the board, or in one sector? Has client traffic decreased compared to a year ago?) and, once identified, gather information from all relevant sources (e.g., doctors, administrator, technicians, receptionists, clients). If your sale of pet foods is down and the determined cause for the loss of revenues, it probably can't be explained by the x-ray machine breakdown that took a week to be fixed. The cause that best explains all of the facts observed is most likely to be the right one (e.g., a new receptionist was hired but not mentored on pet foods carried and how to counsel clients on dietary issues).

Decision Trees

Sometimes we need to make decisions for which there are no clear answers, or an amount of uncertainty (probability) that still needs to be accounted for. In these cases, decision trees can be a useful tool in planning. For instance, perhaps in an entrepreneurial frame of mind you consider building a state-of-the-art veterinary hospital. The anticipated cost of your clinic is $1 million and your contractors are 75% sure that it can be delivered at that price, but there is a 25% chance that it will come in way over budget at $1.3 million. Hoping to hedge your bet, you also do an analysis that says that if your project comes in on budget, there is a 60% chance that your clinic will break even at two years, an incredible 25% chance that it will net + $0.75 million in that time, but also a depressing 15% chance that it will be $0.5 million below break even at that point. The figures look worse if the project comes in over budget, but that's not very likely (only 25%). In that instance, there is a 25% chance that the clinic will still net +$0.25 million at that time, a 30% chance that it will break even, and a dismal 45% possibility that it will be down $0.6 million at the two-year mark. So, what do you do?

Hopefully, you will contact your financial consultants to advise you on the venture, but in the interim, we can use a decision tree to help us. In a decision tree, a chance node (designated by a circle) indicates outcomes that occur with certain probabilities. The decision node (designated by a square) indicates a point at which a decision must be made. In our example, we are only prepared to go ahead with the project if there is a very good possibility that it will break even in two years. Accordingly, the decision tree might look like this (amounts are based on present value of future cash flows):

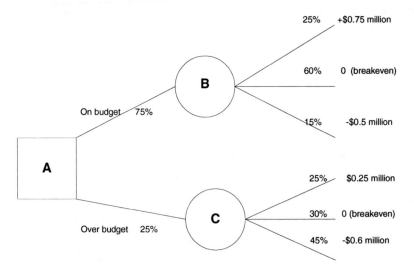

Box A is the decision node, where we are going to decide whether or not to proceed with the construction of our hospital. We are only prepared to do this if we can break even (net $0) or better at two years into the venture. To determine this, we need to calculate the likely "net" values if the project comes in on budget, versus over budget. Our first calculation is the net expected value of chance node B (in the upper circle), the outcome if the project comes in on budget. This is just the sum of all the probabilities:

25% of $+0.75M + 60% of (0) + 15% of -$0.5M = $0.1125M

According to this statistical exercise, if the project comes in on budget, we should net about $112,500 above breakeven after two years. However, there is still a 25% chance that the project will come in over budget, so we need to address this possibility as well. This is the probability that we need to assign to chance node C. This is the sum of those probabilities:

25% of 0.25M + 30% of 0 + 45% of -$0.6M = 0.0625 + 0 - 0.27
= - 0.2075M

According to this statistic, if the project comes in over budget, you will likely be $207,500 below break even by year two, something that you find unacceptable.

Now, the final decision will be made on the basis of whether you can break even by year two, accounting for the probability of both scenarios, on budget versus over budget. Once again, this is simply the sum of the probabilities:

75% x $112,500 + 25% x -$207,500 = $84,375 - $51,875 = $32,500

Thus, according to this exercise and the assumptions made, you should fund the project since it appears that you will better than break even (by $32,500) by year two. The final decision tree would look like this.

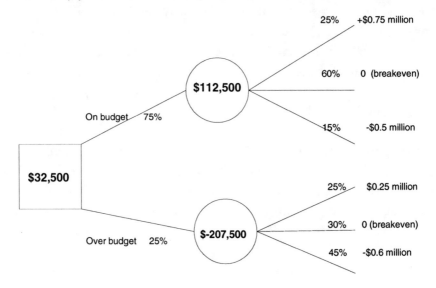

Market Planning—SWOT Analysis

A useful strategic exercise that works as well for planning as it does for marketing is to perform a SWOT analysis. This stands for:
Strengths
Weaknesses
Opportunities
Threats

It is a way of looking at a situation, sizing it up objectively, and then deciding how best to proceed. In our decision tree analysis, we looked at the possibilities of success for a new hospital venture based solely on statistics and contrived probabilities. A SWOT analysis can be very helpful at sizing up the situation to enable those probabilities to be realistically based. For example, our SWOT analysis for a hospital at this location might reveal the following:

Strengths	Clinical excellence offered
	State of the Art Technology
	Empowered staff
	Service-oriented priorities
Weaknesses	Not an existing entity yet
	Difficulty acquiring quality staff
	Veterinary services are undervalued by public
	High overhead in new building
	Pet population stable in area
Opportunities	Neighborhood can afford fees to be charged
	High-tech services not offered elsewhere in area
	Marketing and promotion opportunities
	Already approached to do local newspaper column
Threats	Existing practices in area are competitive and established Fear of recession making consumers more price-conscious
	Rumors that Pet Superstore practice is going in nearby
	Other hospitals in area could easily copy service model
	Services might be too expensive given cost of building, forcing clients to utilize other clinics in area
	Internet and superstores cutting into sales revenues

Once the SWOT analysis has been completed, it is sometimes useful to summarize the situation in a 2 x 2 comparison chart.

	Opportunities	Threats
Strength	This is a great time and a great location to showcase what veterinary medicine is all about	We have the ability to defend our position in head-to-head competition on the basis of great medicine and client service
Weakness	Will acquire strength through marketing and excellent client experience	Must determine if other new practice is on horizon; strategize to gain competitive advantage

Of course, the decision-making is still done by you. The SWOT analysis just gives you a forum to look at all sides of the situation.

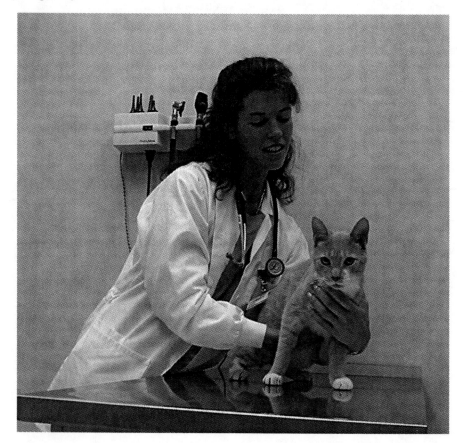

Business Plans

This chapter is not the place for an in-depth discussion of business plans (see business plan section in the appendix), but is an appropriate venue for some of the "planning" aspects that go into such a document. There are a variety of software options (such as BusinessPlan Pro or PlanWrite) to take you step by step through the process of writing a business plan. Regardless of your venture, though, take the time to work through the planning aspects of your actual business plan.

The sad truth is that while few veterinary hospitals fail, not many are highly profitable either. Unless veterinary medicine is a hobby for you, you should plan a hospital (or any venture) with the notion that it will provide a respectable Return on Investment (ROI). That doesn't mean that when everyone else is paid and there is something left for you that the hospital is profitable. When you've paid all expenses and paid yourself a reasonable salary for both clinical and management duties, and there is still money left over, then you can consider the hospital profitable.

Imagine it this way. Let's say you have inherited one million dollars and you are trying to decide whether to invest it in the stock market or in a veterinary hospital. If you invest in the hospital and can afford to pay yourself a $100,000 salary (which is what you believe you are worth in the veterinary market) and still have a few thousand left in the bank, you are probably profitable, right? Not really. If you invested your million dollars in the stock market and it had a 10% return, you'd make $100,000. The difference with the hospital is that you invested your money to buy a place where you could work for free. While you paid yourself a salary of $100,000, you would have made that money without working by investing it in a venture that actually had a decent rate of return on investment. If you invested your money in the stock market (assuming that it would likely have a 10% rate of return) and took a veterinary job elsewhere at the

$100,000 you believe that you are worth, you would have ended up with $200,000. The lesson to be learned—plan so that your venture is profitable all on its own. Plan on it delivering a reasonable return on your investment AND paying you a reasonable salary. Sometimes the easiest way to look at the hospital as an investment is to consider the likely return if you weren't working there yourself. If you had to hire another veterinarian and/or additional staff to do the job that you anticipate doing yourself, would the venture still be profitable. After all, if you paid yourself a reasonable salary and then learned that the hospital had a 2% return on your investment, you would realize that your investment probably could have been easily reproduced with a bank account, and without the risk you assumed with the hospital.

For a hospital to be truly profitable and worth the risk of operating it, it must have sustainable growth potential, and hopefully an exit strategy for you, the owner. If you had invested in a stock or bond, in addition to the benefit of receiving periodic dividends, the instrument itself has value, which can be sold. While there is a large market for the sale of stocks and bonds, there is a very limited market for the sale of veterinary hospitals. If you build a small hospital sufficient to maintain one or two doctors, you probably won't have much to sell when you retire. New graduates want to work regular hours, have many other doctors around and lots of new medical gadgets, and make enough money to pay off their student debts and lead a decent lifestyle. Fewer and fewer want to own small practices that involve long workweeks and management headaches.

Once again, the moral of the story is to plan. When you write a business plan, realize that the mission statement and vision are important, and so are the pro-forma financial statements. But the most important aspect is often the objective analysis that you can do to protect your investment. Don't be swayed when the bank accepts the business plan that you propose. They will likely fund your project, not because it is superior, but because veterinarians rarely default on bank loans. Veterinarians may pay themselves poorly and have an abysmal rate of return on their investment, but they do tend to pay their loans on time.

Accordingly, spend appropriate amounts of time on creating the value proposition for your business plan. In this section, you look at the "value" that you are creating for all parties—for shareholders, for clients, and other interested parties (stakeholders). What makes your notion so superior? Why will clients be better served at your establishment and be prepared to pay a premium to go there? What is it that is going to make your staff so motivated to deliver the utmost in client services? If you are truly creating "value", raising money is rarely a problem. If you were presented with this business plan, would you invest with the idea of making a decent rate of return?

Similarly, when you select an area in which you would like to practice, take the time to do your homework on the area and its veterinary needs. While many veterinarians are fiercely independent and want to stake out their own territory, medical doctors learned long ago that cooperation is a better alternative. Group practices are the norm, offering superior client service, better lifestyle options for physicians, and economies of scale and scope. Consolidation of practices is coming to veterinary medicine, but it is doing so slowly. Whatever you decide to do, don't just set up a "copycat" clinic in an area already well served by veterinarians. It only serves to cut up the client revenue pie in ever-smaller pieces. Check the demographics of the proposed area with a service such as CACI (www.caci.com) or Equifax (www.equifax.com) and make sure it can sustain additional veterinary services.

Evaluating an area involves more than sizing up your competition. First, the other practices in the area need not be your competition. There might be like-minded colleagues in the community who would be interested in merging practices to form a large group practice. Imagine having an imaging center, rather than individual x-ray machines in every practice. Imagine being able to concentrate more on surgery if that is your interest, rather than doing a mediocre job with medical cases. And, imagine being able to take regular vacations while your clients remain well served. It's worth planning for, isn't it?

Planning Rules to Live By

In practice, 80% of your revenues will come from 20% of your clients. Also, 80% of profits come from 20% of products or services (Pareto's law). The corollary to this is that 80% of all complaining in the practice will be done by 20% of the client base.

Within 3 years of graduation, your total debt, including unpaid balance on student loans, credit cards, car loans, lines of credit, but NOT mortgage payments, should be less than 20% of your annual take-home pay.

When leasing, companies often refer to a money factor rather than an interest rate. If the money factor is expressed as a percentage, convert the percentage to the money factor by dividing the number by 24. For example, a 7% (0.07) interest rate converts to a 0.0029 money factor.

Don't finance long-term projects with short-term debt. Since interest rates vary, the period of financing should approximate the useful life of the asset being financed. You don't finance a house with a 5-year mortgage unless you are preparing to move or you don't mind the risk of potentially refinancing when rates may be much higher.

To find out how fast your savings will double, divide 72 by the annual interest rate. For instance, if you invest $100 at a return rate of 10%, the amount will double every 7.2 (72/10) years. If you can find an investment that pays 15%, the principal will double every 4.8 (72/15) years.

You should save at least 10% of your take home pay each pay period for your long term needs (i.e., retirement). If your take home pay was $52,000 per year, and you invested $100 weekly ($5,200 annually), in 30 years you'd be a millionaire. And that doesn't even factor in any raises for the next 30 years! Unfortunately, it also doesn't factor in inflation or tax consequences.

You should spend no more than 30% of your monthly take-home pay on rent or mortgage. This can be difficult if you are living in an expensive city, but by the same token, you should be aware that you actually need to make more money in these locations just to keep up with your peers. To compare, try a salary calculator such as those available at homefair.com (www.homefair.com/homefair/calc/salcalc.html) or on Monster (www.monstermoving.com/Find_A_Place/Calculators/SalaryCalc/).
According to the Social Security Administration, by the year 2025 the median price of a single-family home in the United States will hit $400,000. Plan for it!

Maintain an emergency fund equal to 3-6 months of living expenses. Do not invest this money in instruments that are not immediately liquid.

Fund your retirement from income, not from the equity of practice ownership. Do not mortgage veterinary facilities beyond what the practice can support. In other words, do not expect to finance your retirement with the sale of a veterinary practice. Few practice owners do so successfully.

There is a 3-year deadline from the filing date for the IRS to audit your return if it suspects good faith errors, or for you to submit an amended return if you discover a mistake that entitles you to a refund. The IRS has six years to challenge your return if it thinks you underreported your gross income by 25 percent or more. There is no time limit if you failed to file your return or if you filed a fraudulent return.

Recommended Reading

Heller, R (Ed). Manager's Handbook. DK, London, 2002. 256pp.

Smith, CA: Career Choices for Veterinarians. Smith Veterinary Services, Leavenworth Washington, 1998, 254pp.

BUDGETS AND BUDGETING

Kurt A. Oster, MS, SPHR

Kurt A. Oster, MS, SPHR has worked as a Hospital Administrator in a variety of practice formats and is currently a practice management consultant with Veterinary Healthcare Consultants, LLC of Haverhill, Massachusetts. Mr. Oster consults regularly with veterinary practices on human resources, operations, demographics and financial issues.

A few short years ago, you probably would not have seen a chapter on budgeting in a business book for veterinarians. However, the environment that all businesses, including veterinary hospitals operate in today is more complex than ever before. This requires veterinary practice owners and veterinary practice managers to have greater financial skills in order to be successful.

Budgets are a topic plagued by a lot of myths and misinformation. Budgets are planning tools, not weapons. Budgets have had a negative history in veterinary medicine because many practice owners and managers used budgets as weapons against staff members. If an associate asked a manager for a raise, or to purchase a piece of equipment they did not wish to purchase, they may have been told, "Sorry, it's not in the budget." This tactic was most frequently used in practices that did not even have a budget in place. This behavior leads to a misconception that budgets stifle creativity and limit responses to the business environment.

Instead, if the practice had a budget in place and used it correctly, they would know that a budget is a fluid object. Budgets should be revised on a regular basis in response to internal and external influences (such as a new practice startup down the road) or a change in practice priorities. For example, providing team members with adequate healthcare coverage is a high priority for many employers. A sudden increase in healthcare costs may necessitate a decrease in lower priority spending somewhere else in the budget. Maintaining a current budget supports informed decision making in a timely manner.

Another popular misconception is that budgets are purely a business tool. In reality, the need for veterinarians to develop personal budgets is greater than at any time in history. A recent study by the General Accounting Office (GAO) in 2002 (www.gao.gov) found that the average college graduate had three credit cards with an average credit card debt of $7,900. Many of these college seniors were unemployed full time students with no source of income. Yet the aggressive lending habits of financial institutions flood student mailboxes with pre-approved credit card offers.

Students cannot resist the temptation of these credit offers. Easy credit allows students to purchase many of the comforts they denied themselves during the earlier years of their education. With graduation on the horizon, many students (especially seniors) begin shopping sprees believing that the debt they are accumulating will not be a problem once they are gainfully employed. This seemingly simple misconception can produce catastrophic results. For the first time in history, new veterinary school and medical school graduates are declaring personal bankruptcy. Although the GAO study did not specifically address these types of students, these advanced degrees require an additional four years of study, which makes it highly probable that their debt levels will be higher than those students receiving Bachelor degrees.

A credit card can be a real lifesaver when an emergency situation arises and you are at college, far away from home. Automobile repairs are the most common use, or the ability to reserve airline tickets for the long trip home during break. If the balance is paid in full upon receipt of the billing statement, you usually will not be assessed finance charges. If your card has no annual fee, this convenience costs you very little. If however, you charge up a large balance and only make minimum payments, you could literally spend years trying to get out of debt. Most credit cards only require you to pay a minimum payment of 2% of the current principal. Add to this the impact of the finance charges and the average card takes as many as seven years to become paid in full. Many card offers come with an enormous amount of fine print including sizeable late fees and interest rate hikes for payments as little as an hour past due. One or two late payments later and your costs will begin to go up, as your credit rating begins to go down.

Once your credit rating begins to be impacted negatively, the effect can be far reaching. A lower credit score can cost you lots of money down the road with higher interest rates for car loans, home mortgages and business loans for such things as acquiring a veterinary hospital. In contrast, maintaining a personal and practice budget demonstrates a higher degree of financial skill to a lender and may actually result in a lower interest rate.

If you don't trust your personal will power when it comes to managing credit, use a debit card or obtain a secured credit card. A debit card gives you the acceptance of a credit card (very helpful if you travel), but they deduct money directly from your checking account. This means you do not accumulate a balance that needs to be paid later and it is impossible to spend beyond the available funds in your checking account. Secured credit cards are cards that you obtain after you have given the lending institution a deposit in advance. For example, paying the bank a $500 deposit allows you to have a credit card with a $500 credit limit. The tight control of your credit limit keeps you from charging up debt beyond your ability to pay.

Controlling your spending habits is a key first step in successful personal financial management, but in order to exercise total control of your personal finances, you must develop a personal budget. Most practice management classes within veterinary schools walk students through the creation of a personal budget. This is an extremely important exercise, which can be a real eye opener for students that have previously relied on mom and dad for financial guidance. The earlier in their academic training students complete this exercise, the more likely they are to make realistic and responsible financial decisions.

During personal conversations with several instructors of veterinary practice management at the 2001 American Veterinary Medical Association (AVMA) annual meeting, it came to light that senior veterinary students completed budgets that required an average of $70,000 in annual income to meet their projected financial needs. Unfortunately, a survey of recent graduates by the AVMA during the same year indicated that female graduates that accepted positions in private clinical practice reported a mean starting salary of $39,120. Male graduates faired only 2.4% better, reporting a mean starting salary of $40,052. The only good news is that the gender gap in wages continues to close, but the gap between what new graduates need to survive and what the market is willing to pay them continues to be as wide as the Grand Canyon.

Students and associates alike that do not complete a personal budget exercise, risk financial hardship at the least and a damaged credit rating and personal bankruptcy at the most. Until the veterinary profession as a whole changes so that veterinarians are paid what they are truly worth, veterinarians will need to learn how to survive on a tight budget. How tight? The information above indicates that in 2001, the typical new graduate received approximately $40,000 in wages during their first year of employment, despite their perception that to meet "reasonable" living expenses they needed to earn $70,000. On average, new graduates only earned about 57% of the wages they felt they needed to survive. Even if the average associate veterinarian received a substantial raise of $5,000 for their second year of practice, their income still falls below the 2/3 level of what they need to live comfortably. Without a well thought out budget and a large dose of will power a young professional can make just a few poor financial decisions that can take literally a lifetime to recover from. The good news is, despite the myth that budgets are difficult to create, they are in reality easy to prepare and there are a lot of free resources available to help.

If you are still a veterinary student, or if you are a recent graduate, most practice management instructors already have a personal budget handout and template available for your personal use. If you have your checkbook and credit card statements handy, you can probably complete your budget in a couple of hours. A well thought out personal budget is a small investment in time that will reap huge dividends.

Among the many resources available for helping you create your first personal budget is a simple personal budget template located below. It is by no means a complete in-depth model, but it does cover all of the basic components that are required. You can add or subtract specific categories or line items as needed. Instructions and tips for completing the template simplify the budgeting process by breaking it down to seven easy-to-follow steps. Other resources that are available include a variety of personal finance software programs such as Quicken® by Intuit and Money® from Microsoft. These relatively inexpensive programs have personal budget templates as well as money management tools such as a debt calculator that allows you to chart your total indebtedness so you can monitor the results of your spending and payment habits.

Many free resources are also available on the web as well. Entering terms as simple as "personal budget" into any popular search engine will provide you with a pretty extensive list of free sources (such as www.nolo.com) of how-to articles and publications.

Budgeting is synonymous with planning. Developing a budget is really an exercise in strategic planning rather than a "numbers" exercise. In many cases, forcing yourself (or your practice team if it is a practice budget) to go through the strategic planning exercise required for budget preparation is the most rewarding part of the process. It essentially outlines strategic objectives and operating plans for the next year. Once you have planned for the year ahead, there are fewer surprises as the year progresses. Contrary to popular belief, filling in the numbers is the final step in the preparation of a budget.

Steps to Budgeting

The seven steps outlined below for completing the personal budget template are in many ways interchangeable with the steps necessary to complete a business budget. To complete the exercise, you may choose to photocopy the sample templates and fill them in the appropriate information in pencil, or you may choose to make similar templates in a spreadsheet program such as Excel®. This simple budget example utilizes only a few basic spreadsheet functions, so it would be fairly easy to recreate.

1. **Estimate your income.** If you are currently employed, or you have accepted employment, you can enter your wage information. If you are still a student, you can use the average salary obtained by last year's graduating class.

Wages comprise only a portion of many veterinarians' incomes. If you are eligible to receive production bonuses, compensation for emergencies or other income (such as child support), please list your best estimate for these amounts in the appropriate boxes in Table 1 below.

The amount of taxes deducted from your gross wages will vary based on the information you provided on your W-4 form. If you are currently employed, you can estimate your percentage of taxes from your most recent pay stub. If you are not currently employed you can use either 25% or 30% as a reasonable estimate until you have more accurate information. Do not worry about specifying federal taxes versus state taxes or Social Security. For this example, you can lump all of theses "tax" deductions together as one value. For many students entering the workforce, the reality of payroll taxes hits them like an oncoming train. An annual salary of $40,000 per year only puts about $30,000 per year in your pocket after taxes.

2. **Determine expenses.** Now that you have developed an accurate estimate of your income, it is time to begin reviewing expenses. If you have historical expense information available, this greatly simplifies your planning. You must analyze the historical information to determine if it is likely to reoccur the same this year, or if specific expenses were unique occurrences. An example may be significant car repair that is not likely to reoccur again this year. Historical expenses should not be taken at face value. A reasonable inflation factor needs to be added to last year's amount. Expenses that may grow faster than inflation such as automobile or health insurance need to be researched before assigning a dollar value.

There are about a dozen major expense categories in a personal budget. For those living on a very tight budget, it may be wise to list them in order of decreasing importance. This places housing and food near the top of the list and entertainment at the bottom. Table 2 contains a sample of the most common personal expense categories. The more complex categories have several items listed under the primary heading. These examples are oversimplified for this exercise. Adding greater detail to your real budget would increase its effectiveness. For simplification, savings and pension contributions have been omitted, but are a very important part of personal financial planning and should not be overlooked for too long. You won't be able to save if you don't budget for it!

3. **Manage cash flow.** The timing of cash flow management is a critical financial skill that budgeting can help you master. Timing frequently affects both income and expenses. For example, if you receive a quarterly production bonus, your first quarter bonus will probably be paid sometime in April after the first quarter has been completed.

Expenses can be even more complicated and thus, there are multiple methods for managing them. For example, assume you pay $540 in car insurance every 6 months. One method is to allocate this expense equally over the time period that it covers. Utilizing this method, you would allocate $90 each month for car insurance. At the end of the month, you should have $90 reserved for your upcoming insurance premium. A different method is to place the entire amount in the actual month it is due. If you pay the $540 once in January and again in June, you would place zeroes in the months in which you are not making payments. You may wish to experiment with each of these methods until you determine which one works better for you personally.

The impact of student loans can also be a huge factor in cash flow timing. Some loans have a grace period (often six months) after graduation before you are required to make the first installment, while others do not. Some loan programs will allow deferments while you further your education such as participating in an internship or residency programs, while others do not. It is advised that the earlier you inquire about these types of restrictions the better off you will be. For example, some loan programs only recognize internships at universities and do not grant deferments for internships within private practices. If you are considering an internship, you need to understand the terms of your loan(s) before you enter the matching program.

Practice budgets typically include many transactions that are sensitive to timing issues, such as bulk purchases of heartworm preventatives, or flea and tick products. These products can be purchased today, but their payment does not come due for several months. This is known in financial jargon as trade credit, but most veterinarians refer to it as delayed billings. Delayed billings can total in the tens of thousands of dollars in a typical small animal practice; failure to properly manage these transactions has caused practice owners and practice managers significant financial hardship.

4. **Balance your budget.** Once you have made your best estimates for income and expenses during the year, you will need to continually revise the numbers until you have more income than expenses. If you have already accepted a position, it may be difficult to increase your income significantly. Therefore, your greatest gains will be made by attempting to lower your projected expenses. The size of the gap between your projected income and expenses will determine just how deep the sacrifices need to be.

5. **Record actual numbers in a timely manner.** Upon completion of your budget projections, you can make an additional set of templates for recording the actual amounts each month.

6. **Calculate budget variances.** Upon completion of entering each month's actual data, comparisons can be made to the original projections. The difference between these two amounts is called the variance. If the amounts are identical, the variance is zero. If the amounts are not identical, the variance may be classified as favorable, or unfavorable. Income that is greater than you planned for, such as an unanticipated raise, is a favorable variance. A higher than anticipated expense is an unfavorable variance.

7. **Revise your plans to overcome unfavorable budget variances.** Learning how to manage your budget variances is a critical budget skill that you will perfect with experience. The first question you need to ask is if the variance was caused by a singular occurrence unlikely to repeat itself, or is it a predictable change over time? An example of a singular occurrence may be an unexpected bonus (e.g., a hiring bonus), which is not expected to recur. A predictable change may be an increase in your base pay for the remainder of the year. The frequency and magnitude of predictable changes determine how often you will need to revise your original projections. Most budgets are typically revised once each quarter.

Budgets should always be thought of as fluid objects that can be reshaped at any time. One of the great rewards of budgeting is their ability to quickly alert you to deviations from your strategic plans. The month your car breaks down unexpectedly may force you to lower your entertainment budget for the next several months to compensate for the increased expense. However, your entertainment expense will not drop on its own if you do not make a plan. For example, you may decide to rent videos instead of going to the theater. You may go out on lunch dates instead of dinner dates. You may even have to cancel your cable television or internet subscription. Having all of your data in front of you at one time helps facilitate this type of decision making.

Table 1: Income

Category	Jan	Feb	Mar	Apr	May	Jun	Jul	Aug	Sep	Oct	Nov	Dec	Total
Income													
Wages													
Bonuses													
Other Income													
Taxes													
Net Income													

Table 2: Expense

EXPENSES	Jan	Feb	Mar	Apr	May	Jun	Jul	Aug	Sep	Oct	Nov	Dec	Total
Home													
Rent													
Telephone													
Electric													
Heat/ Other Utilities													
Food													
Transportation													
Car Payment													
Insurance													
Gas													
Repairs													
Debt													
Prior Credit Cards													
Student Loans													
Personal													
Health Insurance													
Doctor/Dentist													
Medications													
Cosmetics/Haircuts													
Children/Spouse													
Events													
Birthdays/Weddings													
Related Travel													
Pet Care													
Clothing													
Entertainment													
Meals out													
Movies and concerts													
TOTAL EXPENSES													
NET INCOME													
Extra, or (deficit)													

Administering a Budget

Your ability to develop and administer budgets will grow with experience. Practice managers typically require three to five years of experience in order to master budgeting. This learning curve is similar to those associated with other practice management disciplines such as human resources or marketing.

The steps outlined previously will walk any novice through the preparation of their first budget. However, some additional advice may be helpful to the beginner. First, always begin your budgeting process in the same level of detail you are used to working in. Many beginners try to create the "greatest budget ever" their first time. If you track five profit centers in your practice, do not create a budget with twelve profit centers. The day-to-day demands of managing a practice can be significant. If you do not have the time to properly develop the mechanisms to allocate all of your income and expenses to twelve profit centers, the odds are that your budget will sit in a desk drawer. If you cannot enter meaningful data into the budget, you will not be able to calculate meaningful variances. The preparation of this "detailed" budget soon becomes wasted time and effort. Instead, a budget with only five profit centers that is updated in a timely manner will generate meaningful results. Greater detail can always be added to the budget next year.

Second, with the possible exception of your personal budget, the more people involved in the creation of the budget, the better the result. Budget preparation should not be a secret event carried out by one individual. Staff participation is critical to the development of a realistic and practical budget. Staff members can help identify potential income opportunities as well as possible areas where expenses may be controlled.

Most veterinary practices will have multiple months in which the budget predicts negative cash flow. These negative months are typically the result of a combination of factors such as changes in seasonal caseload, increased heating or cooling costs and delayed pharmaceutical billings. A practice staff that is aware of a budget prediction of a poor month may rally to drive income and control expenses in order to make the month profitable. This makes the budget a terrific tool for human resource planning and goal setting.

It is also important to document all of your assumptions when you are developing your budget. Brainstorming sessions during the development of a budget can be pretty intense. It is often difficult to remember exactly how you arrived at a specific number, four, seven or ten months down the road when you are analyzing budget variances. If for example you predicted a 10% increase in laboratory income, you should document that 4% was from scheduled fee increases, 5% were from increased frequency of collecting pre-anesthetic blood work, and 1% was from an increase in fecal examinations during annual physical examinations. If your laboratory income falls below the target, which goal (or goals) did you fail to meet?

Keep your budget current. You must discipline yourself to make regular entries each month. Setting dates to make variance results available to others is a great tool for keeping you on schedule. Promising the practice owner a variance report by the tenth of each month prevents the budget from being placed on the back burner as you tend to other practice needs. A first quarter variance report issued in September has very little management value because too much time has elapsed without corrective action. A first quarter unfavorable variance that is spotted in April, gives you the spring and summer to take corrective action.

The sample budget in Tables 3 and 4 below represent the first six months of a simple practice budget. The samples illustrate several of the concepts mentioned above. First, despite the efforts of many practices to level out the revenue stream throughout the year, this sample practice still generates significantly less revenue during the winter with peak revenue production occurring in the spring and summer months. This variation is important to recognize so the practice can properly manage its seasonal cash flow.

Table 3. Sample Animal Hospital Revenue

Sample Animal Hospital
Operating Budget
For Year Ending December 31, 2002

Acct Name	January	February	March	April	May	June
REVENUE						
Office Procedures/Immuniz	45410	46735	54277	62845	60726	53183
Pharmacy	42628	39841	49283	67798	67283	53631
Prescription Diet	4762	4623	5816	5691	6146	5960
Lab In-house	13455	12094	17055	17102	18155	15778
Lab Send-out	18066	19105	23015	22772	23298	20488
Radiology	10763	7973	10150	9090	10739	10207
Hosp./Inpatient	12925	10537	15766	15214	15626	12871
Surgery	12210	10888	15960	18310	14796	11898
Dentistry	1980	2548	3100	2410	1904	1306
Anesthesia	5365	4919	5324	7369	6256	5213
Ancillary Serv.	7341	6230	10417	11153	7255	10171
Discounts	(154)	(478)	(1752)	(906)	(770)	(306)
Total Income	174,750	165,015	208,412	238,847	231,413	200,401

During the six-month period represented in the sample budget, it is important to note that the month of February is forecasting revenues of $165,015 and expenses of $165,303, a loss of $288.00. Therefore, there will need to be enough cash reserve to handle the anticipated loss. This is a common scenario so practice managers must plan ahead for these shortfalls.

The expense data in Table 4 illustrates a common phenomenon in staff payroll. The sample practice budget illustrates a typical bi-weekly pay period. This means there will be 26 pay periods throughout the year. In May, the payroll projections are substantially higher than in the other months. This is because May is one of the two months during the year that has three pay periods instead of two. Since payroll is typically the single greatest practice expense, the dollar increase in these months is substantial. Prior planning is again needed to avoid a possible cash shortfall.

Table 4 Sample Animal Hospital Expenses

EXPENSES	January	February	March	April	May	June
Drugs/Medical Supplies	28834	27227	34388	39410	38183	33066
Lab Costs Send Out	4368	5640	5297	7416	5421	6567
Animal Disposal	330	33	195	324	157	401
Comp./ Vet. Officers	13500	13500	13500	13500	13500	13500
Comp./ Other Vets	23410	23410	23410	23410	35130	23410
Relief Vets/ Specialists	1999	1935	2565	4090	3202	5110
Technicians	16636	16636	16636	16636	24965	16636
Receptionists	11520	11520	11520	11520	17288	11520
Ward	6168	6168	6168	6168	9256	6168
Administrative	7886	7886	7886	7886	11835	7886
401K Match/Administr	2145	2145	2145	2145	2145	2145
FICA Employers Portion	5098	5098	5098	5098	5098	5098
Fed Unemployment Tax	154	154	154	154	154	154
State Unemp. Tax	740	740	740	740	740	740
Workers Comp Insur	(1416)	779	880	880	880	880
Other Taxes	18	0	0	18	558	0
Health Insurance	6301	3190	5331	5552	3899	5397
Laundry and Uniforms	0	2425	2704	1786	(14)	93
Vehicle Expense	1165	1232	1104	1983	1235	1224
Continuing Ed/Vet Pub	175	0	1000	0	0	1000
Prof and Bus Dues	233	157	346	294	27	27
Rent on Bus. Property	0	0	0	0	0	0
Maint & Serv. Comp & Med	556	1700	1903	1483	57	41
Repairs	0	0	0	0	0	0
Insur Pkg. Umbrella	229	304	574	304	304	304
Real Estate Tax	0	0	0	3574	0	0
Rent and Lease Equip.	314	521	869	733	522	623
Pers.Property Tax	0	0	0	0	0	0
Utilities	2833	4394	3285	3685	4901	2461
Telephone	1160	1328	1022	1326	1011	1105
Advertising	1557	1823	1434	1588	1434	1919
Computer Supplies	746	428	628	139	3653	376
Office Expense	4946	6383	5005	2370	1313	2309
Postage Expense	740	808	779	1068	614	667
Legal Services	1829	618	782	618	618	618
Charitable Contributions	155	206	103	0	1030	0
Bank Charges	1306	1344	1328	1349	1809	1658
Collection Expense	206	0	0	0	0	0
Misc. Expenses	1096	893	2190	1060	1499	914
Depreciation Expense	4411	4411	4411	4411	4411	4411
Penalties	0	0	0	103	0	0
Int Exp Bank Fin Loan	10984	10267	10178	10575	9548	9824
Subtotal Misc Expenses	162332	165303	175558	183398	206382	168253
Total Expenses 2001	110484	134192	104613	100615	109451	81259
Net Income Before Tax	12418	(288)	32854	55449	25031	32147
Cum Net Income	12418	12130	44983	100432	125463	157611

Finally, if you are still apprehensive about starting this process, find a mentor. Most managers that have been through the budget learning curve are very willing to help others develop the same skills. Once you have created and faithfully maintained your first budget, you will wonder how you ever lived without one!

ECONOMICS

Lowell Ackerman DVM DACVD MBA MPA

Dr. Lowell Ackerman is a Diplomate of the American College of Veterinary Dermatology and in addition holds an MBA from the University of Phoenix and an MPA from Harvard University. He is involved in clinical practice as a clinical assistant professor at Tufts University School of Veterinary Medicine as well as helping to develop the business skills curriculum there. In addition, Dr. Ackerman is affiliated with Veterinary Healthcare Consultants, primarily dealing with practice administration and management issues. Dr. Ackerman is the author/co-author of 74 books to date and numerous book chapters and articles. He lectures extensively, on an international basis.

An Introduction to the Topic of Economics

While you probably won't use economic formulas in your day-to-day activities, learning the basic tenets of the discipline is important because it guides the fundamental ways that money changes hands. In this chapter, we're not going to assess the gross national product (GDP) or the impact of abandoning the gold standard, but you hopefully won't be too surprised to discover that we use the principles of economics on a daily basis.

So, what exactly is economics? Economics is the study of how society allocates scarce resources and goods. It is the element of scarcity that is critical to the discussion, since this is key to how society allocates resources, goods and services. For most of us, that scarce resource is money. If we could afford to buy anything that we wanted, economics wouldn't have much impact on our lives. However, when our wants and needs surpass our abilities to procure them, then economics is very important on how we make choices for what we can have.

Macroeconomics is concerned with the study of the market system on a large scale, evaluating the role of consumers, businesses and government. While this is an important topic, there isn't much that we as individual veterinarians can do to change the macroeconomic picture affecting us. That is, we can't individually impact the gross national product of the country, or monetary policy, or the effect of a recession. Microeconomics, on the other hand, is concerned with the study of the market system on a small scale, looking at individual markets, consumers, businesses and government agencies. It is this branch of economics that we will explore, because it very directly affects our lives and our livelihoods.

To begin our study, it is important to understand some basic definitions, terms, and conditions. The term market refers to any arrangement that allows people to trade with one another. That could be the market for veterinary services in the country, in your community, or in an individual practice. There's another very common term used in economics that is just as aptly used in medicine. *Ceteris paribus*—which is Latin for "all else held constant," conveys the assumption that only a few of many factors are being examined. For example, looking only at starting salaries and veterinary school enrollment (but not all of the other possible factors), one might conclude that a slow stagnant increase in veterinary starting salaries over the past five years has led to reduced veterinary school applications, *ceteris paribus*. The *ceteris paribus* is there to state that we only looked at two variables in this case, in isolation. Perhaps veterinary school applications are down because the population of veterinary school-aged applicants is lower now than 5 years ago, or that undergraduate guidance counselors are pushing scientific-minded students towards computer studies, or that potential applicants fear exposure to biological agents and are selecting other careers. In the same vein, when we find evidence of glucose in the urine, prevailing evidence might suggest diabetes mellitus, *ceteris paribus*, but there could be a variety of reasons for the glucosuria. That's the trouble with rigid medical protocols, and the trouble with rigid economic models. There are lots of exceptions in both disciplines.

A simple economic model to start with is the Production Possibilities Frontier (PPF), used for economic analysis of production decisions. It measures the quantity of two goods (or services) that an economy is capable of producing with its currently available resources and technology. It is just a simplistic model examining and restricting two possibilities, not everything that might be relevant.

While the classic example in economics is guns and butter, it is just as easy to illustrate with a veterinary example. For instance, imagine a fixed budget and only two options in a veterinary hospital: seeing appointments, or doing surgery. For now, imagine that there was nothing else and the veterinarians in the hospital could only see appointments, do surgery, or a combination of the two. The Production Possibilities Frontier (PPF) is a graphical depiction of an assumption of "efficient production," in which the economy is always using its resources and technology to produce the maximum number of goods possible. Look at Figure 5-1 with Units of Surgery on the x-axis and Units of Appointments on the y-axis. At the point touching the x-axis, all of the resources in the hospital are being used for surgery and no appointments are getting done. All of the clinic's resources (money, staff, equipment) have been dedicated to surgical procedures. At the other end of the spectrum, there is no surgery being done, only appointments. At all other points on the PPF, there is a combination of appointments and surgical procedures being done. Points falling inside the PPF (e.g., doing two surgeries and seeing 10 appointments per day) represent inefficient production because the facility is capable of doing more (this is the unused capacity that is so prevalent in veterinary hospitals). At points outside the PPF (e.g., doing 6 surgeries and seeing 20 appointments) we are faced with unattainable production, regardless of how efficiently one tries to run things. These things could only be obtained by pushing out the PPF (such as by hiring another veterinarian or working longer hours), but are not possible with the existing situation.

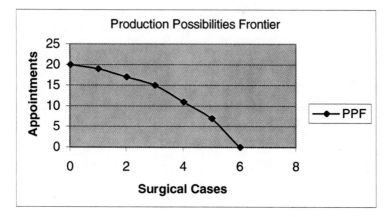

Figure 5-1. The PPF for a practice offering only appointments and surgery

You might wonder why the PPF is bowed and not a straight line. It has nothing to do with the relative importance of either discipline, but the fact that resources are not equally well suited to the production of both. For example, some resources may not be very useful for surgery (an ophthalmoscope) but are very useful for appointments. The same would be true of orthopedic fixation gear. If surgery is slow, the fixation equipment can't be shifted over to appointments to start making money there. What could you do with an anesthetic machine in the exam room? Staffing can also be an issue. If you gear up for surgery-only and have trained technicians doing anesthesia, assisting and surgical prep, it is hard to switch over efficiently to an appointment-only system. Can you efficiently switch over the trained surgical technicians to reception and checkout where they would be most needed in an appointment-only system? Only when departments share resources that are equally well suited to the other (or when staff is effectively cross-trained) would the PPF be a straight line. This becomes important when there is a fixed budget and the hospital needs to decide what to purchase or who to hire. Obviously, equipment or services that can be shared by multiple departments are better options.

The PPF also serves to illustrate another important economic concept— opportunity cost. The opportunity cost of an investment is the next best option forsaken or the highest valued alternative that could have been chosen, but wasn't. For instance, you made a conscious decision to read this book and improve your business skills. You could have gone to a movie, spent an evening with friends, or read a book on another topic. While you had many opportunities and choices available to you, you placed the highest value on reading this book and did so. The next valued choice that you gave up in order to read this book became the opportunity cost of actually reading this book. In the example above, you could have seen 15 appointments and done three surgeries in your day. To do one more surgery, you would have to give up 4 appointments. Thus, your opportunity cost for doing the fourth surgery is 4 appointments (and all the revenue that they represent).

When we take a look at the PPF, we also see the effects of opportunity cost. To do progressively more surgical cases means that fewer appointments can be seen. In fact the opportunity cost of producing one more unit of surgery increases as more surgery is produced, because some of the resources used to service appointments are not as well suited to surgery. So, as more and more resources are devoted to surgery, the opportunity cost of lost appointments will be increasing. This is referred to as the Law of Increasing Opportunity Cost.

Demand and Supply

Demand and supply are the cornerstones of a capitalist marketplace. There are many examples of this in our everyday lives, including buying and selling stock in the stock market, the real estate market, and many retail opportunities. Let's look at an example involving the sale of a veterinary practice. You have a practice to sell and want $500,000 for it. However, you list the practice and there doesn't seem to be any interest in it at that price. You can't understand it, because you added a new x-ray machine a year ago and painted the reception area recently, and yet the offers don't come in. Finally, someone places an offer at $300,000—and you are insulted. You counter with $490,000 and the buyer loses interest and moves on. You scold the listing agent for not adequately marketing your practice. In time, you take the agent's advice to lower the price and you reluctantly list it at $450,000, sure that you are getting robbed at that price. Still the offers don't come in. But, an offer eventually comes in at $330,000 and after a lot of countering back and forth, the practice sells for $400,000. You think you got too little, the buyer thinks they paid too much, but the practice does sell. The lesson to be learned—the value of any commodity is what the market will pay for it, not what you think it should be worth.

Demand

According to the law of demand, an inverse relationship exists between the price of something, and the quantity bought. That is, as the price goes up, that quantity bought goes down; when the price drops, more is bought. A demand schedule provides a tabular illustration of the process. Let's see what happens when we experiment with pricing for a dental prophylaxis procedure.

Price	Quantity performed
$0	10
$50	8
$100	6
$150	4
$200	2
$250	0

Table 5-1: The effect of price on client requests for dental prophylaxis procedures.

As we can see, when we are giving away prophies for free, we get requests to perform ten a day. We perform fewer and fewer procedures as we raise the price until, at $250, we're not doing any on a regular daily basis.

We can illustrate this graphically with a demand curve as well (Figure 5-2).

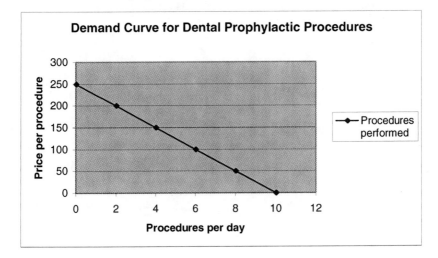

Figure 5-2: Graphical representation of the data in Table 5-1.

One of the most convenient things of a demand schedule/curve, is that we can use it to predict quantities of goods or services demanded for any given price. To do this, we need to use a concept that you might not have used since high school—calculating the slope of a line (and you thought you'd never ever use slope again). The slope of a line is equal to the rise divided by the run, or the change in the y-axis divided by the change in the x-axis. In this example, the change in the y-axis between any two consecutive points is the same, because we are dealing with a straight line. So, when the price rises from $100 to $200 (+100) the quantity demanded drops from 6 to 2 (i.e., -4). The slope of the line is therefore equal to +100 divided by -4, or -25. [Note that in a demand schedule, the slope is always negative, since quantities demanded drop as prices increase].

The equation for a line may be written as $y = mx + b$, where
y = the value on the y-axis,
x = the value on the x-axis,
m = slope and
b = y-intercept (where the line hits the y axis and x=0)

In this example,
$m = -25$
$b = 250$

Therefore, if we know the price, we can determine how many procedures we are likely to do in a day. So, if we set our prophy price at $175, we can expect to do the following number of procedures per day, on average:

$$175 = -25x + 250$$

Solving for x,

25 x + 175 = 250   [adding 25x to both sides of the equation]
25x = 250 - 175   [subtracting 175 from both sides of equation]
25 x = 75   [subtracting 175 from 250]
x = 75/25   [dividing both sides by 25]
x=3   [dividing 75 by 25]

Therefore, if we set our prophy price at $175, we would expect to do about 3 procedures per day.

It is important to mention that this is a simplified model in which the formulas are straightforward because the curve is linear (i.e., a straight line in which the slope is constant). Economists can and do work with non-linear curves, but more complex formulas are needed to represent them.

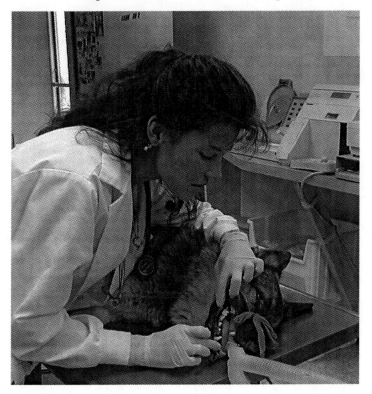

We get a *change in the quantity demanded* when we change price, but when any other relevant factor is changed, the entire curve shifts and we get an actual *change in demand.* This is because our two-dimensional curve can only capture the relationship between price and quantity, *ceteris paribus*, holding all other factors constant. When other factors change, the linear relationship between price and quantity is usually preserved, but the entire curve shifts in response to the other factor. For example, if there is a news story that covers the impact of dental disease on pet health (or you circulate a newsletter that accomplishes the same thing), you increase demand at all price levels, effectively changing the demand schedule to the following, for example:

Price	Quantity demanded
$0	12
$50	10
$100	8
$150	6
$200	4
$250	2
$300	0

Table 5-2: The effect of price on client requests for dental prophylaxis procedures after a promotional news story.

This also effectively "shifts" the demand curve out (Figure 5-3), which is termed a "shift to the right" in economics. In this example we have a demand curve where

b = 300

m (slope) = -25 (when price rises from $100 to $150 (+50), quantity demanded decreases from 8 to 6 (-2) [50/-2 = -25]

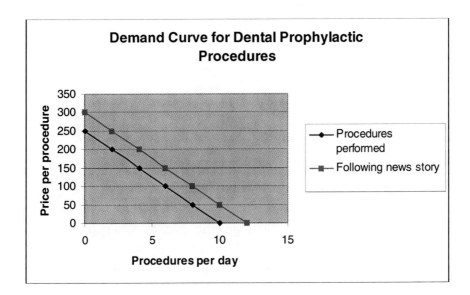

Figure 5-3. Change of Demand for dental prophylaxis following a news release

Now, if you wanted to keep performing 3 prophies a day, you should price the procedure as follows:

Price (y) = mx + b
$$= -25 (3) + 300$$
$$= 300 - 75$$
$$= \$225$$

On the other hand, if you didn't want to change your price, at the original prophy price of $175 you could expect to do the following number of procedures (on average) a day.

y = mx + b
175 = -25x + 300

25 x + 175 = 300
25 x = 300 - 175
25 x = 125
x = 125/25
x = 5   •

Why would demand change?

Things that cause shifts to the demand curve tend to be very important economic factors, and it is worth reviewing some of these now.

When people have more disposable income, they tend to spend more on everything. This shifts the demand curve to the right in most cases. We refer to goods for which increased income translates to increased sales as **normal goods**. For instance, premium dog foods are considered normal goods. When people make more money, they tend to buy more premium dog foods. On the other hand, goods for which demand varies inversely with income are known as **inferior goods** (at least in economics). An example might be generic pet foods. So, for this so-called inferior good, when incomes rise, overall purchases of generic diets fall (probably because people can afford to purchase better quality pet foods).

A related topic has to do with expectations for the future. If you are relatively stable in your career and salary expectations, then you are more prepared to make financial decisions over the long term. For example, if you are happy with your professional situation, you are more likely to buy a house nearby, create equity in your practice, etc.

When prices change for goods that are related to the item of interest, this also affects the demand curve. The two most important categories for these related items are **substitutes** and **complements**. A substitute for any good is something that satisfies the same requirements for the consumer.

The classic example of substitutes is Coca-cola and Pepsi-cola. If the price of Coke rises significantly, people might turn to Pepsi, brand preferences notwithstanding. They both fulfill a similar need, and so one cannot price itself significantly above the competition if it wants to maintain sales volumes. In this case of substitutes, an increase in the price of Coke leads to an increase in the sales of Pepsi. No doubt you can think of pet food brands that have the same constraints.

On the other hand, a complement (not compliment) is a good that is consumed in some proportion of another and is thus directly affected by it, good or bad. A complement may be dogs and dog food. If the licensing laws change and dog ownership require expensive licensing such that the increased cost prompts people to stop acquiring dogs as pets, there will be less need for dog food. Thus, when two goods are complements, then as the price of one good rises, the demand for the other decreases and the demand curve shifts to the left. When the price of the complementary good falls, the demand for the other good increases and the demand curve shifts to the right.

While it is safe to say that pets will likely always be a part of many households, things can and do change, and these changes can affect demand schedules. For instance, the number of dogs in North America is fairly stable now, but cats have increased in number to become the most populous pet. This has increased the demand for feline goods and services, and decreased (on a relative basis) the demands for canine goods, *ceteris paribus* (there's that term again).

There can also be events that change pet ownership preferences dramatically. For instance, 40 years ago it wasn't unusual for kids to have pet turtles. Several outbreaks of salmonellosis changed that demographic in a very short period of time.

There is also an important exception to the Law of Demand that does have some relevance in veterinary medicine. A **Giffen good** is such that demand increases as prices increase. This typically happens because of "snob appeal" but might have other motivators. For example, laser surgery might have appeal to consumers beyond its utility for a specific procedure. In this case, clients may pay more for a procedure partly because of its increased cost (and hopefully because of its merits as a surgical modality).

The Supply Side of the Equation

Demand isn't the only thing to be considered in deciding what goods and services to provide. After all, while you could do many dental prophies for free and have clients love you, how many veterinarians really want to "supply" service at this price.

While consumers buy more when prices are low, suppliers are prepared to sell more when prices are high. So, if clients were prepared to pay $300 for a prophy, you'd probably be more than willing to gear up to do at least 12 a day. The law of supply says that as the price of a good or service increases, the quantity supplied will also increase.

Let's take a look at the supply schedule (Table 5-3) for the dental prophy service that we are offering:

Price	Quantity supplied
$0	0
$50	2
$100	4
$150	6
$200	8
$250	10
$300	12

Table 5-3. The number of dental prophylactic procedures that veterinarians would be prepared to supply at different prices.

This can also be illustrated with a supply curve.

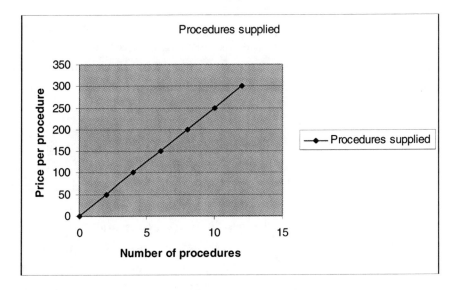

Figure 5-4. Graphical representation of the data in Table 5-3.

In this case, there is a direct relationship between the price of a good and the quantity supplied and sellers are prepared to supply more as prices rise. In a supply curve, the line rises to the right and the slope is always positive.

Now we have the following components of the linear equation:
b = y-intercept = 0 (i.e., the line crosses the y-axis at zero)
m = rise/run = 50/2 = 25; when price rises from $50 to $100 (+50), the quantity supplied increases from 2 to 4 (+2)

So, y = mx + b becomes
Y = 25x (+0)

So, if the going rate was $175 per prophy, you'd be prepared to provide $175/25 or 7 procedures a day.

Just as there were differences between changes in quantities demanded and actual changes in demand, there are also very real differences in quantities supplied and actual changes in supply. Changes in the determinants of supply, other than price, shift the supply curve inwards or outwards, depending on their effects.

Changes in supply may occur for many reasons. One of the most important is a change in the price of inputs. For example, if the cost of anesthetic goes up (or technicians' salaries), the curve will shift as you decide that $300 isn't such a windfall any more, given your expenses. Supply curves can also fluctuate with the changes in other goods and services. For instance, if you determine that you can actually make more money by doing laser procedures, or even just seeing more clients, than you do from dental prophies, you will elect to do fewer procedures for the same amount of money. Finally, changes in technology can also affect supplies of goods and services. If a new dental device could provide effective prophylaxis in less time, without anesthesia and at reduced cost to veterinarians, practices would be willing to supply more service at all price levels.

Supply meets demand

Lots of clients would be prepared for you to do prophies on their pets for free, and you'd be happy to do them all day if they were priced high enough, but the number that actually gets done on a daily basis only happens when the number demanded by clients meets the number supplied by the practice. This **equilibrium quantity** occurs at an **equilibrium price**. This equilibrium analysis can be performed algebraically with our demand and supply formulas, or graphically by depictions of the intersection of demand and supply curves.

If the demand equation is: y = 300 - 25 x

and the supply equation is y = 25x

we can substitute and solve as follows:

25 x = 300 - 25 x
50 x = 300   [add 25x to both sides of the equation]
x = 300/50 = 6

Thus, the equilibrium quantity is 6. Substitute this into either the supply or demand equation to get the equilibrium price:
y = 25 (6)
y = 150

So, in this example, both parties are best satisfied with doing six procedures a day at $150 per procedure (Figure 5-5).

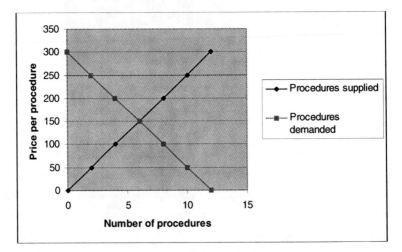

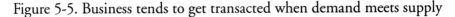

Figure 5-5. Business tends to get transacted when demand meets supply

Elasticity

We often don't have all of the information necessary to calculate an entire demand curve, in most instances. An additional piece of information that would be useful is understanding how responsive demand and supply are to changes in prices or incomes. As business people, we are interested in how small or large changes in price affect the demand for our services. For example, we want to know what impact a 10% increase in our fees will have on clients requesting our services. A useful indicator is the **price elasticity of demand**, the percentage change in quantity demanded divided by the percentage change in price.

Price elasticity of demand = <u>percentage change in quantity demanded</u>
Percentage change in price

If changes in prices don't affect the quantity demanded much (absolute value of elasticity < 1), we say they are price inelastic. For example, if you were treating a diabetic cat with insulin, and you increased the price of insulin by 30%, do you think that there would be a significant decrease in the number of owners prepared to pay for the insulin for their pets? Not likely. Similarly, the demand for cigarettes is also relatively price inelastic, because for addicted smokers, increasing the price by any percentage causes decreased consumption by a lesser amount.

If a percentage change in quantity demanded is greater than the percentage change in price, then demand is said to be price elastic. In other words, the demand for a good or service that is price elastic is very responsive to changes in price. For example, mortgage refinancing is quite price elastic. As mortgage rates increase, refinancing volume drops precipitously. When rates drop, refinancing becomes more brisk.

The elasticity of demand for a particular good or service offers important clues regarding total revenues. If a good is price inelastic, you can increase revenues by raising price! If a good is price elastic, you will decrease revenues by raising price. Most veterinary prices are relatively price inelastic. That is, if you raise your prices by 10%, you should expect that quantities demanded will drop by something less than 10%. That's why raising prices may scare away some clients, but total revenues tend to increase such that they more than compensate for lost quantity.

Let's illustrate with an example. Say you work in a 10-doctor practice that does 25 dental prophies a day at $150 each. That translates into $3,750 (25 x $150) of revenue daily from dental prophylaxis in the practice. You've been told that the elasticity of demand for veterinary services is about 0.4, meaning that demand drops by 4% when you raise fees by 10%. Sure enough, you raise your fees be 10% to $165 and demand drops by 4%, so now the practice is only doing 24 prophies a day. Should the practice drop its price to attract back the clients they are no longer servicing? Not for financial reasons. Raising the prices to $165 did scare off 1 client a day, but led to revenues of $3960 per day instead of $3750, while doing one less procedure. You decide.

Utility

Utility is sometimes a hard concept to grasp, but important nonetheless in any study of economics. Utility is the pleasure or satisfaction derived from consumption of goods and services and while difficult to measure, economists sometimes try with their own contrived units, called utils. We measure weight in grams and economists measure utility in utils. Just as your preferences dictated the opportunity costs of reading this book, so does utility measure the value of your choices regarding goods and services.

Utility may sound like a bizarre topic to introduce into the scientific world of veterinary medicine, but hang in there for a few paragraphs and see if it doesn't make a lot of sense in the care of pets.

The utility received from consuming a certain amount of anything is defined as the total utility. The marginal utility is the addition to total utility achieved by consuming one more unit of that good or service. This concept is very important in practice, as is the Law of Diminishing Marginal Utility, which states that the marginal utility that one receives from consuming successive units of the same good or service will decrease as the number of units consumed increases.

While we can represent utility using numbers, it is probably much more important to conceptually appreciate what is going on and realize that consumers always act to maximize their total utility.

Suppose you went out jogging on a hot day and when you returned you could think of nothing other than a nice cold beverage. You drink one glass and feel refreshed, but you are not completely satisfied, so have a second glass. You drink the second glass over a period of time and find it satisfying. A while later you even drink part of a third glass. This illustrates nicely the Law of diminishing utility. That first glass brought you a lot of pleasure. The second glass was good too, but you didn't appreciate it as much as the first glass when you were really parched. The third glass was OK, but not enough to make you feel compelled to finish it.

When we have to pay for goods and services, we subconsciously try to calculate the marginal utility of the purchase. Assigning utils to our choices would help quantify them, but most of the time we make the decision intuitively, without calculation.

Suppose you had a free evening and had just $10 to keep you entertained. You decide to rent a movie, and there is a deal that if you rent two movies at $4 each, you can rent a third movie for half price ($2). It also strikes you that you have no food in the house, and you could get some inexpensive take-out for $6. What do you do? You really have 2 options if you plan on spending all of that $10 and intend to watch at least one movie:

- Get three movies for your $10, and starve
- Get one movie and some food

What is your best choice? If you are a real movie hound you may have the highest total utility from option 1. However, if you're like most people, you'd take option 2 because the marginal utility of the second and third movie is not as valued as getting something to eat, too. However, total utility is entirely in the eye of the beholder.

What does dinner and a movie have to do with veterinary medicine? Surprisingly, a lot. You might recommend two prophys a year for your dental patients. Certainly that first prophy at $150 has a lot of value for owners, as they are aware of the importance of such dental care. However, the second prophy each year may not seem as critical to the owner. Perhaps they actually have $450 in disposable income available, but a child needs $300 in dental care, and the car needs servicing that will cost around $135. That first dental procedure was definitely valued by the client at $150, but if they value the second one at less, say $125, then that procedure will likely need to be postponed. Once again, we can't determine total utility for our clients. That's why some clients will stop at no expense for the care of their pets, and others will complain at the smallest of charges. Blame it on utility, which is a personal choice that we all make. All we can do is assert the value of our services, and the client will presumably make decisions to maximize their total utility and we need to deal with that.

Insurance

Another factor that influences utility is risk. If you have anything of value (house, car, jewelry, veterinary practice), you will choose to insure it. Why? Do you really think that there is a likely chance that your house will burn down? No, but your total utility is maximized by protecting against that risk. Most people are risk-averse and prefer certainty of protection against risk rather that gambling on outcomes. It's worth something to you to know that if something unforeseen happened, you wouldn't lose everything that you had. In the case of pets, the utility has to do with ensuring that a pet will receive needed care if medical costs are much higher than anticipated. Indemnity insurance also keeps veterinarians relatively uninvolved with the entire insurance process, other than signing forms and providing clients with itemized bills.

It is that risk management component that makes insurance universal. By having many people pay premiums and only paying out for a predictable percentage of them, insurance companies make their profits and individuals sleep better at night. Of course, insurance companies have to do a lot of work for their money and the premiums need to be fair and reflect the true risk of loss as well as compensation for bearing that risk. The **actuarially fair premium** is the portion of the premium that is likely to be paid out. If the insurance company didn't charge more than this, it would not be able to cover its administrative costs and would go out of business (as many pet insurance companies have done). The policy must also carry a **risk premium**, which is the insurance company's reward for bearing a client's risk for them. A client is only prepared to pay a total premium that matches his or her utility for covering a pet's cost in case of emergency.

This is significant in veterinary medicine, but there often seems to be a disconnect between veterinary impressions and those of clients. Pet health insurance, especially true indemnity insurance, is woefully underutilized, not because clients don't see the utility of it, but because veterinarians often don't. If clients appreciated that a trip to an emergency clinic, a referral to a specialist, or treatment for a serious condition could cost them thousands of dollars, they'd be clamoring for a way to maximize their utility and manage their risk. It is typically at this juncture, faced with a large, unanticipated expense that clients ask why their veterinarians never told them about pet insurance. When clients perceive that their annual veterinary bills will typically always be less than $200, it is hard to justify the insurance premium. If clients were aware that the prices that veterinarians charge for a spay (ovariohysterectomy) are not representative of typical surgeries, and that animals often require some very expensive intervention at some occasions during their lives, then insurance would be a more common way of clients to maximize their utility. The bonus for veterinarians would be that when clients have insurance, they are much less resistant to having a problem appropriately managed, and can afford to do so.

There are two problems with insurance that are appreciated from an economic standpoint and which are mentioned here simply for educational value. The first concern is known as **moral hazard**. It is a concept based on the possibility that someone with insurance will take more risks than someone without. For instance, say a client had a rocky yard and didn't typically let the dog out for fear of it breaking a leg and then having to deal with a costly surgical repair. If the pet was insured, might the client let the dog run in the yard, knowing that if an accident did happen, at least it would be covered by insurance?

The second concern is one of **adverse selection**. It reflects asymmetric information between the person buying the insurance and the insurance company. In this scenario, the insurance company charges a single premium for a dog or cat health insurance policy, being unable to distinguish between high-risk and low-risk individuals. However, owners may know that their dog or cat is likely to have health problems, and therefore insure them. In fact, owners may go to one veterinarian, find out their pet has problems, and then apply for insurance (without mentioning their last veterinary visit) and go to a new veterinarian once the new policy is in effect. The new veterinarian makes the diagnosis, treats the condition, and signs the forms, the client pays the bill, and then collects from the insurance company. This, unfortunately, drives up the actuarially fair premium for all pets, sometimes to the point where the utility of insuring animals that seem quite healthy may not be worth it to owners.

Indemnity insurance is a very important commodity for clients and for veterinarians. Keeping the process fair is in the best interests of everyone.

Theory of the Firm

While consumers will always try to maximize their total utility, businesses try to make decisions that maximize their profitability. This is important, because veterinarians need to decide how many hours each day to be open, how many employees to have on staff and available, and how much inventory to keep on their shelves.

Whenever we look at the economics of a business model, we have to be concerned about fixed costs and variable costs. These are covered in more detail in the accounting and finance chapters, but are worth introducing here. The **fixed costs** of running a business are those costs that are unavoidable, based on contractual obligations. **Variable costs** are those that vary with the amount of business being done. So, things like rent, a proportion of utilities, assets such as a surgery table or radiography machine are fixed costs. Some employees are also fixed costs if you can't send them home without pay when they are not needed. When you first open a business, it seems like everything is a fixed cost, because everything must be ready and available even before the first client walks in the door.

Variable costs are those that increase proportionately to business being done. An example might be suture material; it only increases costs as surgeries are being done and more needs to be ordered.

It's easy to illustrate fixed and variable costs with a telephone system. When you get your telephone hooked up, you have a base monthly fee whether you use the telephone or not. That's the fixed expense. As you make long-distance calls and utilize other telephone services, you incur additional costs associated with your usage of the system. That's the variable expense.

Along with fixed and variable costs, we also deal in time horizons, and discuss plans in terms of the short run and the long run. How short is a short run? How long is a long run? When we talk about our costs in the short run, it implies not a period of time (such as 6 months), but the time in which our factors of production are considered fixed. If you decide that your treatment room is too small, that's too bad in the short-run, because it will take time (and money) to change it. If you work in a practice and realize that it was a big mistake to have taken a job there, you have few options in the short-run, because you will have a contractual obligation to remain for the contractually specified time. Even if you own a practice and business is terrible, you can't just pull up stakes and move along. You have obligations for rent, employment, utilities, etc., in the short run. However, in the long run, all factors of production can be varied. If the clinic was too small in the short run, that can be corrected in the long run by building a new facility. So, a factor of production that cannot be varied in the short-run is called a fixed factor of production. Variable factors of production are those that can be varied in the short-run.

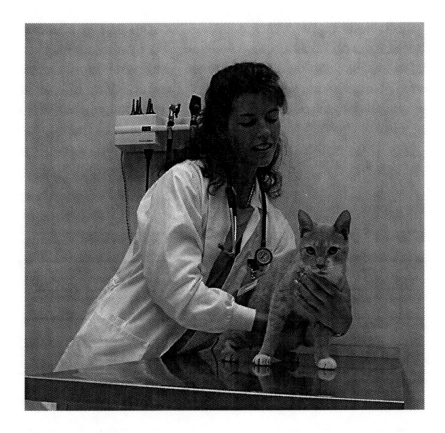

Diminishing Returns

There is no doubt that trained staff make a hospital run smoother. For example, if you try to run a hospital with one staff member, that individual has to play the role of receptionist, technician, clinical assistant, and every other non-veterinary position in the hospital. As you might imagine, this is terribly inefficient. Add another staff member and efficiency increases as duties are shared. The end result is that more work gets done with the two people. Now there is someone to answer the telephone and book appointments, while the other runs laboratory tests. Add another staff member, and now things really start to happen. Two of the staff members might put in a catheter, saving the doctor the time and effort of doing so, and allowing another appointment to be seen instead. However, at some point, we start experiencing inefficiencies, which in economic terms we describe as **diminishing returns**. The **marginal product of labor** refers to the increase in total production that can be achieved by adding one more staff member. Eventually, adding staff members doesn't make things more efficient; it just adds cost and doesn't increase profit.

Here are some formulas for some useful economic terms:

Marginal Cost	$\frac{\Delta Cost}{\Delta Output \text{ by 1 unit}}$	Per unit change in cost with a change in output
Marginal Revenue	$\frac{\Delta Revenue}{\Delta Output \text{ by 1 unit}}$	Change in revenue from increasing output by 1 unit
Marginal Product of Labor	$\frac{\Delta Output}{\Delta Labor \text{ by 1 unit}}$	The change in output from adding one more unit of labor
Average Total Cost	$\frac{Total\ Cost}{Output}$	Total cost on a per unit basis
Average Variable Cost	$\frac{Total\ Variable\ Cost}{Output}$	Variable cost on a per unit basis
Average Fixed Cost	$\frac{Total\ Fixed\ Cost}{Output}$	Fixed cost on a per unit basis

There are some good reasons for calculating such figures. In a perfectly competitive market, the marginal revenue is the price of the service or good. For example, if we are discussing a hospital situation, the marginal revenue may refer to the revenue derived from seeing one more patient. If we state that the average transaction for each office visit is $115, then the marginal revenue from seeing another appointment is also $115 (i.e., the marginal revenue equals the market price). When the marginal revenue exceeds marginal cost (i.e., each additional unit sold adds more to total revenue than to total cost), the firm will increase output and earn greater profits. When marginal revenue is below marginal cost (i.e., each additional unit sold adds more to total cost than to total revenue), the firm is losing money and should reduce its output. The important conclusion is thus that profits are maximized when the firm chooses the level of output where its marginal revenue equals its marginal cost (Fig. 5-6). In our example, we may chart out the number of appointments (or surgeries, or prophies or any other procedure) where the marginal revenue equals the marginal cost, and that is the most profitable level of output to achieve. In Figure 5-6, the most profitable situation is performing approximately 8 procedures at a cost of about $115 (i.e., the point where marginal cost equals marginal revenue).

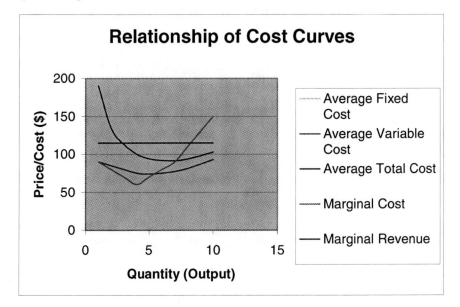

Figure 5-6: Relationship of cost curves. Profit is recognized when the price is higher than the point at which marginal cost and average total cost intersect. Profit is maximized where marginal revenue (price) and marginal cost intersect. This is the point at which total revenue exceeds total cost by the greatest amount.

Once we know the level of output, and the price of the service, there are some interesting conclusions to be drawn by looking at average costs.

When the price of the service is higher than the average total cost of offering the service, it pays to continue doing business both in the short run and in the long run. When the price of the service is less than the average total cost, but greater than the average variable cost, you will continue in the short term because you are at least covering a portion of your fixed costs. However, don't renew your lease because the business is losing money for you. If the price is actually less than the average variable cost, you might as well close the doors now, because if you can't even cover your variable costs, you're losing more money with every day you continue to be open.

Recommended Reading

Case, KE; Fair, RC: Principles of Microeconomics ActiveBook. Prentice Hall, 2002, 368pp.

Mankiw, NG: Principles of Economics. South-Western College Publishing , 2000, 888pp;

McEachern, WA: Economics, 5th Edition. South-Western College Publishing, 2000, 816pp.

Pindyck, RS; Rubinfeld, DL: Microeconomics (5th Edition). Prentice Hall, 2000, 699pp.

THE ABC'S OF ACCOUNTING

Amy K. Thieling, CPA

Amy Thieling received her accounting degree from Indiana University and is currently the manager of the Veterinary Practice Division of Thieling Co, CPA. Thieling Co., CPA has worked with veterinarians for approximately 30 years and now specializes in providing accounting, tax, management, and financial advice to the veterinary profession. Ms Thieling is a graduate of AAHA/Purdue University Veterinary Management Institute, and is a member of American Animal Hospital Association, Veterinary Hospital Managers' Association, American Institute of Certified Public Accountants, Association of Certified Fraud Examiners, Indiana CPA Society, and the Indiana CPA Society Young Professionals development team.

People have been using accounting in one form or another to record business transactions since 3500 B.C. Our present accounting method, the double-entry system, originated during the Italian Renaissance. It was during this time that the terms debit (Dr.) and credit (Cr.) were first used. Debit is from the Latin for left and credit is from the Latin for right. The double-entry system requires that the left-sided entries, or debits, equal the right-sided entries, or credits.

Why is the double-entry system an advantage over other methods? The true advantage is that it is a balanced system. Every transaction has a balancing and offsetting transaction (or transactions) that allow us to keep track of our finances. For example, if you buy some tablets to be used in the dispensing pharmacy, you debit the inventory account and credit the cash account. On the other hand, if the medication was delivered and you received an invoice with the amount due in 30 days, you debit inventory and credit accounts payable (the account that includes all your business creditors). When you finally write that check to the seller, you credit cash and debit accounts payable.

Figure 6-1. Using T-accounts to illustrate debit and credit transactions. (Note: T-accounts are a time-proven method of illustrating the concept of debits and credits and ensuring that all necessary entries are made. They are not, however, commonly seen.)

In this example, $100 worth of tablets are purchased. Figure 6-1a shows the transaction as if cash were paid. Figure 1b shows the two-part transaction if the tablets were purchased on credit, and then payment was made.

a) T-accounts when inventory is purchased with cash

Inventory		Cash	
Dr.	Cr.	Dr.	Cr.
$100			$100

This effectively subtracts $100 from our cash account to purchase inventory valued at $100.

b) T-accounts when inventory purchased on credit, then invoice finally paid.

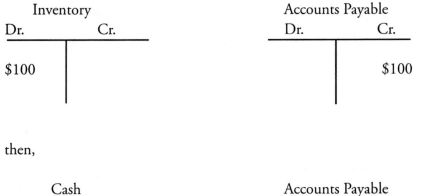

then,

In this exercise, the inventory is immediately increased by $100 and we create an obligation to pay that $100 in the future (an accounts payable). When we write the check to pay for the inventory, we now reduce our accounts payable by $100 and reduce our cash as well.

If you are inclined to think of debits as good and credits as bad, fight that temptation. Really, they only imply that you are adding to the left side or the right side of accounts and are neither good nor bad. Let's illustrate with an "accounts receivable" example, which represents monies that are owed to us, such as when a client receives services but doesn't pay for them at the time of the visit (but hopefully they will be paying for them in the near future). We might credit an income account called Revenues for services (recognizing that the client has received services for which payment is expected, which is a good thing), while debiting accounts receivable (acknowledging that somebody owes us money, which is better than us owing someone else money). When the client pays, we credit the accounts receivable account (an even better thing in this example), because we debit the cash account (the best thing).

The best part of this double-entry bookkeeping is that, for the most part, you don't need to worry about it. If you utilize a computer program for practice finances, it is set up to automatically know which accounts are appropriate and whether to debit or credit. These programs also generate financial statements and statistics. The main reason for having an appreciation for basic accounting is to understand what these programs and your accounting professional are doing for you and how to interpret the reports generated. You should also be familiar with a chart of accounts, which is a listing of all the different accounts and categories. Some standardization is important so you can compare your numbers with others in similar situations (benchmarking). So, whether you have your own business, or are researching companies to include in your investment portfolio, understanding a little bit about accounting can actually take you quite far.

It shouldn't be surprising to anyone that, in the subject of accounting, money is key. So if you have a practice that has $250 in the cash drawer, 60 bottles of various shampoos, several partially used bottles of medication, an otoscope, an ophthalmoscope and a portable endoscopy unit, you might have some difficulty determining the value of this practice. The cash part is easy. If we know the cost of the shampoos, that part isn't too tough either. To get a better perspective on the number of tablets, we periodically need to count inventory so we know how much is there and calculate the value sitting on the shelves and the cost of goods already sold. As far as the equipment, we can determine how much they were worth when we bought them. As time passes, we depreciate the value of those assets and claim the decline in value as a business expense. This merely represents the money-measurement concept of accounting. Whatever else we do, accounting has to represent the entity only in terms of dollars and cents.

Financial Statements

While the double-entry system has remained basically unchanged for centuries, the methods of reporting information generated by the double-entry system have evolved considerably. The reports currently used to present financial information under generally accepted accounting principles (GAAP) include the balance sheet, statement of operations (income statement, profit-and-loss statement), statement of cash flows, and explanatory disclosures. Together, these comprise the financial statements of a company and provide a summary of its financial and operating decisions and the success of those decisions.

Balance Sheet

The balance sheet is a snapshot of the financial position of the entity at one moment in time. There are three main categories to the balance sheet: the assets (things owned by the entity); liabilities (things owed by the entity), and; owner's equity (contributions by owners/investors and the amount retained from earnings). Assets are the valuable resources owned by the entity, such as cash in the till, accounts receivable (money owed by clients), inventory on the shelves, the building itself and the equipment in it. Liabilities are monies owed to creditors, whether they have provided cash (the bank, in the form of a loan or credit line), product (companies or distributors who have sent us product but have not yet been paid), or services (e.g., the utility bill). The title "Balance Sheet" comes from the requirement that Assets = Liabilities + Equity. This reflects the fact that the value of everything on the asset side was either paid for by debt (liabilities), owner's investment, or earnings from the business.

While there will be variations, a balance sheet will look like this:

"Good will is only recorded once a business has been purchased. It represents the amount paid above the net value of the other business assets purchased."

ABC Veterinary Services, Inc.
Balance Sheet
As of December 31, 200x

ASSETS		LIABILITIES	
Current Assets		Current Liabilities	
Cash	$xxxxx.xx	Accounts Payable	$xxxxx.xx
Accounts Receivable, Net	$xxxxx.xx	Bank loan payable	$xxxxx.xx
Inventory	$xxxxx.xx	Accrued liabilities	$xxxxx.xx
Prepaid expenses	$xxxxx.xx	Estimated tax liability	$xxxxx.xx
Total Current Assets	$xxxxx.xx	Current portion of long-term debt	$xxxxx.xx
		Total current liabilities	$xxxxx.xx
Property, Plant & Equipment - Net	$xxxxx.xx		
		Noncurrent Liabilities	
Other Assets:		Long-term debt, less current portion	$xxxxx.xx
Investments	$xxxxx.xx	Deferred income taxes	$xxxxx.xx
Goodwill	$xxxxx.xx	Total noncurrent liabilities	$xxxxx.xx
Total Other Assets	$xxxxx.xx	Total liabilities	$xxxxx.xx
		EQUITY	
		Common Stock	$xxxxx.xx
		Additional paid-in capital	$xxxxx.xx
		Retained earnings	$xxxxx.xx
		Total equity	$xxxxx.xx
TOTAL ASSETS*	$xxxxx.xx	TOTAL LIABILITIES & EQUITY*	$xxxxx.xx

*These numbers should be the same, so that total assets equal the sum of liabilities and equity

Assets represent resources that a business owns and uses to provide services and meet its obligations to creditors, employees, and suppliers. They are typically grouped into three categories—current, property and equipment, and other. Current assets include cash and items like accounts receivable, inventory, and prepaid expenses (e.g., insurance paid for the year but not all used up yet)—anything that can be reasonably expected to be utilized or converted to cash within one year. Property and equipment (fixed assets) include the long-lived real estate and buildings, vehicles, equipment, and similar items used by a business to provide goods and services. Other assets are long-term resources such as purchased goodwill, investments, and the cash surrender value of company-owned life insurance. If the business holds any patents or trademarks, they belong here too.

Liabilities are the business's obligations owed. Similar to assets, liabilities are generally separated between current and non-current (i.e., greater than one year) timeframes. Current liabilities include trade accounts payable, amounts owed to employees, tax obligations, line-of-credit advances, and the portion of long-term debt due within one year. Long-term liabilities include mortgages, equipment financing contracts, and similar arrangements that provide for any portion of the debt to be paid more than a year after the balance sheet date. The amount of long-term liabilities payable within one year is called the current portion and is included in current liabilities rather than long-term liabilities.

Owners' equity represents the investment that owners have in the company. Depending on the business structure, it may be given titles such as Partners' Capital (in a partnership); Capital Stock, Additional Paid-in Capital, and Retained Earnings (in a corporation—see above example); or Unrestricted and Restricted Net Assets in a government or not-for-profit entity. Equity is the difference between assets and liabilities, and may be either a positive or negative amount. It is also called the "book value" of a business.

"The par value of a stock is just the value printed on the certificate. It does not reflect the true value of the stock or the price for which it could be sold"

Partnership equity accounts generally do not distinguish between the initial investment that the partners made in the business and equity attributable to operations or financing and investment decisions made during the

life of the company. Partners' equity accounts include the initial investment in the company, profits and losses generated since inception, and
withdrawals that partners have taken.

Corporations will report the value of the initial investment shareholders
have made in the company. Stock is issued in units called shares, and each
share may be given a stated or par value. This value will be the same for
each unit of stock issued. If 1,000 shares of $1 stated or par value stock are
issued, then the value of the Capital Stock account will be $1,000. Funds
contributed in excess of the stated or par value are called Additional Paid-
in Capital. If the shareholders of the company initially invested $11,000
for the 1,000 shares, there would be $1,000 of Capital Stock (the "face
value") of the certificates) and $10,000 of Additional Paid-in Capital
(reflecting the value of the stock beyond its par or stated value). The value
of these accounts will not change (even if the value of the stock changes)
unless the corporation issues additional stock or redeems and cancels previously issued stock.

Equity that is the result of a corporation's activities is called Retained
Earnings. As the name indicates, these are business earnings (profits) that
the owners have elected to retain within the corporation. Business earnings (profits) that the shareholders receive as a return on investment are
called Dividends and reduce Retained Earnings.

Government and not-for-profit entities use fund balances (Net Assets) to
account for equity. Fund accounts may be classified as either restricted or
unrestricted. Restricted funds are amounts that may be used only for a
specific donor-designated purpose. For example, many not-for-profit
organizations will receive donations that are to be used for a certain cause.
The assets received would be put into a restricted fund and could only be
used for the specified purpose. Unrestricted funds are used to pay overhead expenses as well as for other purposes of the entity. Organizations

that utilize the fund method of accounting do not make distributions to the members as a return on equity; rather, they distribute funds to further their organizational purpose.

Before we leave the discussion of equity, it is important to note that the equity or book value does not represent the amount the owners should expect to receive if the business liquidates all of its assets and pays all its liabilities. Current accounting principles require that most assets are valued at the amount actually paid for the asset (also called historic cost) less accumulated depreciation or amortization, which does not necessarily represent current market value. Therefore, the book value of a company would only coincidentally equal the actual amount received by owners in the event of liquidation.

Statement Of Operations

The statement of operations is your scorecard for the period (month, quarter, year, etc.). It shows income generated and expenses incurred during a period in time (for example, a one-month or one-year period) and is the basic measurement of profitability and financial health. This statement is also called the income statement, revenue-and-expense statement, or profit-and-loss statement. There are several components reported in the statement of operations including revenues, cost of sales, gross margin, operating (or general and administrative) expenses, operating income, other income and expenses (including income taxes, if applicable), and net income. Together, these items give information about the company's success (or lack thereof) in generating a profit. A typical statement of operations will look something like this:

ABC Veterinary Services, Inc.
STATEMENT OF OPERATIONS
For the Year ended December 31, 200x

Net Revenues	$	x,xxx,xxx
Cost of Revenues		xxx,xxx
Gross Margin		xxx,xxx
Operating Expenses		xxx,xxx
Operating Income		xx,xxx
Other Income and Expenses		x,xxx
Income Before Income Taxes		xx,xxx
Income taxes		(x,xxx)
Net Income*	$	xx,xxx

Net income (or loss) for the period is carried from the Income Statement to the Owner's Equity section of the Balance Sheet, where it will appear as retained earnings, added to the balance from the previous period.

Revenues represent gross amounts earned in the normal course of business operations. They include fees charged for services performed and amounts from sale of goods. The total is then reduced by discounts, returns, and refunds given during the period to arrive at net revenue.

Cost of revenues represents the expenses directly attributable to the generation of revenues. They include the cost of merchandise sold, supplies utilized to generate revenues, wages and salaries paid to employees who directly produce income, and other costs that can be attributed specifically to the production of income.

The difference between net revenues and cost of revenues is called Gross Margin. This figure is significant because it represents funds available to pay overhead expenses, financing costs, and returns on owners' investments. The gross margin also shows how effectively income-producing resources were utilized during the period.

Operating expenses are the general and administrative costs that are necessary to run a business but do not directly generate revenues. These include things like management and clerical wages, telephone expense, cleaning costs, advertising, and similar expenses. Operating expenses represent a significant cost to a business, but only relate indirectly to the generation of revenues. For this reason, they are separated from cost of sales in the statement of operations.

Operating income is the difference between gross margin and operating expenses. It represents the income generated by a company in the normal course of business operations.

Items like interest expense, gain or loss recognized on the sale of long-term assets, interest income, and income taxes are considered Other Income and Expenses. These items are the result of financing and other non-operating decisions or events and therefore are separated from operating results.

Net income is the final result of a business's activities during the reporting period. This is the "bottom line" and represents the final amount that is theoretically available to owners as a return on their investment.

Debits And Credits Revisited

Before we continue our discussion of the basic financial statements, we will briefly return to the function of debits and credits. As discussed earlier, these terms simply indicate left and right, and the total of debit entries must equal the total of credit entries. However, the fact that debits equal credits does not mean that all accounting entries have been properly recorded. In general, debit entries increase the balance of asset and expense accounts and decrease the balance of income, liability, and equity accounts, while credit entries increase liability, equity, and income accounts and decrease asset and expense accounts. With certain limited exceptions, neither asset nor expense accounts should have a credit balance. Likewise, liability and revenue accounts should not have a debit balance. These unusual results generally indicate an error made in recording accounting entries and should be investigated.

Statement Of Cash Flows

The Statement of Cash Flows takes information reflected in the balance sheet and the statement of operations and presents it as the sources and uses of business cash. There are three sections to the statement of cash flows—net cash provided by or used in operating, investing, and financing activities. A typical cash flow statement will look like this:

ABC Veterinary Services, Inc.
STATEMENT OF CASH FLOWS
For the Year ended December 31, 200x

CASH FLOWS FROM OPERATING ACTIVITIES:		
Net Income	$	xx,xxx
Adjustments to Reconcile Net Income to		
Net Cash – Operating Activities:		
Depreciation		x,xxx
Decrease (Increase) in Operating Assets		
Accounts Receivable		xxx
Inventories		(x,xxx)
Increase (Decrease) in Operating Liabilities		
Accounts Payable		(xxx)
Total Adjustments		x,xxx
Net Cash – Operating Activities		xx,xxx
CASH FLOWS FROM INVESTING ACTIVITIES:		
Capital Expenditures		(xx,xxx)
Net Cash – Investing Activities		(xx,xxx)
CASH FLOWS FROM FINANCING ACTIVITIES:		
Short-term notes activity – net		(x,xxx)
Long-term borrowing		xx,xxx
Long-term repayments		(x,xxx)
Dividends paid		(x,xxx)
Net Cash – Financing Activities		xx,xxx
NET INCREASE (DECREASE) IN CASH		x,xxx
CASH – BEGINNING OF PERIOD		xx,xxx
CASH – END OF PERIOD	$	xx,xxx

Net cash from operating activities reconciles the net income for the period to the cash received or used by operations. This is accomplished by adjusting net income for expense items that do not require an actual cash outlay—such as depreciation expense (this will be discussed in more detail later). For example, if you own an expensive piece of equipment, it appears on the Balance Sheet as an asset. Each year you depreciate the asset and claim that amount as a business expense. However, since no cash changes hands (it's just a paper transaction), the depreciation expense doesn't really lower the cash account (but it is offset by lowering the recorded net book value of the equipment). Further adjustments reconcile revenues reported to cash received and reported costs and expenses to amounts actually paid. These adjustments are made by adding or subtracting changes in non-cash assets and liabilities including receivables, inventories, payables, and accruals.

Net cash from investing activities often represents a net cash outflow. Investing activities include the purchase of real estate or other fixed assets, the sale of fixed assets, loans made to other parties, and the purchase or sale of investments.

Financing activities are the amounts borrowed or paid on loans and distributions to owners.

The Statement of Cash Flows provides valuable information which helps management analyze the clinic's overall financial health. For example, cash may have decreased significantly during the year. This may be due to any number of things—significant fixed asset purchases, investments, debt repayments, dividends paid to owners, operating cash outflows exceeding inflows (business operations utilized more cash than they produced), or any combination of the above. The Statement of Cash Flows allows management to determine the source of the decrease in cash and plan corrective actions, if appropriate (a net cash outflow solely as a result of debt reduction most likely is not a critical situation; a net cash outflow as a result of operations may very well be).

Explanatory Note Disclosures

A complete set of financial statements includes notes to provide the user with sufficient information to understand the numbers presented and various financial items not apparent from looking at those numbers. They include a general description of a business's activities, market, goods or services, and accounting policies. Other disclosures include details of certain assets and liabilities, debt covenants, lease obligations, changes in equity, and any additional information necessary to better understand the company's financial statements. For example, if you decided to buy a magnetic resonance imaging unit for your hospital and financed the cost of $1.5 million, an explanatory note would be included to provide details of the financing arrangements—the lender, terms, collateral, covenants and restrictions, required principal payments for the next five years and in total, and other related information.

Supplemental Financial Information

Financial statements often include supplementary schedules that provide details of items included in the basic financial statements. Supplementary information may include revenue details, a breakdown of cost of revenues or operating expenses, and any other details useful for management decisions.

Other Comprehensive Basis Of Accounting (OCBOA)

The above discussions have dealt predominantly with GAAP-based financial statements and utilized the titles of financial statements prepared using generally accepted accounting principles. However, it is important to note that many clinics utilize one of the other comprehensive bases of accounting in their financial statements. In addition to different timing of recording transactions (please see the section about cash vs. accrual accounting for further discussion of this), financial statements prepared in OCBOA format will have different titles (the Balance Sheet may be called the Statement of Position, Statement of Assets, Liabilities, and Equity, or other similar title; the Statement of Operations may be called the Profit-and-Loss Statement, Statement of Revenues Collected and Expenses Paid, or other similar titles) and normally exclude the Statement of Cash Flows.

Capitalization And Depreciation Of Fixed Assets

Fixed assets are used in production, distribution, and to provide services for business enterprises. They include land, buildings, furniture and fixtures, machinery and equipment, and vehicles. Fixed assets have two primary characteristics—they are acquired for use in operations (and only indirectly generate revenues as they are not sold as a normal part of business), and they have relatively long lives. For example, a clinic's x-ray machine will be utilized in practice but there is no intention for the clinc to sell the x-ray machine as part of its operation. The x-ray machine will also be used over a period of years. Because it is used in operations and has a relatively long expected life, the x-ray machine is a fixed asset. In contrast, items that will be used within one year (such as radiographic film and developing fluid) would not be considered fixed assets because, while they are used in operations to generate revenues, they would not provide continuous utility over an extended time period.

It is because of the long-life nature of fixed assets that they are treated differently than "ordinary" business expenditures. These assets are capitalized (placed on the balance sheet as an asset) and depreciated over their expected useful lives (the period over which the asset is expected to be used in production of revenue). Depreciation is the term used to describe the systematic and rational method of "writing off" the cost of the asset as it is used. The amount to be depreciated over the equipment's stated useful lifespan is the purchase price of the equipment less any salvage value expected at the end of the depreciation period. For instance, if you bought a laser surgery unit for $45,000 that you anticipated would have a useful life of 5 years and at the end of those five years the unit could still be sold for $5,000, you would depreciate the $40,000 (initial price less salvage value) over 5 years.

Why not just pay for the asset and claim it as a business expense? We certainly do this for staplers and trash containers, even though we expect them to be around for more than a year. While that is true, proper profit measurement requires that the cost of an expensive piece of equipment be spread over the useful life of that equipment. However, staplers, trash containers, and similar items are insignificant in cost and are functionally more like operating supplies than long-lived equipment.

Generally, a company should maintain separate depreciation schedules for financial and income tax reporting. In addition, it must maintain one for alternative minimum tax purposes, and may need one or more to meet state income tax requirements. We will briefly discuss common methods of depreciating assets for the first two schedules, as alternative minimum taxation requirements are an issue best left to tax professionals, and state requirements vary.

The Internal Revenue Service has specific guidelines that give the depreciable lives of different types of assets and the methods that should be used to depreciate each asset. The Modified Accelerated Cost Recovery System (MACRS) currently in use allows businesses to deduct the cost of most fixed assets at an accelerated rate during the early years they are in service. This is beneficial for a company that has large cash outflows to purchase an asset because it provides income tax savings. However, the fixed nature of the MACRS depreciation lives and methods generally do not result in recording depreciation expense in a manner consistent with the actual use of the asset. For this reason, most companies should maintain a separate "book" or "internal" depreciation schedule.

You will recall that a depreciation system must be systematic and rational. While MACRS depreciation meets these guidelines, it does not necessarily reflect the actual amount of time an asset will be used or the manner in which it will be utilized. For example, an x-ray machine is seven-year

MACRS property. It would be depreciated over seven years, with a higher deduction during the first few years and lower depreciation in later years. However, the company that has purchased this machine may believe that it will, in fact, last ten years and be used approximately the same amount in each of those years. It is thus more realistic to depreciate this x-ray machine evenly over the ten years it will be in use for financial reporting purposes. In this case, the business will have more meaningful information about the asset in question if it maintains a depreciation schedule for financial reporting purposes in addition to the required MACRS schedule. This depreciation schedule will provide more accurate information about the cost associated with using the asset than the IRS-established system.

Methods Of Accounting—Cash Vs. Accrual

There are two basic methods commonly used to account for a business's transactions—the modified cash method and the accrual method.

Businesses that use the "cash method" of accounting actually use the modified cash method to account for their business activities. They capitalize and depreciate long-term assets and record short-term and long-term borrowings as liabilities. Revenues are recorded when payment is received, and expenses are recorded when payment is made. The modified cash method does not allow for accounts receivable, inventories, or accounts payable.

The accrual method of accounting is also called the GAAP method because it follows Generally Accepted Accounting Principles. These principles ensure that there is a consistent method of reporting the actual net income for a company. Using GAAP, revenues are reported when they are earned, whether or not payment has been received. For example, if Mrs. Smith takes her pet in for its annual vaccinations but doesn't pay before she leaves, a bill will still get generated and the amount of the bill would be included in revenues because the veterinarian has performed the services (earned the income) and does expect to get paid. Additionally, GAAP requires that expenses be recorded when incurred. Continuing with our example above, the cost of any vaccinations given, tests performed, any supplies used, and the veterinarian's time would be included in expenses. The costs associated with this transaction would not be included in a prior period's expenses (even if they were paid for then), and they would not be included in the following period's expenses (even if, for example, the veterinarian received his paycheck then). GAAP gives the most realistic picture of the activity that actually took place during a given time period—what revenue was earned during that time, and the expenses incurred while earning that revenue.

Many clinics will choose their method of bookkeeping and accounting based on real or perceived tax advantages. Specifically, many taxpayers report on a modified cash basis because they do not have to report revenues until funds are actually received—they are attempting to minimize taxable income. Is this the proper reason to select a method of maintaining the company's financial records? Let us consider for a moment the reasons we want financial information:

- To provide the bank and other creditors information necessary to obtain financing
- Current owners may wish to sell their portion of a business and will need to provide financial information to potential buyers
- To provide management and other decision-makers with the information necessary to make decisions and plan for the future

Selecting the accounting method that a clinic will use based only on income tax considerations will not be in its best interest as it is counterproductive both to the goal of painting a realistic picture for creditors and potential buyers and to the goal of having accurate and reliable information for making management decisions. For these reasons, GAAP-based accounting methods are generally preferred for a clinic.

During April of 2002, the IRS released *Revenue Procedure 2002-28* which allows most clinics to maintain accounting records and prepare financial reports using a method of accounting that is different from the one used to prepare income tax returns. This means that a business can now have the "best of both worlds"—realistic GAAP-based information for financial reporting purposes and modified cash-based information for income tax purposes.

Debt And Leasing Arrangements

Recalling our discussion of the balance sheet, we said that there are two ways to finance assets—the owners' equity (investment in the business) and debt. In this section we will explore various forms of debt more closely. Additionally, a clinic may acquire fixed assets for use under a lease arrangement.

There are two basic types of debt—short-term and long-term. Short-term debt consists primarily of accounts payable and funds advanced under lines of credit issued by a financial institution. Accounts payable are the amounts owed to vendors and suppliers under credit purchasing agreements. An example of this is that a clinic will purchase drugs and medical supplies from a supplier and place its purchase on account with that vendor. The clinic will then generally have 30 days from the receipt of its supplies to pay the amount owed. Often, vendors will offer an "early payment discount"—it will have terms like 2/10, net 30. This means that the clinic will receive a 2% discount if it pays the invoice within ten days and that otherwise the balance is due within 30 days with no discount after ten days. It is generally beneficial to take advantage of all such discounts since the effective annual interest rate of losing the discounts is 36%! A business may incur a finance charge if it does not pay its balance due within 30 days—a situation in which a well-managed business should never find itself.

A different type of short-tem financing is the line of credit. This is an arrangement with a bank or financial institution to provide operating cash on an as-needed basis. The line of credit is generally a one-year revolving note and requires monthly interest payments with all principal due at the termination of the agreement. The financing institution will review the creditor's financial information on at least an annual basis to determine whether or not to continue the line of credit arrangement. For example, We Love Animals Veterinary Clinic, Inc., may arrange a $10,000 line of credit with its bank on January 1. On January 15, the clinic realizes that it does not have enough cash available to pay its obligations (possibly because it extended free credit to clients and logged accounts receivable rather than cash) and makes a $2,000 draw on its line of credit. We Love Animals will now have a liability of $2,000 on its balance sheet. It still has $8,000 available to borrow if needed. During the remainder of January, We Love Animals collects most of its outstanding accounts receivable in addition to fairly good sales, so it is able to meet all its operating obligations and has additional cash left. They decide to repay part of their line of credit advance, and on February 1, write a check to the bank for $1,007.01—$7.01 in interest plus $1,000 of the principal owed. The clinic now has a $1,000 liability on its balance sheet and $9,000 of available funds. Because this is a revolving credit arrangement, We Love Animals is able to "re-borrow" any funds that it repays.

Short-term financing can be used to pay operating expenses. Some purchases, however, may require that a clinic arrange for longer-term financing on which it makes periodic payments. This type of debt is considered long-term because the final payment (maturity) date is more than one year from the date of the balance sheet. There are two basic types of long-term debt—installment loans and mortgages. Installment loans are generally used when a company wishes to purchase a piece of equipment or a vehicle and does not have sufficient cash to pay the entire purchase price. These loans have relatively short repayment periods (from two to five years is common). They are usually secured by the item purchased with the loan proceeds. The clinic normally makes monthly installment payments of a set amount that includes a portion of the principal owed plus interest.

The other common form of long-term debt is the mortgage. These loans are for the larger sums necessary to purchase real estate. They are for a longer term than installment loans (ten to twenty year terms are typical), and may be paid in equal installments over the term of the mortgage; or they may be paid in smaller installments for the first years of the loan followed by a large "balloon" payment of the remaining balance. Mortgages are secured by the real estate purchased using the loan funds.

Sometimes, a clinic finds it beneficial to lease rather than purchase needed equipment or facilities. This sometimes occurs with a new venture that is unable to secure financing to purchase its facilities. Leasing arrangements can benefit a business that requires expensive equipment that quickly becomes obsolete. A company may also enter lease arrangements as a trial to determine whether to purchase something or to fulfill short-term needs.

There are two basic arrangements—operating leases and capital leases. Many people are familiar with operating leases, as they are an alternate form of vehicle financing. Operating lease payments are calculated based on the difference between the original price of the item and the anticipated residual value at the termination of the lease, plus interest fees. At the end of the lease term, the lessee returns the item with no obligation to purchase. If the lessee wishes to purchase the leased item, the price is negotiated based on the fair market value of the item at that time. Short-term rental arrangements are also considered operating leases. All costs associated with operating leases are treated as expenses, and nothing is included on the balance sheet.

Capital leases are an alternate form of long-term financing. Payments are calculated in a manner more consistent with installment loans than operating leases. At the termination of the lease, the lessee will have the option to purchase the leased item at a bargain purchase price determined at the inception of the lease. When a company enters a capital lease, it will include the asset on its balance sheet and record a liability based on the total anticipated lease payments. The asset is depreciated over its useful life. Lease payments are not treated as an operating expense; rather, they are considered a reduction in debt with only the interest portion of each payment being expensed.

Ratios And Other Financial Measures

A business will often find it useful to compare its financial information with various measures (its own prior-year information, other businesses in the same industry, or industry benchmarks). However, many factors like sales volume differences from year-to-year or company-to-company will make raw financial data difficult to compare. For this reason, there are ratios and measures that take this data and convert it to comparable figures. Following is a brief discussion of some of these measures, what information they provide, and the formulas used to calculate them.

Balance Sheet Measures

Current ratio is the number of times short-term assets cover short-term liabilities. This measure of liquidity shows the company's ability to pay its current liabilities using current assets. The formula is:

$$\frac{\text{current assets}}{\text{current liabilities}}$$

Debt-to-Equity ratio shows relative use of borrowed funds compared to equity financing. This measure shows a comparison of sources of assets. The formula is:

$$\frac{\text{total liabilities}}{\text{total equity}}$$

Number of days' revenues in receivables shows the number of days that accounts receivable are outstanding. This number indicates the business's success in collecting its sales. The formula is:

$$\frac{\text{accounts receivable}}{\text{revenue per day}}$$

The Number of days' merchandise cost in inventory is the length of time product is held as inventory. It can indicate a company's success in maintaining suitable levels of inventory. The formula for calculating the number of days' sales in inventory is:

$$\frac{\text{inventory}}{\text{cost of inventory sold per day}}$$

Operations Measures

<u>Profit margin on revenues</u> is a measure of profitability and an indicator of efficiency. It shows the "bottom line" profit (net income) as a percentage of net revenues. The formula is:

$$\frac{\text{Net income}}{\text{Net revenues}} \times 100$$

<u>Number of times interest earned</u> relates earnings before interest and income taxes to interest expense. This is one measure of a business's ability to pay its debt. The formula is:

$$\frac{\text{Net income before interest and income taxes}}{\text{Interest}}$$

<u>Ratio of net revenues to assets</u> measures the effectiveness of the asset base in producing revenue. It shows the amount of revenue generated per dollar of assets owned. The formula is:

$$\frac{\text{Net revenues}}{\text{Total assets}}$$

<u>Rate of return (ROR) on total assets</u> measures the effectiveness of the company's assets in producing net income. This indicates a business's ability to utilize its assets to produce revenue and pay expenses. The formula is:

$$\frac{\text{Net income}}{\text{Total assets}} \times 100$$

<u>Rate of return on equity</u> measures a company's return on equity. It is an indication of how well the owners' investment is performing. The formula is:

$$\frac{\underline{\text{Net income}} \times 100}{\text{Total equity}}$$

<u>Depreciation expense as a percent of net property and equipment</u> indicates reasonableness and consistency of depreciation expense over time. It can be used to ensure that lives and methods of calculating depreciation are applied consistently to fixed assets. The formula is:

$$\frac{\underline{\text{Depreciation expense}} \times 100}{\text{Net fixed assets}}$$

<u>Repairs and maintenance as a percent of net property and equipment</u> indicates the reasonableness of repairs expense and helps to identify misclassifications between capital expenditures and expenses. The formula is:

$$\frac{\underline{\text{Repairs expense}} \times 100}{\text{Net fixed assets}}$$

Cost Allocation And Management Accounting

Whether direct or indirect, the goal of every business is to make money. Even non-profits need to make "profits" if they are going to continue to provide services. In order to make profits, it is necessary for a company to determine the actual costs it incurs in generating each revenue stream. Fortunately, as long as it maintains good accounting records, a company has available all the information necessary to generate this information.

There are different methods of classifying costs. Two of the more common ones are fixed/variable and direct/indirect. Fixed costs are the expenses a business will incur regardless of revenues generated. Some examples are rent, depreciation, fixed salaries, insurance, and interest on existing obligations. Variable costs, as the name implies, will vary based on revenue streams. These include overtime and temporary worker compensation, the direct cost of items sold, supplies, and production-based bonuses. There are costs that are both fixed and variable. An example that most people are familiar with is related to telephone expenses. Each telephone line will have a monthly base charge that will not change no matter how much or little the telephone is used (the fixed component). There are then additional fees for long distance calls based on the length and number of calls (the variable component). Many expenses behave similarly, and the fixed and variable components of these costs should be separated.

The fixed/variable cost separation is used in breakeven analysis, a method of determining the revenue necessary to pay all expenses. Fixed and variable costs must also be determined for implementing fair allocation of expenses. For example, in a specialty hospital that includes a dermatologist, a surgeon and an ophthalmologist, how would you allocate the expenses of radiology?—the dermatologist and ophthalmologist won't stand for an equal three-way split, although the surgeon would welcome it. Consider even the leased office photocopier. It might be fairest to split the base lease payment equally (the fixed expense) to have the copier available, but then charge the departments a variable expense depending on the number of copies made during a period. Or it might be fairer to split the fixed cost on the basis of number of cases seen, or the square footage of each department, or a variety of other "drivers" that may be considered relevant for cost allocation. As more and more "cooperative" practices are formed, proper cost allocation becomes an even more critical element in effective business management.

Costs may also be divided into direct and indirect expenses. Direct expenses are similar to cost of revenues—they are the expenses that can be directly attributed to generating revenue. Indirect expenses are like operating expenses—necessary costs incurred that do not directly generate revenue. However, we are now allocating the costs to a specific portion of our revenue stream. Therefore, each expense should be attributed to the revenue it generated. For example, the direct expenses attributable to a surgery would include the cost of anesthesia (including any needles, syringes, catheters, tubes, or other items used), surgical sponges, blades, suture material, drapes, gloves, the technician's or anesthesiologist's and the veterinarian's wages and benefits (based on average surgery time plus recheck and suture removal time), pain medication and antibiotics administered, a portion of total rent (or interest and depreciation) and building maintenance attributable to the surgical suite based on average surgery time and to the wards based on average recovery time, depreciation and maintenance of surgical equipment, utilities used during surgery, and any other costs that can be directly attributed to the performance of the surgery. Additionally, there are indirect costs associated with the performance of the surgery. These would include things like a portion of the receptionist's wages (scheduling the appointment, checking the patient in, release procedures, follow-up telephone calls, etc.), waiting room expenses, telephone expense, computer use, office supplies, advertising, parking lot maintenance—any necessary expense that does not directly generate fees but is critical to the clinic's ability to perform the surgery.

It is possible to estimate the cost associated with most direct expenses. In our example above, for example, one can calculate the cost of the supplies used (one surgical blade may cost $.25, a drape may cost $1.00, etc.) fairly easily. The cost of salaries plus benefits can be based on the average amount of time spent performing a surgery as a percentage of time spent working during a pay period. Rent and other facilities expense may be calculated based on both the square footage of the surgical suite and recovery facilities (to arrive at a per-day expense) and on the time spent performing the surgery (45 minutes per surgery out of a 600 minute working day). Equipment depreciation and maintenance costs may be based on the amount of time the equipment is used for the surgery compared to the estimated amount of time the equipment is expected to be utilized during the year. In short, it is possible to come up with a reasonable estimate of the direct costs associated with the performance of a surgery. As long as the measure is objective—the time that the equipment is used or square footage of the surgical suite—one should be able to arrive at a reasonable estimate of the actual costs associated with generating a revenue stream (performing an surgery, in our example).

Allocating indirect (overhead) costs to a specific revenue stream is more difficult. One common method of doing this is to charge a percentage of total overhead to each revenue unit based on an objective measure like the amount of time spent per surgery each month as a percentage of the total amount of time the clinic was operating.

Obviously, cost allocation is a time-consuming exercise. However, it provides invaluable information to the management of an operation. For example, we may determine that the total cost of performing one typical surgery is $178.82. However, the fee to perform the surgery may currently be $175. Assuming that 2,000 surgeries are performed annually, we are currently losing $7,640 per year doing this procedure. If we raise the price of a surgery to $185 (holding all expenses at the same level), those same surgeries will now generate profits of $12,360—a much more favorable situation. This is still a poor return for the expertise provided, but that's the subject of a whole different chapter.

MONEY MATTERS

Lowell Ackerman DVM DACVD MBA MPA

Dr. Lowell Ackerman is a Diplomate of the American College of Veterinary Dermatology and in addition holds an MBA from the University of Phoenix and an MPA from Harvard University. He is involved in clinical practice as a clinical assistant professor at Tufts University School of Veterinary Medicine as well as helping to develop the business skills curriculum there. In addition, Dr. Ackerman is affiliated with Veterinary Healthcare Consultants, primarily dealing with practice administration and management issues. Dr. Ackerman is the author/co-author of 74 books to date and numerous book chapters and articles. He lectures extensively, on an international basis.

Time Value of Money

The time value of money is a simple but important concept that presupposes that getting money in the future is not as good as getting that money now. When a client gets $1,000 worth of medical work done but, because of financial constraints, doesn't manage to pay the bill for an entire year, the costs may be greater than you realize. Not only did you lose the interest on that money, but even the buying power of that money has decreased due to inflation. If you could have used that money to buy equipment or prescription items that would have returned 20% profit in that period, that was also lost. Instead, you bought a new microscope on a line of credit (costing you 9% for the year), you spent time tracking your accounts receivable and sending invoices, and possibly worst of all from a

148

business perspective, you fronted the money for a medical procedure and then accepted all risks for getting paid for it. You may have also set a dangerous precedent in your practice that you are prepared to finance health care for pets, and perhaps even without a credit application. This is a wake-up call. Veterinarians should be engaged in the practice of veterinary medicine. Veterinary practices are not banks. They are not insurance companies. Keep in mind that there are alternatives for credit-worthy clients, such as credit cards, loans, pet insurance, CareCredit, etc.). In many areas, there are also alternatives for truly indigent pet owners to get charitable aid. As a medical professional, it is best to keep the relationship doctor-client rather than bank-debtor.

A dollar today is worth more than a dollar tomorrow

The buying power of the dollar typically declines with time. Given the choice between receiving a dollar now and a dollar a year from now, the choice should be clear. If you have a dollar today, you can invest it or spend it today. A year from now, the dollar will typically purchase less than it will today. If we invest the dollar today, in a year it will have produced interest or profit that hopefully will have greater value than a dollar received a year from now.

If we are going to forsake a dollar today, we had better be compensated more than that in future gains. For example, let's say you just won a lottery. Congratulations! As the prizewinner, would you rather have $750,000 now, or $800,000 a year from now? Ignoring any tax implications, you still need some additional information to make an informed decision. Your opportunity cost depends on what you are going to do with the money and your potential rate of return. The historic rate of return on stock market investments is just over 10% per year. If you could invest with a rate of return of 10% your *future value* in one year would be $750,000 +10% or $825,000. In that case, it's better to take the money now and invest it! If the stock market is in the doldrums and you suspect that a bond or certificate of deposit will give you the best return, say 6%, then your future value would be $750,000 + 6% or $795,000. In this case, it's better to take the $800,000 a year from now. Therefore, the rate of return, r, really depends on opportunity costs (i.e., the next best option available to you).

Most financial decisions are based on this time value of money, from the mortgage on your home, to a car lease, to an insurance policy. So, to compare payouts, one must either convert all returns to present values or to future ones. That is the only fair way to compare.

Present and future values can be easily calculated, given the rate of return (r), but standardized tables can also be used to give close approximations. We will do the mathematics here to illustrate, but in practice, the tables and/or computer software make the process quite easy.

When calculating present and future values, the toughest number to come up with may be the expected rate of return. The rate of return should reflect a reasonable return in the profession. The historic return in the stock market is just over 10%. Inflation has typically been around 3%, although it has dipped to about 1.5% in the recent past. For most veterinary practices, a decent rate of return to plan for is probably 12-15%; in extremely well managed practices, the rate of return might be 18-20%. So, the rate of return mirrors your opportunity cost (i.e., if you weren't using the money for the planned activity, what is the next best return you anticipate).

Future Value (FV) is just the Present Value (PV) *compounded* at the stated rate of return. So,

$1,000 compounded annually at 6% over 2 years
= $1,000 x 1.06^2 = $1,123

The formula to calculate Future Value is:
$FV = PV \times (1 + r)^t$

where,
FV = Future Value
PV = Present Value
r = Rate of Return (e.g., 6% = 0.06)
t = time

Present Value (PV) is just the Future Value *discounted* at the stated rate of return. So,

$1,123 two years from now, at 6% rate of return, today would be worth:
$1,123 / 1.06^2 = $1,000

The formula to calculate Present Value is:
$PV = FV/ (1 + r)^t$

You might be surprised at how often you could use the value of money in practice. Imagine that you are at a veterinary conference and drawn to the laser surgery units. One vendor has a product that costs $30,000 and shows you a chart illustrating how you could conservatively make $60,000 from the unit within 5 years. Is this a quick way to make a profit of $30,000?

Even in this simple example, there is still a need for more facts before you can make a sensible decision. You are informed that the maintenance for the unit will cost approximately $2,000 per year. The vendor has also offered to buy back the unit in 5 years for $500 salvage (you'll want to upgrade by then anyway). Sound good so far?

The beauty of the arrangement is that you do not need to attract any new business on which to use the laser. Based on the laser causing less pain and less tissue trauma, you believe that clients will elect the use of the laser for scheduled procedures, paying a premium for that use, without additional staffing expenses or other costs to the practice. In essence, these are procedures that you would do anyway, but you can collect a premium for using the laser in a percentage of cases. You anticipate that you should be able to convert 2 procedures a week in year one (at a $50 premium per procedure), 3 procedures weekly in year two (at a per procedure premium of $55), 4 procedures weekly in year three (at a premium of $60), 5 procedures weekly in year four (at a premium of $65), and 6 procedures weekly in year five (at a premium of $70). You plan to work 50 weeks per year (2 weeks vacation). Are you rich yet?

The piece of information that you are still missing is the opportunity cost, so you can determine your anticipated rate of return. If you didn't spend $30,000 on the laser, what would you be doing with the money? If you'd invest in another hospital profit center, you'd like your rate of return to be at least 12%. If you'd invest in a CD, your rate of return might be 5%. If this purchase is the moneymaker you hope it to be, you think the return might be in excess of 20%!

To calculate your break-even costs, you need to know your fixed and variable expenses and the unit selling price.

$$\text{Break-even quantity} = \frac{\text{Fixed Cost}}{\text{Unit Selling Price}-\text{Unit Variable Cost}}$$

Since this is an add-on activity, you determine that there is no real variable expense. You have only fixed expenses of the finance cost for the unit and the $2,000 annually for maintenance. In reality, there would be variable expenses, such that maintenance costs and replacement costs would vary with client numbers, but to keep things simple, we're going to treat everything as a fixed cost.

One way to finance the laser is with a bank loan. If you borrowed $30,000 at 9%, over 5 years you will pay back 30K x 1.09^5 or $46,000, including $16,000 in interest. If you paid for the unit with a check, you would probably have foregone a similar amount in lost investment earnings. If those payments were spread evenly over those five years, the annual payment would be $46,000/5 or $9,200 per year. Together with the maintenance fee, if you hoped to break even in year 1, you would need to earn $9,200 + $2,000 = $11,200. How would you do that with your planned 100 procedures a year (i.e., 2 per week for 50 weeks)? Not by charging a premium of $50. If you wanted to break even with 100 procedures, the charge would need to be $112, not $50. Alternatively, if you were charging $50, you should plan on doing 224 procedures each year or 4.5 procedures each week to break even. If you don't need to break even from the start, the project is easier to defend and gives you more time to become profitable. Since we anticipate that the unit's lifespan is five years, and we're financing it for five years, it makes sense to determine whether it will have been profitable over a 5-year time span.

How do we make the determination of whether or not this is a money making deal? We calculate the present value of future cash flows with prospective discount rates, and see if revenues are greater than expenses. If the final number is positive, it means that we have more than met the rate of return stipulated. Let's take a closer look.

Year	Revenue	Expense	Total	PV@20%	PV@12%
0	$0	-$30,000	-$30,000	-$30,000	-$30,000
1	$5,000	-$2,000	$3,000	$2,500	$2,679
2	$8,250	-$2,000	$6,250	$4,340	$4,982
3	$12,000	-$2,000	$10,000	$5,787	$7,118
4	$16,250	-$2,000	$14,250	$6,872	$9,056
5	$21,500	-$2,000	$19,500	$7,837	$11,065
Totals	$63,000	-$40,000	$23,000	-$2,664	$4,900

At the beginning, we are going to write a check for $30,000 before we have made any revenue at all. So, at this point we are $30,000 in debt. At the end of the first year, we have $5,000 in revenue but had to pay $2,000 in maintenance fees, so we had a net positive income of $3,000. At our discount rate of 20% (if this were a huge profit maker), this would be equivalent to having $2,500 today (present value). That is, if you had $2,500 today and could get a rate of return of 20%, you would have $3,000 at the end of a year. At a 12% rate of return, the present value would be $2,679. We repeat this for each year, totaling our revenues, expenses and present values.

In year 5, we make $21,000 in revenues as well as an additional $500 from the distributor as salvage value for buying back the 5-year-old equipment. We will have made a total of $63,000 in revenues over the five years and had $40,000 in expenses. Whether the "net" of $23,000 is good or not depends on our desired rate of return. As we can see from the chart, the present value is negative given a discount rate of 20%, implying that the venture did not achieve this rate of return. However, the present value is positive given the discount rate of 12%, implying that the venture exceeded this rate of return. You can calculate the actual Internal Rate of Return (IRR) with a financial calculator or a spreadsheet program in you need more detail for your analysis. So, was it a good investment? It was if you are happy with a rate of return better than 12%, but it didn't fare so well if you were hoping that it would make you more than a 20% annual rate of return. You decide!

Veterinary Fees

Determining profit from veterinary sales can seem bewildering to the uninitiated. After all, if you buy a product for $10 and sell it for $15, didn't you just make $5 in profit? The pricing model that has been used by most veterinarians in the past is to adopt the pricing model of the last hospital in which they worked. All too often, however, that pricing model failed to reflect the true costs of operating a business.

In the retail marketplace, price is taken very seriously. When all products are considered identical (e.g., farm produce), these products become commodities and sellers become "price takers". If someone has feedlot cattle, there isn't much that can be done to "differentiate" their product from that produced on the next farm. When they go to market, everyone gets paid pretty much the same going rate. In small animal practice, much goes into adding value to services (hospital appearance, expertise of veterinarians, attention by staff, dedication to service, etc.) and so pricing should most reflect actual costs and profits.

For veterinarians and other service providers that are price-setters rather than price-takers, lessons from the retail marketplace are a great place to start. And the very first place to start is to look at the real costs involved with selling a product, or offering a service. The real profit to be made is in services, although veterinarians are increasingly banking on revenues from product sales. In 1992, medical services accounted for 82% of veterinary revenues, with product sales providing 18%. By 1999, revenues from medical services dropped to 75%, while product sales increased to 25%. Unfortunately, product sales can disappear with any real competition (e.g., Internet, pet retail superstores, etc.) and are even very sensitive to competition from other veterinary clinics. Veterinarians had a windfall when companies openly promoted flea control and heartworm products directly to consumers that were only available through veterinarians. What do you think would happen to that revenue stream if those same or similar products started to become available over the Internet or in pet stores at a fraction of the price charged by veterinarians? It's happening today. The services that veterinarians perform allow them to be price-setters. The products that veterinarians sell are commodities, the profits from which could disappear in a heartbeat if the marketplace changed.

Perhaps it is best to start to look at fees by what those fees accomplish within a practice

Where Fees Go

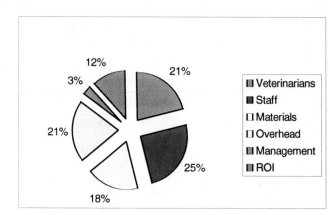

Veterinarians	21%
Staff	25%
Materials	18%
Overhead	21%
Management	3%
ROI	12%

It is sometimes difficult to remember that products and services actually cost significantly more than the materials themselves. The receptionists' pay must be factored in to the goods and service costs. So must the utilities' bills, the cost of the hospital administrator, bills from the accountant, insurance premiums, telephone bills, alarm system monitoring and many other expenses. And don't forget the veterinarians and technicians! In fact, approximately one-quarter of all revenues from goods and services go to pay staff in the average practice, even more than to veterinarians. Paying all hospital workers, veterinarians, technicians, assistants, kennel attendants, and management staff takes about 50 cents out of every revenue dollar. That doesn't account yet for the cost of keeping the hospital open, with rent and utilities and the like, having inventory on the shelves, or making a profit for the hospital owners.

The return on investment (ROI) of 12% is a decent target for a fairly well managed practice, but ROI may be almost non-existent in some practices across the country. All too many veterinarians simply invest money to provide a place for themselves to work, often making less than they would if they had put their money into a bank, money market account or Certificate of Deposit, rather than a veterinary hospital.

Few practices are complete price-setters, immune to the pressures of the marketplace. In general, fees for goods and services do vary with:

- Location and client base
- Fees of competitors
- Actual costs
- Who's performing the service (specialist versus general practitioner
- Perceived value by clients
- Industry "Standards?"

How Fees are Currently Set

Most fees in veterinary hospitals are only very loosely cost-based. Most products on the shelf are priced at 2-3 times cost (a markup of 100-200%). Even at this figure, some products at this markup make lots of money, and some are relative money losers.

Most services are priced on what the market will bear. Unfortunately, this is rarely based on true costs, and most derived from competitive pressure or questionable benchmarks. For example, if a client paid $200 for an ovariohysterectomy, this is the benchmark on which they tend to judge all other surgeries and procedures. How would you expect such clients to react to an $800 charge for an exploratory laparotomy?

Another approach, also involving benchmarking, is evident in the 1999 Well-Managed Practice Study by Wutchiett & Associates. They observed that in the well-managed practices that they studied, many service fees could be represented as multiples of the examination fee. The notion is that most veterinarians establish examination fees that are competitively priced within their communities and that other services could be priced relative to this examination fee. For example, the hourly surgical fee might be 8.32 times the examination fee, and a two-radiograph series might be 2.76 times the examination fee. The same study suggested that the Average Transaction Charge (ATC) for a visit should be approximately 3—3.4 times the Physical Examination fee. Accordingly, if the Physical Examination fee is set at $35, then the Average Transaction Charge for visits should be in the range of $105—$119. According to the 2002 Well-Managed Practice Study, the ATC averages $111 per doctor and non-doctor transactions per client is approximately $40.

Examples of Examination Fee-based Charges*
Recheck exam = PE x 0.85
Surgery charge/hr = PE x 8.32
Anesthesia/hr = PE x 4.64
Radiography (x2) = PE x 2.76
Ovariohysterectomy = PE x 4.29
Ultrasonography = PE x 5.71

* From 1999 Well-Managed Practice Study by Wutchiett & Associates

Pricing

The basic pricing formula that is at work in most retail establishments is:

$$\text{Sales price} = \text{Fixed costs} + \text{Variable costs} + \text{Profit}$$

Another way of looking at the situation is that the final price must reflect all of the specific contributing expenses, such as:

$$\text{Sales price} = \text{Overhead} + \text{Direct Labor} + \text{Materials} + \text{Profit} +/-$$
$$\text{Commissions}$$

Keeping these formulas in mind is important, because veterinary hospitals can't provide services for long that fail to provide a return on investment (Profit). They just become a drain on other hospital operations, and hold the hospital back from paying decent wages, hiring desirable staff, expanding services, and investing in new equipment and facilities.

The purpose of fees is to:

- Cover fair labor costs
- Cover fair materials costs

- Cover overhead costs
- Provide adequate return on investment

Operating a veterinary hospital is an expensive undertaking. On the human side, most general practitioners function with only examination rooms and staff, which they leverage to see as many patients as possible with minimal overhead and materials charges. They don't hospitalize, they don't run the majority of their own laboratory work, they don't take radiographs, and often they don't even collect blood samples. Most veterinary hospitals, on the other hand, have surgeries, radiology departments, laboratories, kennels, rooms for special procedures, and lots of expensive gadgets.

When we look at the above list of reasons for charging fees, veterinarians tend to balance out their higher overhead with lower wages and poor return on investment. This isn't a fair exchange. Even when veterinarians are prepared to charge less for services and compensate themselves less than comparably trained professionals, the results of low fees are that technicians, assistants, receptionists and kennel attendants are also forced to accept low wages for the privilege of working in a veterinary hospital. Without fair fees and fair compensation, staff turnover becomes an issue and the quality of medical care suffers.

Cost-based Pricing

There are direct and indirect costs associated with any business transaction. In general, when we evaluate services, we tend to examine three contributors to cost: overhead, direct labor hours, and materials. For products, we examine direct and indirect costs of product handling and sales. For all sales, there are some fixed and some variable costs that must be factored into the final price.

Let's look at services first. Services aren't performed in a vacuum. There is a need for a facility in which to operate, complete with staff, equipment, and utilities. Overhead is a term used to describe the costs inherent in operating the practice even if no clients come in the door. One still needs to pay rent, have electricity on, receptionists in the front office, functional telephones, supplies and equipment at the ready, and many other things to which costs are attached. This is the "fixed cost" of doing business, and must be spread across all charges generated by the practice.

Variable costs are those costs incurred only when services are rendered. For example, there is a base telephone rate (fixed cost) even if no calls are made. When long-distance calls or other user functions are utilized, additional expenses are generated, as a function of utilizing the service. Suture material is only re-ordered as a consequence of being used up in the performance of surgical procedures. It is a variable cost to the hospital, proportional to the number of surgeries performed.

Profit Centers

The best way of matching hospital costs to overhead is to develop profit centers within the hospital to which these costs can be allocated. For example, rent and utilities can probably be allocated to different profit centers based on their area representation within the hospital. However, it is important to allocate all of these expenses only across centers that can earn revenue. For example, in a hospital of 2,000 square feet, it is not useful to calculate a per-square-foot charge equally across the hospital. How is the reception area to pay its portion of the overhead? Or office and closet space? If 400 square feet of space in the hospital is non-revenue generating, then the overhead charge needs to be divided among the 1,600 square feet (2,000 minus 400) that can generate revenue. For example, if in this hospital rent, utilities and other general expenses (including reception, telephones, security, etc.) were $4,800 a month ($57,600 per year) and we wanted to allocate a fair portion of this expense to the radiology profit center, we could do so. If radiology occupied 200 square feet in the hospital, then their fair share of rent and utilities (etc.) would be 200/1,600 or 12.5% of the total ($7,200 for the year). Note that overhead was not allocated to the exact proportion of the radiology department to the entire hospital (200/2000 or 10%), but only to the proportion of the hospital capable of generating revenues. To that would be added the costs of the x-ray machine (e.g., the annual lease payment and other relevant charges directly attributed to radiology). Dividing this total by the anticipated number of radiographs to be taken provides an overhead figure on a unit basis—the cost of having radiology available in the practice to do the number of radiographs anticipated.

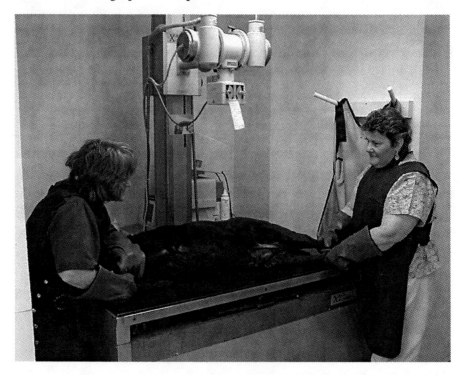

Overhead, of course, is not the only expense to be considered. Radiographs don't take themselves. Technicians are needed not only to take the radiographs, but to position and sometimes restrain the patient and potentially also to develop the films. Should we just charge the technician's time based on hourly wage? Unfortunately, this won't capture all of the expense of having staff available since technicians likely have a lot of related jobs that aren't directly billable (e.g., re-taking films, filing films, ordering radiology supplies, etc.). Once again, it is best to estimate the total time that technicians are spending doing radiology-related activities and then allocate that proportion of total technician expenses (including salaries, benefits, continuing education, uniforms, etc.). For example, if a hospital has two technicians with total technician compensation of $60,000 (including all benefits) and the technicians spend 15% of their time in radiology, then radiology should be allocated $9,000 yearly (15% of $60,000) for technician contribution. This amount spread over the anticipated number of films gives a unit cost for labor. If a veterinarian or another technician is called in to assist, that should be an additional charge in providing the service.

Next, materials need to be accounted for. There is going to be a cost for films and the expense for chemicals and markers also needs to be spread across the number of films anticipated.

Then, profit needs to be factored into the equation. In addition, if associates are compensated on a production basis, that also needs to be considered.

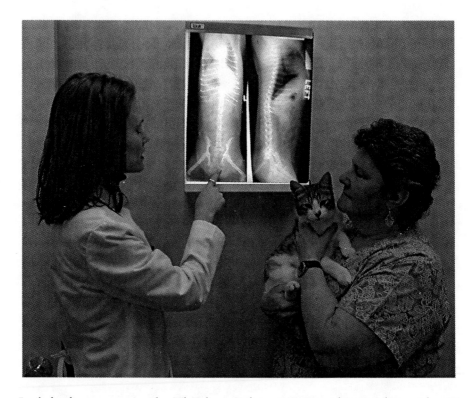

Let's look at an example. This hospital anticipates taking radiographs on 300 patients a year, averaging two films per patient or 600 films per year. The rent and utilities allocated to radiology were $7,200 per year, and the lease on the x-ray machine (with maintenance) was $5,600 per year, so total overhead was $12,800. Technician support was $9,000 for the year and materials (film, chemicals, etc.) were $2,400. Therefore, the total costs attributed to the radiology services were $24,200 and if 600 films were taken, that would amount to $40.33 per film ($24,200/600) or $80.66 per 2-view series. But, wait… we still haven't made any profit! If we would like to make a profit of 15% on radiology, then we would need to charge the following:

C = $80.66 + 0.15C
Solving for C,
0.85C = $80.66
C = $94.89

Therefore, to generate a 15% profit on radiology it would be necessary to charge about $95 for a two-view radiographic series in this hospital.

But, wait… what if our contract with associate veterinarians specified that they are entitled to a 25% commission on services generated, including radiography? In this case, we would not only need to factor in the 15% profit, but a 25% commission as well (40% total). So,

C = $80.66 + 0.40C
Solving for C,
0.6C = $80.66
C = $134.43

In this instance, one would need to charge clients $134.43 for a 2-view radiographic series to cover costs, make a 15% profit and pay an associate a 25% commission. With 300 patients a year, this would yield $40,329 in revenues, with $24,200 in expenses, $10,082.25 in commissions (25%) and a final profit of $6,046.75 (15%)

If you haven't seen this type of algebraic equation before, where the final charge equals the total costs plus a proportion of the final charge, note that this is not the same as a "markup". The goal of this equation is to claim a fixed percentage of the final price. When you mark up a charge, you do so on the initial amount, not the final amount. For example, imagine that we want a 25% profit on the final price of a service that costs us $100. If we mark the price up by 25%, the total is $125. However, 25% of $125 is not $25; it is $31.25. In this instance, we didn't make a profit of 25% of the final price. Our profit was only $25 on a sale of $125, which is only 20%. We just lost 5% of our intended profit!

To claim a fixed percentage of the final charge, C in this example, the equation would need to be set up as:

C = $100 + 0.25C
Solving for C,
0.75C = $100
C = $133.33

Now, to claim 25% profit "off the top" will give $33.33 (i.e., 25% of $133.33), leaving $100 (i.e., $133.33—$33.33) to pay for the costs.

Note that if we need to pay an associate a commission on the sale that the final price increases dramatically more than just the price of the commission. So, if we need to pay a 25% commission as well as make 25% profit (total 50%) and costs are still $100, then the equation needs to be:

C = $100 + 0.5C
0.5C = $100
C = $200

Now, the final price is $200 of which 25% ($50) goes to pay commission, 25% ($50) is profit and $100 is left to pay the bills. Note also that $33.33 was enough to give us a 25% profit margin before we had to pay commission, but that rose to $50 to give the same 25% profit margin once we figured in commission. In addition, in order to accommodate 25% for profit and 25% for commission, the bill to the client had to be increased by 100%!

Establishing profit centers in a hospital makes it a relatively easy exercise to allocate costs. It may be time-consuming to gather all the requisite numbers, but it is invaluable for looking at services provided and determining how profitable they really are.

In this example, we can also use the information to look at potential trends. Perhaps we are contemplating a marketing campaign that involves developing a pamphlet to send to owners of geriatric patients advising a chest radiographic series to help evaluate cardiopulmonary function. The cost of pamphlet development, printing and mailing is $2,250. You anticipate that it might increase radiographic revenues by 20% (radiographing 360 patients a year rather than 300) and, if it does, technician time dedicated to radiology will increase from 15% to 18% and materials charges will increase by 20%. Should you do the mailing?

Your overhead doesn't increase ($12,800), but your technician expense will increase to $10,800 for the year (18% of $60,000). Let's assume that materials increase by 20% to $2,880 and, of course, we need to add the cost of the mailing ($2,250). So, the total costs were $28,730. If our estimates were correct, and we kept our charges the same ($134.43 for a 2-view series), then revenues might be $48,394.80 (360 x $134.43) with expenses of $28,730 and commission of 25% to the associate ($12,098.70), with a net profit of $7,566.10, representing a profit of 15.6%. If the predictions are correct, the mailing sounds like a good idea.

General Activity Centers

While profit center analysis is definitely the proper way to approach activity-based costing, there are times when what is needed is just a time-based formulaic approach to overhead calculation. After all, how would you calculate overhead for placing a catheter, or performing a fecal, or doing a bandage change?

As a rough guide to calculating overhead, Mark Opperman in the Art of Veterinary Practice Management (Veterinary Medicine Practicing Group, 1999) recommends taking all expenses in the hospital except for doctors' wages and materials/drug costs and dividing them by the total number of doctors' hours for the same period. This gives the overhead per hour; dividing by 60 provides the overhead per minute. In most practices, overhead per minute is in the range of $1.50-$2.00, according to Opperman.

We can probably get closer to the true cost of overhead by removing some other costs in the equation, and by stripping out labor costs not just of veterinarians, but any employee who provides services that can be recovered in the direct labor contribution to services. We can also remove costs that are clearly recovered within profit centers, such as lease payments on an x-ray machine, or a laser surgery unit. What we are then left with are the true overhead costs to be shared across all services in the hospital (e.g., rent, utilities, security, telephones, reception, etc.) without including expenses that are covered in other overhead categories (e.g., radiology profit center, surgery profit center, etc.).

To spread these costs only across doctors' hours neglects the real revenue contributions made by technicians and assistants. Since we have stripped the salaries of veterinarians, technicians and assistants out of overhead, we'll spread the overhead charges out over the contributions of all of these professionals and paraprofessionals. Since veterinarians, technicians and assistants are paid different wages, it makes sense to consolidate the work time into standardized units, such as veterinary time equivalents (VTE). As an example, in an individual practice it might be the norm for average technician salaries to be one-third of an average veterinary salary. Perhaps assistants receive pay approximately one-quarter of that of the typical practice veterinarian. To calculate the total VTE for a period, just add up the total number of hours worked by doctors (multiplied by one), the hours worked by technicians (multiplied by 0.33) and the hours worked by assistants (multiplied by 0.25).

There is one other factor that needs to be considered in spreading over-head over the hours that veterinarians, technicians and assistants are *available* in the veterinary practice. The VTE calculated would be fine if all of those hours were considered billable, but the fact is that there are many hours in the day when the actions of veterinarians, technicians and assistants are not directly billable to any client. By some estimates, this can account for 50% of a veterinarian's time at a hospital. The same is true for technicians and assistants, who may be cleaning cages, doing laundry, or taking longer than anticipated doing a procedure (e.g., venipuncture fee based on 4 minutes to collect sample, but it actually takes 20 minutes and two extra people or a particular animal)—with no individual client being directly billed. To deal with this, we need another factor, a billing factor, to adjust the VTE for the amount of directly billable VTE hours. After all, it doesn't make sense to try to spread the overhead over the total VTE, if only half of those hours are billable. So, if the practice concludes that 50% of its time spent in the hospital is not directly billable to clients, then the *corrected* VTE is the total VTE hours multiplied by the billing factor—in this case 0.5.

Now, you can calculate the overhead per hour by dividing the overhead determined previously by the *corrected* VTE total for the same period. Dividing that number by 60 gives an overhead charge per minute. Note that this formula is not comparing how fast a veterinarian could do a task versus that of a technician or assistant. It reflects the difference in costs between having tasks performed by professionals versus different classes of paraprofessionals.

Overhead per hour = <u>Corrected overhead</u>
Total VTE x billing factor

For example, a hospital might have overhead costs (stripping out all of the expenses cited above) of $12,000 for the month. In that month, there are 200 hours of veterinary time (200 hours VTE), 450 hours of technician time (150 hours VTE) and 200 hours of assistant time (50 hours VTE) amounting to 400 total VTE hours (i.e., 200 + 150 + 50). The practice believes that 50% of its available professional/paraprofessional time is "billable", so the *corrected* VTE is 200 hours. The general overhead rate would then be $60/hour ($12,000/200 hours) or $1 per minute. Each practice will be different, depending on their fixed expenses, the number of staff that they employ, and how "billable" their time.

Note that using this model for calculating overhead gives a practice the opportunity to re-engineer its processes to become more efficient and more profitable. If overhead prices are established with the notion that only 50% of professional/paraprofessional time is directly billable to clients, this gives great incentive to improving this figure and capturing the difference as profit, rather than expense. For example, technicians may be able to handle more client callbacks, freeing up the veterinarians to see more patients. Technicians may handle more responsibilities within the hospital, such as anesthetic induction, bandage changes, and suture removal, all freeing up the doctors to be more productive with their time. The result may be that the overhead expense is calculated on the basis of 50% billable time, when more efficient use of staff time has allowed the correction factor to actually be 75%. This translates directly to increased profit for the practice.

Now that overhead has been addressed, the next component of pricing is labor. Since we have stripped all of the compensation for veterinarians, technicians and assistants out of overhead, these wages must be compensated for in the direct labor calculation. Once again, it is easiest to standardize wages with veterinary time equivalents (VTE). Most veterinary time is currently billed at a rate of $4 to $6 per minute. If a veterinarian's time is billed at $4 per minute ($240 per hour) and a veterinarian is paid 20-25% of revenues generated in production, then compensation to the veterinarian is approximately $50-$60 per productive hour. Unfortunately, only about one-half of a veterinarian's time is fully billable, with much time spent talking with clients on the telephone, providing technical services for which a technician could be better utilized, or sitting idle with holes in the schedule. This explains why current surveys cite associates as only making about $25 per hour! So, when veterinarians provide service, the direct labor contribution should be at least $4 to $6 per minute; it doesn't translate to as much as you might initially think. Using the previous example, you would bill the time of technicians at roughly $1/3^{rd}$ that of veterinarians, and assistants at ¼ that of veterinarians. For example, if veterinarians in the practice bill at $6 per minute, then placing a catheter utilizing one technician and one assistant (and NO veterinary time) can be easily calculated depending of the time contributions of participants. In this case, you predict that the average time requirement for placing a catheter utilizing one technician and one assistant should average 6 minutes. The labor charge should be $12 for the technician (6 minutes x 1/3 x $6) and $9 for the assistant (6 minutes x ¼ x $6), suggesting a labor cost of $21.

The cost of materials must also be reflected in the final price. This necessarily includes not only the direct cost of the materials, but the indirect costs of ordering and maintaining them.

Indirect Costs

The price to the consumer must realize the direct and indirect costs of products and materials, and a fair profit margin. If veterinarians are paid a commission of the basis of the product sale, this must also be factored into the equation. In addition to the actual cost of the products, one needs to also appreciate that there are very real indirect costs.

Ordering costs include the employee's time spent shopping for the product, comparison shopping with other distributors, the associated payroll taxes and benefits for that time, the time spent receiving and unpacking the order and comparing the order with the bill of lading, maintaining documentation for the order, making any notations in the computer program and putting the products on the shelves or in storage. This can account for 15-20% of the total unit cost!

On the other hand, holding costs reflect the monetary value tied up in inventory (which is often considerable for most veterinary practices), personal property taxes paid on the inventory, the space occupied in the hospital that could be otherwise used (opportunity cost), wastage of product, insurance premiums, and even regulatory compliance and documentation for products. This can account for 8-15% of the total cost of the product.

Shortage costs result when demand exceeds supply (e.g., client wants to purchase product but there are none on the shelves). There are opportunity costs of not making the sale, but also loss of goodwill and the real risk that the client will go elsewhere for their pet-related needs. Accordingly, indirect costs of products comprise 25-40% of the direct product cost and reflect real costs, not profit markup. If pilferage is a problem in a practice, indirect costs can exceed 50% of product costs!

Another indirect cost that will be discussed later in the chapter is payment costs. Since most veterinary hospitals accept payment in the form of credit card or check, there is a direct cost associated with verifying funds and processing, but no reasonable way of recovering it (i.e., consumers don't want to pay a surcharge for the privilege of having their credit assured). Even with an electronic processor, there is time and very real expense associated with the effort. The "hard" cost alone of accepting credit cards may be 1.5-3.5% of the sale.

Value Pricing

One of the most important determinants for fee setting is the perceived value by clients. Clients do understand that extraordinary care is associated with extra expense, but most clients will quickly lose faith in a practice that overcharges for commodities, such as flea control products, heartworm preventatives, or even pharmacy items. Since these are not areas where the veterinarian directly adds "value", overcharging for these items should be considered a significant marketing faux pas. It might cause clients to consider that all charges are over-inflated. As a good general guideline for product sales, the charge to a client should never be such that you would feel embarrassed or guilty if the client were to learn your true cost. Accordingly, it is very worthwhile to understand true costs and to establish defensible and profitable fees!

One of the reasons that veterinarians and veterinary clients are potential targets for retail raiders is that fees to clients don't always represent value-added services. That is, veterinarians tend to mark up prices on things beyond the value that others would consider reasonable for commodities and do so in a relatively protected environment (i.e., prescription item versus non-prescription item). For example, it is not unusual for veterinary hospitals to double or triple the price of a medication to set a retail cost, and then add a dispensing fee. This does help pay the considerable bills of the hospital, but where is the veterinarian really adding "value"? If the professional knowledge of the veterinarian to select a medication is adequately compensated with the office examination fee, and if no compounding is required, then compensation for medication should be based on standard retail markups if veterinarians would like to fend off competition. As an example, if the veterinarian recommends a harness for behavior management, is it reasonable to charge a 100-200% markup on the product when it is available from a pet store at a markup of 65%? If the veterinarian recommends a book on pet health care, can the hospital charge several times what the book would cost at a bookstore or Internet bookseller, just because the veterinary hospital is a professional office? The value is added by the professional consultation, not the commodity itself.

There is another aspect of the current markup strategy that may be considered inherently unfair for consumers. Standard markups most profoundly affect clients whose pets require expensive drugs, tests or products, without providing the client real value for the money. For example, let's look at two laboratory tests and the effects they have on consumers. Dog A has blood collected for a Complete Blood Count (CBC) while Dog B has an erythropoietin assay. Both involve venipuncture and blood collection, completing requisition forms, sample handling and submission to the laboratory, and veterinary assessment of the results. The laboratory charges the hospital approximately $15 for the CBC and approximately $150 for the erythropoietin. The hospital then "marks up" the costs to the clients by a factor of 2.5 (for example), charging the owner of dog A $37.50 for the CBC, and the owner of dog B $375 for the erythropoietin. Note that the CBC netted the hospital $22.50 ($37.50—$15) while the erythropoietin netted $225 ($375—$150) for essentially the same amount of work. The owner of dog B was penalized because the dog required a more expensive test even though the effort by the veterinarian and staff was essentially the same for both. Does that seem fair? How would you defend the hospital's position if the client learned that they had been charged $375 for a test that was performed by an outside laboratory for $150? Did the hospital "earn" $225 for the erythropoietin result, when they were happy making $1/10^{th}$ that amount for performing the same actions with the CBC?

The same injustice often happens with medications. Two dogs come in with urinary tract infections. Dog C is placed on a penicillin-type antibiotic that costs the hospital $0.10 apiece. Dog D is placed on a fluoroquinolone that costs $1.00 apiece. To keep the math simple, let's say that 100 tablets of each are dispensed. The hospital uses a standard markup of 2.5 times cost for each. The owner of Dog C pays $25 for the medication (plus dispensing fee) that costs the hospital $10 (net $15 plus dispensing fee). The owner of dog D pays $250 for the medication (plus dispensing fee) that costs the hospital $100 (net $150 plus dispensing fee). The hospital potentially made ten times as much "net" by dispensing the fluoroquinolone compared to the cheaper medication. This method penalizes owners of pets requiring expensive medicines. This also offers a potential conflict of interest without providing any additional value to the consumer.

A Better Way!

The recommendation is not that veterinarians should lower their prices—quite the contrary. The goal is to allocate charges appropriately, earning professional fees for those services in which the veterinarian adds value, and reasonable retail fees for goods for which no intrinsic value is added other than convenience. Clients will not begrudge spending more at a veterinary office than at a pharmacy for a similar product—within reason. If they perceive that it is more convenient to get the product at the veterinarian's office and it saves them a trip to the pharmacy, they are prepared to spend a small premium for that convenience, time saving, and real or perceived value.

Value Pricing sets service fees using information on relevant labor figures, overhead, materials and profit; product fees based on direct and indirect product costs and profit, and; laboratory fees based on hard costs, professional collection and submission, professional interpretation, and profit.

Here's one way of looking at pharmaceutical sales that is fair to consumers and profitable to veterinarians. For any pharmaceutical dispensed, charge a per-tablet fee (typically $0.10-$0.30) in addition to the direct and indirect product cost, plus a dispensing fee. This equalizes the playing field since the profit is a fixed per-tablet fee, regardless of the actual price of the medication. Let's illustrate using the previous example and a per-tablet charge of $0.25 and assuming indirect costs to be 35% of product costs.

For the penicillin-type capsules, we will dispense 100 and charge $0.25 apiece (our per-capsule profit), plus the actual cost of the drug with its indirect costs (i.e., 35% of total costs of 1.35 times the direct drug cost). This would be:

$$\$0.25 \times 100 + (\$0.10 \times 1.35 \times 100)$$
= $$\$25 + \$13.50$$
= $$\$38.50 \text{ (plus dispensing fee)}$$

Note that our previous model only charged the client $25 for this prescription (plus dispensing fee).

For the more expensive fluorquinolone at $1.00 per pill, we use the same rules, charging $0.25 apiece (our per-tablet profit), plus the actual cost of the drug with its indirect costs (35%, or 1.35 times the direct drug cost. This would be:

$$\$0.25 \times 100 + (\$1.00 \times 1.35 \times 100)$$
= $$\$25 + 135$$
= $$\$160 \text{ (plus dispensing fee)}$$

Note that the previous model would have charged the client $250 for this prescription (plus the dispensing fee). While this model makes less money on more expensive drugs, it is very defensible to clients since the clinic is making the same $0.25 per pill on all products, while covering all of its direct and indirect expenses. At what point does the model switch from bringing in more money on the cheap drugs and relatively less on the expensive ones? We can calculate that easily if we know our standard markup and our desired per-tablet charge. For example, when we typically mark up drugs by a factor of 2.5 and we intend instead to implement a per-tablet charge of $0.25 and a markup factor of 1.35 to cover direct and indirect costs, the break point cost (C) where the two are equal is:

$$2.5C = 0.25 + 1.35\ C$$
$$1.15C = \$0.25$$
$$C = \$0.22$$

Therefore, the hospital will make more using this model for all tablets costing the hospital less that $0.22 (that would typically sell for $0.22 x 2.5, or $0.55 apiece to clients). In fact it will make the hospital considerably more on most prescriptions. If a practice doesn't like that particular break point, they can change the per-tablet cost and/or indirect cost factor to be any point they choose. However, remember Pareto's Law that 80% of profits come from 20% of inventory items. It is not necessary to set a break point so high as to include virtually all drugs on the premises. This model assures the hospital that they will always make at least the per-tablet charge on every prescription, while covering all direct and indirect costs. In fact, this model makes expensive drugs more affordable, so that proper dosing and compliance are less of an issue.

This also removes any potential ethical conflict, since the hospital doesn't make bigger returns on more expensive medications. In addition, it is easy to make changes to the per-tablet charge to reflect inflation and price increases. For example, on an annual or semi-annual basis it is easy to make small increases to the per-tablet charge (e.g., a 12% increase on $0.25 would increase the per-tablet charge to $0.28, hardly noticeable to clients; this increases costs to clients by $3.00 per 100 tablets). Then, the actual drug costs can just be updated as price from the distributor changes.

A slightly different situation exists for prepackaged products such as topicals, pet foods, flea and tick control products and heartworm preventatives. In this case, it is best to set a per-unit charge (equivalent in principle to the per-tablet charge) and then add the direct and indirect costs. For example, with shampoos that have a $2.50 cost, one might add a charge for indirect costs (e.g., 35%) and a per-unit charge (e.g., $3). The product would thus sell for $6.38. For an expensive shampoo that cost $10, the charge to the client would be 1.35 x $10 + $3 or $16.50. If the standard markup factors applied (e.g., multiplying the cost by 2.5), that shampoo would cost the client $25, and that is a hard battle to win with most clients. Similarly for pet foods, it is best to account for direct and indirect costs and add a per-unit charge. How does it work in pet stores? The average markup for products is 67.5% and for pet foods is only 23-25%. There is not a lot of profit to be squeezed out of those sorts of margins!

One could make legitimate arguments on why associate veterinarians should not be compensated on the basis of prescriptions, but if they are, the commission should be based on the per-service/product charge rather than the total charge for the medication itself. Adding charges to the prescription to compensate for commissions greatly inflates the cost to the consumer without providing additional value. They paid for the expertise of the veterinarian during the examination, which included selection of pharmaceuticals. Their physician would have sent them on their way with a prescription. The veterinary hospital made a small but significant $0.25 per-tablet profit, which most clients will find extremely fair. Paying a commission on the final drug charge would greatly inflate the charge to the client. For example, if the final medication charge is $100 and the veterinarian gets a 25% commission, the charge must be adjusted upward by one-third (to $133.33) for the clinic to still make its $0.25 per tablet fee. This is a non-value-added expense to the client, and one that is difficult to justify in most instances. If it is necessary to compensate associates for drug sales, it is best to base it on the per-tablet charge (e.g., increasing it by one-third to pay a 25% commission) rather than the drug charge (which just reflects the actual costs plus the indirect charges, without any profit markup).

What about laboratory charges?

Laboratory charges are similar to pharmaceutical charges in that value is added by the veterinarian in selecting and interpreting laboratory tests, not in the costing of the test itself. By using standard markups, the client is penalized for needing expensive tests without the veterinarian providing additional services.

If the laboratory tests are run in-house, one can account for direct labor hours (DLH) of the veterinarian or technician the direct and indirect materials charges, and an overhead determined for the laboratory profit center. For example, to do a fecal flotation involving one technician and requiring 5 minutes of dedicated time can be calculated if we know the overhead for the laboratory profit center, and the veterinary time equivalents (VTE) of technicians compared to veterinarians. For this example, let's assume that the laboratory overhead is $1.10 per minute, that veterinarians are billed at $4 per minute for general duties, and that the VTE for technicians is one-third that of veterinarians. In addition, the test requires approximately $1.00 in materials (assume at least an additional 35% in indirect material charges, and 70-100% should not be considered excessive). Under these circumstances, the breakeven cost for the fecal flotation would be:

Overhead + Direct Labor Hours + Materials

Therefore, breakeven cost is 5 minutes of overhead at $1.10 per minute ($5.50), 5 minutes of technician time at $6.67 (5 minutes x $4/min x 1/3) and $1.35 materials = $13.52. Remember, this is the cost to the hospital for the fecal without any profit or commission for associates. To provide the hospital with a 15% profit margin would require:

Price = P = Cost + 0.15 P

When the cost is $13.52,

P = $13.52 + 0.15P

0.85P = $13.52

P = $15.91

So, charging $15.91 for a fecal flotation would cover direct and indirect costs and would net the practice a 15% profit margin ($2.39). However, it still wouldn't pay any commission to an associate. If we wanted to pay an associate 25% commission on all fecals ordered, one would need to factor an additional 25% into the equation:

$$P = Cost + (0.15 + 0.25)\ P$$
$$P = \$13.52 + 0.40\ P$$
$$0.6\ P = \$13.52$$
$$P = \$22.53$$

Therefore, in order to cover costs, earn a 15% profit for the hospital, and pay a 25% commission to an associate veterinarian, the charge for a fecal flotation would need to be $22.53! Charging the client anything less directly affects the profit margin, because the rest of the charges represent real costs that the practice will have to pay.

For samples that are sent to an outside laboratory, there is little that the veterinarian does to add value to the testing. Therefore, marking up laboratory costs is a non-value-added exercise. Instead, it makes more sense for the practice to concentrate on the veterinary activities that do make a value-added contribution. For example, sample collection is a very legitimate charge. A venipuncture charge should cover technician time, overhead and materials, perhaps $16 or so in total, based on current overhead, VTE, and materials costs (e.g., fair proportion of overhead, average time for collection is 3-4 minutes each for a technician and assistant and $1-$3 in materials, including indirect costs). If a veterinarian is involved in blood collection, the fee should also reflect direct labor hour charges of $4.00 to $6.00 per minute for professional involvement. The veterinarian should also factor in an interpretative fee for the laboratory tests, reflecting the likely time required for interpretation. For example, if the veterinarian predicts that evaluating the results will typically require 5 minutes of professional time, then that is a legitimate charge as well (e.g., 5 minutes at $4/minute = $20). Finally, there should be base charge for laboratory submission, which should reflect the time required for the samples to be centrifuged (if needed), labeled, packaged, requisitions completed and the samples sent off to the laboratory (e.g., $10 to $20). If samples require special handling or to be delivered by an overnight service, these are also valid charges.

Revisiting our previous laboratory example, it can be seen that this model is more profitable, without creating any markup on the laboratory cost itself. If the client were to learn what the costs from the laboratory were, there would be no surprises. Let's look at how this would work for the CBC and erythropoietin examples. For the CBC, the cost was $15 and the veterinary practice would typically increase it by a factor of 2.5 or so (i.e., $37.50 for the CBC, but $375 for the erythropoietin). Here's a different way of looking at the situation; one that fairly allocates costs and doesn't unfairly penalize clients that need expensive tests.

Charge	CBC	Erythropoietin
Sample Collection	$16	$16
Laboratory interpretation	$15	$24
In-clinic processing	$8	$12
Laboratory charge	$15	$150
Medical Waste fee	$ 4	$4
Total	$58	$206

Notice that, as with the pharmaceutical example, that the inexpensive tests become relatively more expensive, while the more expensive tests become less expensive. This is beneficial in several regards. First, it elegantly addresses a real problem in hospitals in which clinicians heavily discount expensive tests (and drugs) because they feel guilty about the final cost to the clients. In this scenario, there is no markup on the test, so no tendency or reason to discount it. One might choose to discount a laboratory interpretation charge, but all of the other charges reflect real overhead and materials charges within the hospital. Second, it mitigates problems that result when clients know the real cost of the test. For example, for DNA tests and many others, owners may be aware of the *actual* laboratory charge before coming in for the office visit. Often the charges for these tests are posted on the Internet. So, the client knows exactly what your costs are for the test. Alternatively, clients may show up for an office visit with laboratory results already in hand. With this model, one can still charge an appropriate laboratory interpretation fee. Third, it encourages running multiple tests while only marginally increasing the lab charges. Once you have the collection and processing charges, there is only a moderate increase likely in interpretation fees, and only the laboratory costs themselves for the extra tests. Finally, the charges are completely defensible to staff, associates and clients because they reflect real costs in the hospital setting, not a markup of testing done outside the hospital.

Once again, in this scenario, associate veterinarians are best compensated based on professional services alone, not the direct cost of the laboratory test. Otherwise, to pay a commission of 25% or so on actual laboratory costs would add one-third to the price for a non-value-added service.

All that being said, there is still at least one good reason for considering adding a cost markup to the laboratory charge—covering payment expense. Early in the chapter it was mentioned that there is an expense associated with receiving payment at the veterinary hospital. Most clients use checks or credit cards, and it is very difficult to absorb this expense into other services. The cost of a physical examination is relatively fixed based on area competition, so that isn't a good place to tack on fees. Drug charges are also competitive, and already relatively saturated with indirect costs. Radiology charges would be sufficient, but aren't performed regularly enough to recoup these costs from the majority of clients. Laboratory testing is performed on most patients and, in the current model, is devoid of markups. This, then, would give an opportunity to try to recover these indirect costs with a modest markup to laboratory costs.

How much should be added to the laboratory charge to at least partially satisfy this goal? Let's imagine a hospital where the payment expense was running about 3% of the total transaction (this could occur from credit card charges alone) and laboratory revenue was approximately 20% of total annual revenues. To be meaningful, the markup to the laboratory charge should actually cover the entire bill, at least on average across the hospital population (i.e., if the laboratory charge is $20 and laboratory charges typically represent 20% of revenues, then the final client bill will likely be $100). In this scenario, we can then multiply the payment expense (3%) by a factor of 5 (i.e., since 20% x 5 = 100%) to calculate the desired markup (3% x 5 = 15%). Now if the test actually costs $20, it becomes marked up to $23 ($20 x 1.15), the final bill would likely be around $100 (it doesn't need to be $100 since it will average out across the hospital population if laboratory income represents 20% of revenues) and the $3 will cover the payment expense associated with the visit (e.g., credit card or check). While this markup is definitely not value-added for clients, most would not begrudge a 15% markup and it is a convenient way to recover payment expense across the hospital population.

What about services?

For services performed within a hospital, the standard formula to be used is that charges should represent:

Overhead + Direct Labor Hours + Materials (direct + indirect) + Profit
+/- commissions

Once again, for calculation purposes, direct labor hours (DLH) can be calculated on the basis of veterinary time equivalents (VTE). Overhead should be charged at that calculated for the particular profit center. The material costs must reflect the direct costs from the distributor, as well as ordering and holding costs. These indirect costs may add 25-100% to the unit cost.

By way of example, GoodPet Veterinary Hospital has a dental operatory overhead expense of $1.50 per minute, based on profit center analysis. In pricing the dental prophylaxis procedure, they estimated that it would require 35 minutes of technician time (at a VTE rate of $2.00/minute), 5 minutes of veterinary time (at $6 per minute), 30 minutes of anesthesia (at $3 per minute) and $6 of materials (including indirect costs of 35% of unit cost). The base charge should be:

Overhead	$52.50
Veterinary time	$30.00
Technician time	$70.00
Anesthesia	$90.00
Materials	$ 6.00
Total	**$248.50**

Remember, this is a very basic pricing system, and hasn't included a variety of charges that should be there, such as catheterization, monitoring during anesthesia, induction, medical waste, etc. It also doesn't include any profit, or revenue sharing for associates. To build in a 15% profit margin would raise the cost to almost $292.35 (P = 248.50 + 0.15P) and including a 25% commission would raise the tab to $414.17 (P = 248.50 + 0.40P)! Are you charging enough?

Discounting

Discounting may seem like a way of enticing clients to a practice, but is fraught with problems, not the least of which is drastically affecting your bottom line. A 20% discount may not seem dangerous, but a 20% drop in revenues leads to a much greater drop in net profit than you might imagine. Let's see why.

To keep the mathematics simple, let's investigate what happens when a practice that performs 10,000 client transactions a year and has an average transaction of $100, decides to offer a 20% discount. Assuming that overhead is 60% of undiscounted revenues, the practice brings in $1 million in revenues and has $600,000 in overhead. The net profit is $400,000 on revenues of $1,000,000, a respectable profit margin of 40%. If the practice enacts a 20% discount policy, revenues are now $800,000 with the same overhead of $600,000 (the laboratory, drug distributors, and pet food suppliers did not extend you the same discount that you gave to your clients), giving a net profit of $200,000 rather than $400,000 and a profit margin of 25% rather than 40%. You just cut your net profit in half with that 20% discount!

Now, the reality is that discounts would not apply to all clients in this scenario, but the impact of discounts in a veterinary practice can be profound. When a practice has a return on investment of 10% and fees are discounted by 10%, the practice profit from that client transaction is wiped out. For practices with marginal profitability, the results are even worse. Since most veterinary practices are already charging less than they should for services, discounting rarely has the effect that is envisioned—that of increasing profits. On the contrary, for many practices, increasing fees by 20% will have a much more positive effect on net profit, even if some clients leave the practice because of them.

Let's say that we raised fees by 20% and by such action we actually scared away 15% of our clients. Surely that would be catastrophic to our bottom line. Let's see. Now, instead of seeing 10,000 client transactions, the price increase has caused the practice to only see 8,500 transactions, with an average transaction charge of $120 ($100 + 20%). Revenues are now $1,020,000 and overhead is still $600,000 (although it is probably less than that), providing $420,000 net profit. Why would we possibly consider discounting?

Veterinary Compensation for Goods and Services

There is no universally accepted method of veterinary compensation and quite a bit of debate on the subject. The simplest model is straight salary, and this is most appropriate for administrative, teaching, and commercial positions. In practice, however, paying a standard salary provides no incentive for the associate to increase revenues. Most veterinary practice models feature at least some production-based pay, which implies that associates are compensated based on the amount of revenue they earn for the practice. For new graduates, it is recommended that compensation include a base plus production. This assures the new graduate of a guaranteed amount to be able to pay expenses, including student loans. For instance, if an associate has a base salary of $60,000, there will be a base monthly pay of $5,000 and then the chance to earn a percentage of revenues beyond that expected. On average, the percentage paid in this model is about 20%. Accordingly, it is expected that the associate will bring in revenues of at least 5 (100/20) times the base pay (e.g., $25,000 per month or $300,000 per year) or the practice is losing money on that individual. The AVMA Economic Report on Veterinarians and Veterinary Practices (2001) reported that small animal exclusive practices earned revenues averaging $305,161 per doctor. If associates are prepared to take all the risks associated with production, they are entitled to a premium over base plus production, perhaps 22% or so. For associates that are employees rather than independent contractors, benefits usually reflect an additional 2-3 percent of pay.

Of course, these suppositions are based on averages. Veterinary compensation can be dramatically affected by excess capacity. As a rule of thumb, it should be possible to schedule approximately 3,500 transactions per full time veterinarian per year, and close to half that number in non-doctor visits, approaching 5,000 to 5,500 transactions per year per full time equivalent (FTE) doctor. Production per FTE doctor needs to be at least $300,000 to justify even the low salaries currently paid to veterinarians, so it is important to only hire new associates when they can realistically support $400,000—$500,000 in revenues. Otherwise, the new doctor only dilutes the revenue pool from existing doctors.

There is a problem associated with strict production based pay that was alluded to earlier. There are very different margins in practice for services versus the sale of goods. Paying a veterinarian $4 to $6 per minute to perform medical procedures is associated with few "hard" costs, while crediting a veterinarian with markup on food, drugs, laboratory tests and retail products is associated with very real "hard costs". Is there a way that practice owners can get a break on products and services with low margins, and associates can get a break on products and services with high margins? Happily, yes!

In the model suggested, it was recommended that veterinarians not be compensated (at least not at typical levels) for pharmaceuticals, outside laboratory tests, and packaged retail products. The motive is not to deprive associates of legitimate compensation, but to redirect their efforts towards value-added services that can be much more generously rewarded. As discussed, there is no value added for the client to add a commission to a good or service that has no direct veterinary involvement.

While most associates are compensated at a rate of 18-25% of total revenues generated, the practice experiences cost pressures from the "hard" costs of outside laboratory costs, pet food sales, and packaged pharmaceuticals. There just isn't the "margin" for associate pay, unless associates generate more revenues from goods and services with "soft" costs. Hard costs are associated with an absolute per-unit charge, such as a pharmaceutical tablet. Soft costs are services or raw materials that are used in the process to generate additional revenues. Most services are soft costs, because they involve mainly time rather than materials. An exception would be the itinerant surgeon or radiologist that comes in to perform a procedure and then leaves. Generally this is a fixed "hard" cost, since the specialist must be paid, regardless of the situation. Goods such as anesthetic are charged based on the process (anesthesia) and not on the direct cost of the product, so it is a soft cost for most practices.

Goods and services that have soft costs allow the practice to have more flexibility regarding compensation. For example, a practice that typically pays its associates 22% of total revenues could easily increase that rate by 30-35% to reward associates 28-30% of revenues, excluding the hard costs of pet foods, pharmaceuticals, retail items and send-out laboratory tests. Of course, for laboratory testing, there is still profit sharing from sample collection, processing, interpretation and all other value-added veterinary services.

Another option is differential commission, in which associates are paid a higher commission of professional services and a lower commission of pet foods, pharmaceuticals, retail items and send-out laboratory tests.

This compensation scheme accomplishes two things—it rewards veterinarians appropriately for performing value-added services for which they truly deserve more compensation, and it allows practices to deal effectively with the competitive nature of retail sales in which there really isn't room for professional commissions. For example, most pet food stores sell pet foods at a 23-25% markup; grocery stores have an even tighter margin. How can a veterinary practice hope to be competitive with veterinary commissions in the same range as total markup in the pet store, even before indirect costs are assessed, or profits? The answer is that most practices will take the relative loss in retail sales and make up the difference by saving on the service side. Since services account for 75% of revenues in a veterinary hospital, associates are foregoing higher payouts on the service side to protect their meager income stream on the retail side. This isn't a great strategy.

In fact, productive associates will make much more money being paid a relatively higher percentage based on services. It also provides associates with the incentive, not to rack up drug sales, but to provide professional services and ensure that they appear on the bill. What makes more sense— paying an associate a commission based of the cost of a high-priced drug, or rewarding that associate based on seeing clients and providing services?

To maximize associate revenue, it is necessary to understand how to effectively generate revenues. The main revenue "driver" of services is veterinary attention—spending time with clients. Time spent in the back restraining a dog, drawing blood, or doing laboratory work doesn't count in the pet owner's perception of value. Spending critical appointment time with the client and giving that client and patient needs your full attention is what keeps clients coming back time after time, and paying the bills that are generated. Accordingly, it is imperative to let the paraprofessional staff do all back-office work, if possible. Seeing appointments, talking with clients, and doing veterinary-specific procedures are the duties of a service-oriented veterinarian. While talking with clients is one of those non-billable duties that are hard on a veterinarian's time, client education is critical since clients won't buy what they can't understand. On the other hand, having veterinarians perform the duties of veterinary technicians and assistants is a poor use of training and expertise, and may antagonize the technical staff by devaluing their training and expertise.

Human physicians make their money by seeing patients, and seeing a lot of them. The human general practitioner does not engage in sophisticated diagnostics or treatments, but relies of a support system of specialists. The same holds true for the veterinary general practitioner, who has the skills to tackle hard cases, but from a profit perspective would do better to refer and start seeing the next case. It is just not possible to work up a behavior, dermatology, internal medicine, neurology, or ophthalmology case in a 10- or 20-minute appointment. It also makes no sense to invest in internal fixation equipment to perform surgery on only the occasional orthopedic patient. The point—don't offer services for which you cannot bill accordingly, and don't take on challenges beyond your capabilities. While these cases may be an exciting challenge, the time required to diagnose and manage them appropriately may be negatively valued by the client. For instance, if the case is not resolved expeditiously in the general practice, the client may wonder why their time and money was "wasted" at the general practice when a specialist was available. It's not an accident that human general practitioners refer so quickly. They can't compete cost effectively with specialists who have superior knowledge and experience in a discipline, and they increase their liability the further into the case they delve without coming up with answers. Specialists aren't there to compete with general practitioners, but to support their efforts to offer clients exceptional service and outstanding quality of care. While veterinarians and human physicians have many practice differences, both profit by learning to practice smarter, not harder.

Recommended Reading

Bower, J; Gripperm J; Gripper, P; Gunn, D: Veterinary Practice Management, 3rd Edition. Blackwell Science, Oxford, 2001, 254pp.

Cummings, R: Choose the right path when joining a practice. Veterinary Economics, 2002: May: 58-67.

Heinke, ML; McCarthy, JB: Practice made Perfect. A Guide to Veterinary Practice Management. AAHA Press, Lakewood Colorado, 2001, 459pp.

Levoy, B: Bluelight specials devalue your practice. Veterinary Economics, 2002; May: 42-48.

Lofflin, JL: Protecting your pharmacy business. Veterinary Economics, 2002; April: 34-44.

Nagle, TT; Holden, RK: The Strategy and Tactics of Pricing: A Guide to Profitable Decision Making (3rd Edition). Prentice Hall, 2002, 432pp.

Opperman, M: The Art of Veterinary Practice Management. Veterinary Medicine Publishing Group, Lenexa Kansa, 1999, 248pp.

Wise, JK: Gonzalez, ML: Employment of male and female graduates of US veterinary medical colleges, 2001. J Am Vet Med Assoc, 2002; 220(5): 600-602.

Wise, JK; Gonzalez, ML: Veterinary Income per hour, 1999. J Am Vet Med Assoc, 2002; 220(8): 1157-1158.

MARKETING

Sarah Taylor DVM MBA

Dr. Sarah Taylor is a 1997 graduate of the Ontario Veterinary College and earned her Master of Business Administration in 2001 from Bryant College. She is currently employed as a Professional Services veterinarian with Novartis Animal Health, US, Inc.

Veterinary practitioners and students alike invariably react negatively to the 'M' word as it applies to veterinary medicine. The 'M' word, of course is Marketing. Veterinarians command respect throughout the general population and the fact that marketing would ever invade this noble profession is offensive to many. It may conjure up images of the slick salesperson hocking unnecessary products and services to the unsuspecting public, or commercializing veterinary medicine to the point of being a commodity. However, marketing, in its purest sense, goes hand in hand with practicing the best and most ethical medicine possible. The objective of this chapter is to introduce basic marketing concepts and provide real-life applications of these principles in veterinary medicine.

Marketing Mix—The Four P's of Marketing

The marketing mix refers to all of the various activities that comprise a marketing plan and has, over time, become regrouped into the "4 P's" of marketing. The "4 P's" have come to represent Product, Price, Promotion and Place.

Product

In the veterinary practice setting, product refers to either a consumable item like prescription pet food or medications, or more importantly but less tangible, the service(s) provided by the veterinarian and veterinary staff. It is crucial to view the product not as a physical entity or a service but rather from the viewpoint of the total value delivered to the client and their pet. Veterinary owners must use this product definition as a basis for deciding how value will be delivered to their clients and this becomes intertwined with the clinic's philosophy or vision. Specifically, the answer to the following question must be clear: What is the goal of this veterinary practice? Is it to be the low cost provider of veterinary care, the high tech/early adopter clinic practicing the latest medical techniques or the client-friendly, average cost/good medicine clinic, to just name a few. Once the clinic vision has been identified, it is easier to identify the value-added products and services one can offer clients as well as plan for the integration of new products and services.

Price

Price may seem self explanatory; however, some common misconceptions will be explored with regard to what should be charged for services, what is actually captured in the transaction, and why cutting fees will not bolster the bottom line (see Economics chapter). Generally speaking, cost acts as a floor on pricing. Veterinary medicine, like any industry cannot survive and thrive if products and services are "sold" below cost. This again refers to the perceived value of the product/service provided to the client. Historically, the client cost of veterinary medicine has lagged behind the cost of inflation and not surprisingly, as a result, veterinarians' salaries have been held at low levels and are dramatically different than dentists' or medical doctors' salaries. There are several theories to explain why this is the case—poor management and thus wastage of money carrying excess inventory, and/or veterinarians not charging appropriately for the services rendered. Veterinarians enjoy a fair degree of autonomy on what they charge for veterinary services. Often, fees are too low or, if pricing is appropriate, the charges may fail to be appropriately captured on the client's bill. Veterinarians may also find themselves lowering fees on certain procedures (e.g., spays and neuters) to compete with nearby clinics. As illustrated in the economics chapter, everyone loses when price-cutting occurs. Economically, it is not feasible in the long term. Practically, logically and ethically, it is damaging to the profession in the short term. Veterinary medicine is a highly specialized, customized service industry, and there is danger in *commoditizing* the process. Price cutting diminishes the perceived value of the service provided and consequently requires a higher volume of clients and their pets to be seen in order to maintain the same level of profitability.

The American Animal Hospital Association has compiled extensive price lists for veterinary services throughout the United States based on geographical location (Veterinary Fee Reference, 2nd Edition, 2000). The charges are delineated at different price breaks to show what are the minimum and maximum fees charged for particular services for a certain area as well as the median, 25th and 75th percentile charges. Charging appropriately for every service and product delivered to the client is imperative if veterinary medicine and veterinarians are to grow and prosper in the future.

There are four basic pricing strategies used in veterinary medicine: competitive pricing, value-based pricing, cost-based pricing, and variable pricing.

Competitive pricing is used for goods and services that are shoppable, such as spays, neuters and vaccinations. It is vital that the price structure on these procedures is not markedly different than the neighboring practices in order to avoid losing potential clients. It is likewise important to not undercut these services in order to attract new clients who tend to be the bargain basement hunters. These clients will likely not be loyal to your practice and defect to a competitor in order to save a few bucks. This statement is assuming that your practice is striving to provide high quality pet care to clients who value your services and thus are willing to pay appropriately.

Value-based pricing refers to pricing services and products that are at a premium and that are exclusive with respect to the veterinarian's specialized expertise required to perform the service (or advise on the use of the product). These prices need to reflect the inherent value in the specialized training and expertise that every veterinarian possesses.

Cost-based pricing has been a mainstay in veterinary practices because it is simple. The cost of the product to the clinic is multiplied by a factor to get the retail price that the client will pay. Simplicity aside, this strategy is not as effective as it may have been. With the explosion of other channels (Internet, catalogs and retail outlets) by which clients can procure pet products and food, veterinary hospitals need to be cognizant of what products they carry, why they carry them, and at what price. Again, value must be analyzed. Stocking products for which clients need professional advice will help to cement the concept that you are providing a superior product when you are also providing technical expertise and assistance with its use. This kind of advice is a powerful service that cannot be duplicated by other retail channels and should not be under-valued.

Variable cost pricing is one strategy that is effective in capturing all the costs associated with offering a product. It takes into account such factors as inventory turnover rate and profit per square foot. If one is able to increase product volume without increasing the available labor and facility space, then this method works well.

In the final analysis, veterinarians need to start or continue (if they have already adjusted their fees) to charge what they are worth. It may go too far to quote Gordon Gekko's "Greed is Good" speech, in the film, Wall Street (20th Century Fox, 1987), but charging appropriately for your highly specialized knowledge and skill when treating the four legged family members of your clients is certainly reasonable, fair, and dare it be said, long overdue.

Promotion

Promotion simply means communication to the client, the pet owner, by both <u>interpersonal</u> and <u>non-personal</u> techniques, of what services are offered and the benefits and features of your veterinary practice. It is basically an extension of client education to raise awareness of the value of your veterinary practice. In veterinary medicine, promotion can span a variety of activities, but generally speaking, it can be classified into either personal or non-personal efforts. In most industries, non-personal promotion refers to advertising, sales promotion and public relations. Veterinary medicine does not participate in advertising and sales promotion, in the conventional sense, due to legal and professional ethical constraints. Public relations, on the other hand, can be an invaluable tool to promote the clinic and its valuable services. Examples of public relations activities are diverse—speaking on a weekly radio talk show, writing for the local newspaper column that discusses pet health issues, participating in career day at local high schools, talking to elementary school children, or hosting an annual open house of the clinic. (See Real World Marketing Ideas)

Place

The key to marketing 'Place' in veterinary medicine is really quite straightforward—think client perception and first impression. Obviously, location of the veterinary practice is one important component but not as vital as one might think. A visible and easily accessible facility is ideal but other marketing strategies can overcome the challenge of a less convenient location. Location ranked #6 in importance in a consumer survey studying factors considered when choosing a veterinarian (Brown & Silverman, 1999). One may not have much control over a practice location, but one can exercise a great deal of influence over the physical building and surrounding area of the practice. Never underestimate first impressions. Providing ample parking, easy access to the building, and a clean, bright, odor free facility is essential to indirectly communicate the high quality practice. If the front office/reception/waiting areas (the 'frontline' of what the client sees) are dirty, malodorous, or excessively noisy then how can a pet owner perceive that what goes on in the treatment or surgery area is any different? You may be the best diagnostician, display the best surgical technique in the most aseptic surgical suite, but this is all wasted since the client is not able to appreciate or judge that. Clients judge on what they can see and experience—the front office surroundings and staff. They will assume the back office will operate the same way the front office does.

Consider consulting your staff for ideas on decorating the front reception area and the exterior of the practice. Simple ideas such as educational bulletin boards, client-pet and staff-pet photo boards, a fresh coat of paint for the interior, and planting some flowers or hanging bird-feeders and baths outside are relatively inexpensive yet make any practice more welcoming. Additionally, anticipating and considering clients' needs in the reception and waiting areas exemplifies a customer service focus. For example, providing a phone designed for local calling, a restroom, child-safe play area, even a complimentary gourmet coffee service go a long way to adding to clients' perception of value.

Customer Service

Whatever the reason any of us chose to become veterinarians—love of animals or the attraction to medicine—the truth of the matter is that veterinary medicine is a people oriented business and thus, a service driven industry.

Exceptional customer service starts with the attitude and principles that are usually outlined by the leader of the practice, but it does not end there. Creating a customer-driven service culture takes commitment from the whole team, and it is important to ensure that everyone "buys into" the practice philosophy. This requires good leadership on the part of the owner to embrace and practice the philosophy daily. Every member of the health care team from the part-time animal caretaker to the receptionist, veterinary nurse, and veterinarian has opportunities everyday to delight clients with outstanding customer service. The base for how these opportunities are handled is ATTITUDE. No matter what kind of clientele you service or what kind of veterinary medicine is practiced, attitude will drive how different clients' needs are handled and how problems are turned into opportunities for "moments of truth" (i.e. customer service success).

The first step in serving any clientele successfully is to get to know them. This is obviously an ongoing work in progress but, in the meantime, one needs to develop and maintain methods of servicing, and thereby retaining, those clients as well as attract new clients.

Know Thy Customer and Pareto's Principle

A well known marketing principle, Pareto's Law states that 80% of one's revenue is generated by 20% of one's clientele. This is a comfort when a 'less than ideal' client routinely haggles with you on the cost of your professional veterinary services and you consider the drastic measure of 'firing' that client. Typically, this type of client costs you and your staff more in time, resources, and let's face it, frustration, and consequently it is worth pursuing the 'firing' route sooner rather than later. This is not to say that all of your clients have unlimited financial resources and will never question costs, but in general and ideally, one needs to be aware of when, despite your best efforts, your practice is not fulfilling the expectations and needs (however unrealistic they may be) of a client and the costs are outweighing the benefits.

So, how does a veterinarian get to know his/her clients and figure out how to provide outstanding client service? First, it is necessary to identify what types of clients you serve, also known as segmenting the market. Veterinary clientele are increasingly heterogeneous and diverse; however, some general market analysis can assist in the segmentation process. According to a recent study carried out by Pfizer Animal Health, and summarized in the Veterinary Economics February 1999 issue, the average pet owner in the United States is approximately 46 years old and female (81% of clients). Only 35% have children living in their households, and the average household income is $54,400 per year. Of this, the average client expenditure on veterinary services per year is $307. Obviously, regional differences will affect these figures so a local analysis of your area of practice is warranted. One approach is to conduct a market analysis for your particular geographic area so as to ascertain such socioeconomic data as population and demographics (age, gender, education level, average household income etc.) You can choose the range of the region based on reasonable assumptions of client distance from the practice. The national mean is 5.4 miles; however, if your practice is in a rural location, extending the range will be necessary. According to Johnson in the February 1999 Veterinary Economics, the majority of clients are located between 2 to 5 miles from their veterinary practice of choice (42%). If you are already in an established practice, an easy way to locate your clients is to have an area map in the front office with pins and have each client identify their home in relation to your clinic.

The easiest method for conducting this general market analysis is through searching the U.S. Census Bureau web site (www.census.gov). Furthermore, it is possible to use this data to estimate the number of pet owning households including dog, cat, bird, or horse owners by using the following formulas as described on the American Veterinary Medical Association web site:

All Pets	Number of pet-owning households = 0.589 x total number of households
Dogs	Number of dog-owning households = 0.316 x total number of households
Cats	Number of cat-owning households = 0.273 x total number of households
Birds	Number of bird-owning households = 0.046 x total number of households
Horses	Number of horse-owning households = 0.015 x total number of households

This web site also describes additional methods of estimating the numbers of each type of animal and provides the additional information source on state and regional demographics through the U.S. Pet Ownership & Demographics Sourcebook.

This kind of analysis is a useful starting point for one considering a location to 'hang out their veterinary shingle.' But what about the established practice? Part of the answer lies in surveys. Client surveys can be invaluable in providing information as to how the practice's services are being utilized, what services should be added or deleted, and what services need to be marketed more aggressively. These surveys don't have to be extensive and cumbersome. A one page survey form can be handed to every new client to fill out with the initial client form, sent as a mass mailing to the present client base, or even just to your target *Pareto* clientele.

Surveys are one relatively simple way of segmenting your clientele and thereby identifying each segment's needs through their feedback, or predicting future needs through projections based on their demographic data. Another method of identifying and segmenting clients, specifically your Pareto or "Gold" clients, is by analyzing computer transaction data and identifying those pet owners who generate 80% of the practice revenue. Many software packages are now able to track and report which clients spent $500 to $1,000, or more during the past year. The number of these gold clients may be fewer than you would expect. For example, a practice that generates $1 million a year may have a client base of 2,600 clients. Of those, only 520 clients generate $800,000 of the practice's income—each of these clients averages approximately $1,538, while some may spend considerably more (Dooley, 1998). Interestingly, these gold clients often are not the top income households, and thus, may be inappropriately segmented if one were to identify client types on the basis of income reported on a survey.

So, the gold clients have been identified—what now? First, mark the records and educate the hospital team as to how these clients may be serviced to acknowledge their special status. What sorts of extras could these clients enjoy? Basically anything that one can imagine short of cutting fees. These clients do not choose the hospital because of low cost fees— they come to you because of the service they receive. Some examples of value added services for gold clients: bending hospital rules to accommodate their schedule—scheduling an appointment during the lunch hour, allowing for boarding discharge on a Sunday, or offering house call service or delivery of pet food/medications.

The same method can be employed to the second tier of client—the "silver" client. These clients are those that spend a substantial amount on their pet(s) every year but do not qualify for the gold client status—yet. These are clients that can be targeted by giving special attention and 'samples' of star treatment whenever the opportunity presents itself.

Indeed, every client deserves to be treated with polite, courteous service and obviously reliable veterinary medical care for their pet; however, it is invaluable to identify and cater to those clients who value exceptional health care for their pets and who are willing to pay for it. Client segmentation allows for even greater customization of veterinary services to specific clientele. It is also important to market the practice's services to potential clients and existing clients who may be unaware of valuable services the clinic offers. Many marketing techniques exist, ranging from the simple and inexpensive to the high cost marketing plan and strategy. For the purpose of this discussion, some of the basic marketing tools such as the clinic web site, logo, educational literature, yellow pages, newsletters, word of mouth referrals, open houses, and community programs will be outlined.

Real-World Marketing Ideas

Using the Internet and The Clinic Web Site

Today, a web site is considered an integral part of any business and often the clinic's web site may be a potential pet owner's first exposure to the hospital. Web sites can range from the simple to the highly interactive, and likewise, the cost to design and maintain a web site ranges markedly. Thankfully, web design has become much easier and does not require a high degree of computer savviness. In fact, some veterinary industry business partners can provide all the resources you need to produce a web site. Novartis Animal Health, US Inc., in conjunction with Intelligent Content Corporation, has developed a package called VetSuite™. This tool, in addition to providing web site development, provides a comprehensive research library similar to the 5-minute veterinary consult text, benchmarking tools and practice management information, and an online ordering system for any veterinary medications and supplies from any manufacturer or supplier. This package is available through either company

for a monthly charge, or at no charge for Novartis' customers who participate and meet certain requirements as part of the company's Growth
Alliance program. One of the outstanding marketing features in
VetSuite™ is the Vet Locator that is found on the Pet Place web site. When
a consumer types in their zip code, it will list VetSuite™ veterinary clinics
in that area first.
Additionally, Vet Centric.com provides its customers with the capability
to build a web site to which you can direct clients.

Another Internet site, VetInsite, offers Personal Pet Portals™. This is a set
of Internet tools to "help veterinarians educate clients and staff, market
veterinary services and products and communicate efficiently with clients
and staff." The tools work in concert with existing practice management
systems and allow both veterinarians and clients to use Web-accessed
resources.

Web sites can be tremendous tools for computer savvy clients. Web sites
act as a cyber billboard by displaying clinic and veterinary staff information and services, featuring client education items and links to legitimate
pet information sites. Additionally, communicating with clients can
become simpler and more convenient through e-mail. A word of caution
as this can be a double-edged sword—more time may be spent reading
and answering e-mails everyday as well as phone calls to clients. Sending e-
mail reminders for preventive services, medication refills and/or monthly
heartworm medication administration or refills however can result in substantial savings in terms of postage and staff time. One can provide online
new patient forms for potential clients to download and complete prior to
their first visit, or even allow them to take a virtual tour of the hospital.
Undoubtedly, there are many possibilities for web site use that will
increase with future technological enhancements.

Educational Literature

Virtually every veterinary clinic uses client handouts and brochures to enhance client education of preventive medicine and disease processes. These, too, are marketing tools as every piece of literature or pet merchandise leaving the clinic will bear all of the clinic data and the clinic logo. A clinic logo is commonplace among veterinary clinics and having an eye-catching, yet simple logo can enhance the hospital's image, and ought to be incorporated into all clinic correspondence.

Yellow Page Advertising

Yellow page ads are a "24/7" method of marketing the clinic's services. In one survey, 7% of respondents said they chose a practice from the yellow pages (Grubb, 1999). Client surveys or team member inquiry of new clients as to how they heard about your particular facility is helpful to gauge effectiveness of your particular yellow page ad. It is recommended that yellow page advertising comprise 1% or less of practice revenue (Grubb, 1999). Some tips from Dr. Ross Clark's Mastering the Marketplace: Taking Your Practice to the Top are: use high quality graphics and color to grab readers' attention, use strong borders and make sure important data like accreditations, board certifications and awards received by the hospital or staff are highlighted. Yellow page advertising is a valuable marketing tool but should be re-evaluated annually to ensure that the return in attracting new clients justifies the cost.

Newsletters

A clinic newsletter done on a monthly or quarterly basis is another valuable method of staying connected with your clientele by communicating clinic services and providing educational material as well as entertainment segments. Newsletters do require a great deal of planning and time, particularly the initial issue, but provide a valuable way to bond clients to your practice. It is helpful to leverage the rest of the hospital team in the endeavor to brainstorm newsletter educational subjects as well as fun 'soft-side' stories of veterinary medicine and/or the staff and their pets. To ensure a successful, widely-read newsletter, it is helpful to follow a few helpful hints: resist the urge to use a pre-made newsletter format—write it yourself, use large size typeface with wide margins on high quality paper, use the easy to read three column format and include lots of photos, drawings or cartoons to maintain reader interest. Newsletters do require some work but the rewards can be outstanding.

Word of Mouth Referrals

It may seem rudimentary to consider referrals from present clients as a marketing tool but word of mouth should not be underestimated—as much as 53% of respondents in one survey chose their veterinarian based on referral by a friend or relative (Johnson, 1999). Word of mouth is powerful and is virtually free advertising. Best of all, all you did was your job, practicing the best medicine possible so as to best serve your client and their pet. Encouraging referrals by present clients by sending thank you cards and/or gifts should not be neglected. It may be beneficial to institute a clinic policy for certain gifts for a certain number of referrals so that there is some uniformity in rewarding client's positive word of mouth.

Clinic Open House

Open houses provide an ideal and informal setting for you to show off your clinic's facilities and to answer questions about the various veterinary services offered not only to your own clientele, but to the community as a whole. Open houses need not be confined to a clinic's grand opening—many clinics hold annual or semi-annual open houses. Hosting an open house requires planning and budgeting but using the ideas and effort from the hospital team will make the process less daunting. With respect to financial assistance, look to industry partners. Sales representatives from pet food, pet supply, and drug manufacturing companies are more than happy to help sponsor an open house. Many representatives are also willing to participate in person to help with client education seminars and distribution of literature or promotional items. Open houses provide a win-win situation for everyone—clients, the hospital team, and the community.

Community Programs

Another way of ethically publicizing your name and your clinic is to volunteer within your community. Community involvement can be anything from lecturing at the local school career day to speaking on a weekly radio pet show or writing in the local newspaper pet advice column. Taking the opportunity to educate the general public on pet health issues will always benefit veterinary medicine and it is an effective method to get your name into the public forum.

Conclusion

Hopefully, this chapter has allayed the fear of marketing one's practice and has provided some useful real-world marketing ideas. Of course, marketing one's veterinary practice is not limited to these concepts and every marketing plan will be unique. Keeping the four P's of marketing as a basis of the plan and maintaining a clear focus on what kind of clinic you envision and what kind of clientele you will serve will ensure a sound foundation for any marketing plan and its execution. Marketing is a vital component to the present and future success of the profession and one of the key areas upon which veterinary medicine needs to improve.

Recommended Reading

Albers, JW. The Veterinary Fee Reference, 2nd Edition. AAHA (American Animal Hospital Association). 2000. 272 pp.

Bly, RW. Selling Your Services. Henry Holt and Company. New York, NY. 1991.

Brown, JP, Silverman, JD. The current and future market for veterinarians and veterinary medical services in the United States. JAVMA 1999;215(2):161-183.

Clark, R. Mastering the Marketplace: Taking Your Practice to the Top. Veterinary Medicine Publishing Group. Lenexa, KS. 1996.

Dickson, PR. Marketing Management, 2nd Edition. Harcourt Brace College Publishers. New York. 1997. 813 pp.

Dolan, RJ. Note on Marketing Strategy. Harvard Business School Publishing. Boston, MA. 1997. Rev. November 1, 2000.

Dooley, D. Reward your gold clients. Veterinary Economics 1998;39(5);88-90.

Grubb, DJ. Four tips to impress clients. Veterinary Economics 1999;40(3):64-70.

Hansen, DR, Mowen, MM. Management Accounting. South-Western College Publishing. Boston. 2000. 850 pp.

Johnson, A. Who's your target client? Veterinary Economics 1999;40(2):62-66.

Johnson, A. Marketing your practice. Veterinary Economics 1999;40(7):46-51.

Lee, DE. The Balanced Practice®. Presented at 94th Annual Conference for Veterinarians, Cornell University. March 15-17, 2002.

Lofflin, J. Tapping the web's potential. Veterinary Economics 2000;41(4):4-9.

Rotundo, KJ. Energize your Enterprise. From Rhode Island Veterinary Medical Association Team Building Day. Animal Health Center & Capital Consulting Group. Clifton Park, NY. 12-14.

Roy, K. Will a newsletter help you? Veterinary Economics 1998;39(6):56-59.

Supplement to DVM Newsmagazine: New Product Preview. July 2002.

Tumblin, DL. Pricing strategies that make sense. Veterinary Economics 1999;40(10):40-49.

Verdon, DR. How do you 'sell' preventive medicine? DVM Magazine April, 2002. p. 10.

Ward, EE. Hosting an open house. Veterinary Economics 2000;41(5):48-51.

Werber, J. The client is king! Firstline, Veterinary Economics Apr/May 1999:16-18.

www.avma.org/cim/estimate

www.census.gov

www.petplace.com

www.vetsuite.com. Intelligent Content Corporation, Will King: 954-
659-8338.

www.vetcentric.com

FINANCIAL MANAGEMENT

Karen Felsted CPA MS DVM CVPM

Dr. Felsted graduated from the University of Texas at Austin with a degree in marketing. She spent 12 years in accounting and business management, six of it with the "Big-8" accounting firm of Arthur Young (now Ernst & Young.) During this time, she also obtained an MS degree in Management and Administrative Science (concentration: accounting) from the University of Texas at Dallas.

After graduating from the Texas A&M University College of Veterinary Medicine, Dr. Felsted began her career as a veterinary practitioner in both small animal and emergency medicine while maintaining her existing veterinary accounting and consulting practice. In 1999 she opened and became Manager-in-Charge of the Dallas office of Owen E. McCafferty, CPA, Inc., a national public accounting firm specializing in tax, accounting and practice management services for veterinarians. During this time she received her Certified Veterinary Practice Manager certificate. In 2001, she joined Brakke Consulting, Inc., where she continues to offer practice management consulting services to veterinarians. She also runs her own accounting firm specializing in financial services for veterinarians.

Dr. Felsted has been published in numerous national and international veterinary journals including Veterinary Economics and Texas Veterinarian. She has spoken at many local, national and international veterinary meetings.

Introduction

Good financial management of any business is critical to its success. This is particularly true of a small business that often does not have the resources to sustain itself during poor economic times or during periods of change in the specific industry or profession involved.

For example, a giant company such as IBM or General Motors may have the cash and investment reserves to meet payroll, continue production, market their wares and invest in research and development even during periods in which the company is losing money.

Many small businesses, such as veterinary practices, do not have these resources whether through poor planning and management or through outside influences. For example, one of the issues facing the veterinary profession today is the profitability of product sales. No one will dispute that many outstanding products have been developed for the animal health market and have increased veterinary practices' gross and net income. However, the profit margins on these products are far less than those of medical and surgical services and a practice that sees product revenue increasingly substituted for medical and surgical service revenue will ultimately see a decline in profits. Does this practice have the cash reserves to continue paying its staff and providing a reasonable level of compensation to its owners while they go through the transition necessary to offer a greater range of medical and surgical services? This transition will almost certainly include the acquisition of new equipment and supplies as well as the training of doctors and support staff, all of which will also require resources.

One of the reasons small businesses lack strong financial management is that the owners of these businesses lack training and experience in business management. Though more business courses are being offered to veterinary students, most newly graduated veterinarians lack the training and knowledge necessary to run a practice well. This problem is complicated by the fact that most newly graduated veterinarians (or dentists or physicians, for that matter) don't have a real interest in the business side of their practices. These individuals want to practice medicine, not run a business. Unfortunately, many of these practitioners do not see the connection between solid business management and their goal of practicing good medicine. A practice that generates lackluster profits doesn't have the resources to invest in the new technology and products necessary to practice the most current medicine and surgery, it doesn't have the resources to provide the amount and level of continuing education to its doctors to enable them to stay abreast of current techniques and it doesn't have the resources to hire and train the quantity and level of support staff necessary to provide first class medical care.

Financial management encompasses a broad range of topics including the following:

- Financial statement ratio analysis—understanding the relationships between various items on the financial statements and using this information to improve profits and efficiency in the business
- Profit center analysis—analysis of profits or losses generated by individual income centers in a business
- Time value of money—understanding the value of cash held today versus that generated or paid in the future and using this information to make better financial decisions
- Breakeven analysis—understanding the relationship between revenue and expenses and using this information to determine the feasibility of expansion programs
- Capital budgeting and capital asset acquisition—financial tools to help determine if facility expansion or the acquisition of new

equipment will be profitable for the business in a reasonable amount of time
- Investment risk and uncertainty—understanding the impact of risk in financial decision making

Elsewhere in this book, basic accounting topics have been covered. Confusion exists in some people's minds about the differences between accounting and finance. After all, they both involve money, don't they? Accounting, according to the Merriam-Webster dictionary is "the system of recording and summarizing business and financial transactions and analyzing, verifying, and reporting the results." Whereas accounting produces the financial information necessary for the successful operation of a business, it is the financial management tools and techniques that actually allow this information to be used to produce good financial decisions.

Obviously the entire spectrum of financial management cannot be covered in one chapter of an entry-level book; however, we will attempt here to cover basic concepts and tools that will be useful in managing a successful small business.

Financial Statement Ratio Analysis

Ratios derived from information included in a business's balance sheet and income statement can be very useful in analyzing how well a business is doing in various areas and in identifying areas of concern.

Ratios may be calculated using only balance sheet information, only income statement information or a combination of both.

Ratios can be more useful in analysis and planning compared to reviewing actual numbers for several reasons:

- Relationships between various pieces of information are often more clearly apparent
- Trends over months or years can be more easily analyzed
- Businesses of different sizes can be more easily compared

As with most kinds of analysis, ratios also have limitations. First of all, the results they give are only as good as the information used to calculate them. If the financial statements are erroneous, old or are not prepared on a useful basis, the ratios derived from this information will also be problematic. When analyzing information for the same business but at different points in time, it is important to have an understanding of the changes that have been going on within the business in order to correctly determine the importance of the change. When analyzing ratios between different companies, it is important to remember that differences in accounting methods or operations may create differences in ratio results. The results of ratio analysis aren't always a measure of good or bad management but indicate areas that should be more fully investigated.

Balance sheet ratios

There are four basic kinds of ratios using information from the balance sheet and many individual ratios within the categories. Only those most useful to veterinary medicine are discussed here.

Liquidity ratios measure a business' ability to pay its short-term liabilities. For example, a veterinary practice may have current assets consisting of cash, accounts receivable, and inventory. Remember that current assets are those that are expected to be converted to cash within a one-year period; i.e. the practice expects to sell its inventory for cash within one year and to collect its accounts receivable within one year. It will have to use this cash to pay off its current liabilities such as accounts payable, retirement plan contributions, note payments due within a year, etc. Liquidity ratios give an indication as to whether the practice will be able to do this and how slim the margin is.

The two most commonly used liquidity ratios are the current ratio and the quick ratio.

The current ratio is defined as:

$$\frac{\text{Current assets}}{\text{Current liabilities}}$$

If a practice has a current ratio of 4:1 that means it has 4 times as much cash and other current assets than will be needed to meet its upcoming short-term obligations. If a practice has a current ratio of 0.8:1, that means it will be unable to meet its upcoming short-term obligations with assets currently on hand.

Current ratios for veterinary practices per the American Animal Hospital Association (Financial and Productivity Pulsepoints, AAHA Press 1998) are as follows:

U.S. total (Mixed and small animal practices)	1.14	Median
	2.42	Average
Mixed practices	1.78	Median
	2.83	Average
Small animal practices	1.08	Median
	2.31	Average

A variation on the current ratio is the quick or acid test ratio.

The quick ratio is defined as:

$$\frac{\text{Current assets less inventory}}{\text{Current liabilities}}$$

Inventory is not included in this ratio because it is sometimes less "liquid" than other assets—i.e. there may be more difficulty in converting it to cash than other current assets. Therefore the quick ratio is a more stringent test of a business's ability to pay off its short-term obligations.

Quick ratios for veterinary practices per the American Animal Hospital Association (Financial and Productivity Pulsepoints, AAHA Press 1998) are as follows:

U.S. total (Mixed and small animal practices)	0.83	Median
	1.81	Average
Mixed practices	0.83	Median
	2.06	Average
Small animal practices	0.81	Median
	1.73	Average

Leverage ratios compare and contrast the portion of a business financed by owner contributions and profits versus that financed by an outside source such as a bank or other lender. The two most useful in veterinary medicine are the debt to asset and equity to asset ratios.

The debt ratio is defined as follows:

$$\frac{\text{Total debt}}{\text{Total assets}}$$

The equity ratio is defined as follows:

$$\frac{\text{Total equity}}{\text{Total assets}}$$

In all businesses, the total of the debt used to finance the business plus the equity contributed or earned by the owner equals the total assets of the business. Therefore, the total of debt and equity ratios for the business should be 1.0. A business with a high debt ratio is generally considered to be riskier than one with a lower debt ratio because more of the business is financed with outside money and more of the practice's earnings must go to pay off debt. A practice with no debt, however, may be foregoing opportunities to expand and increase profits through the acquisition of new equipment or a new facility. For the same reason that most people need a mortgage to buy a house, most practices need some debt, from time to time, to finance expansions and major capital acquisitions.

Equity to asset ratios for veterinary practices per the American Animal Hospital Association (Financial and Productivity Pulsepoints, AAHA Press 1998) are as follows:

U.S. total (Mixed and small animal practices)	0.56	Median
	0.47	Average
Mixed practices	0.62	Median
	0.49	Average
Small animal practices	0.53	Median
	0.46	Average

Activity ratios compare the level of sales versus the level of investment in certain asset accounts in order to see if resources are being utilized effectively. Two of the ratios most commonly used in veterinary medicine are the inventory turnover and the average collection period for accounts receivable.

Inventory turnover is defined as:

$$\frac{\text{Cost of goods sold}}{(\text{Inventory at beginning of year} + \text{inventory at end of year})/2}$$

This ratio shows the average number of times a business sells its entire supply of inventory and replaces it. Since a high level of inventory ties up cash that could be used for other purposes, it is generally desirable to have a high turnover number. The number should not be so high, however, that the business runs out of items frequently or forgoes volume or order size discounts because they are ordering in such small amounts. Most practices have a turnover ratio of between 5-6; practices with very efficient inventory systems often increase this ratio to 8-12.

Average collection period for accounts receivable is defined as:

$$\frac{(\text{Accounts receivable at beginning of year} + \text{accounts receivable at end of year})/2}{\text{Annual sales purchased on credit}/360 \text{ days per year}}$$

The annual sales purchased on credit figure should include only those sales that the practice finances via its own accounts receivable; this number should not include amounts financed by credit cards or other outside credit programs. The result of this ratio calculation is the number of days it takes clients to pay the amounts they owe the clinic. For example, if the resulting ratio is 35, this means it takes 35 days for the practice to collect its money after the client purchased goods or services from the clinic. This is cash that cannot be used to purchase supplies or equipment or earn interest in an investment account.

Profitability ratios compare the profits of the company to other financial items such as sales or total assets. (See the income statement ratio section for the profits to sales ratio.)

Return on total assets is calculated as:

$$\frac{\text{Annual net profit}}{(\text{Total assets at beginning of year} + \text{total assets at end of year})/2}$$

In many industries the net profit figure used is that "after taxes". Because most veterinary practices do not pay taxes at the entity or business level, but only at the personal level, a before tax net profit figure is more useful for comparison with other practices.

The return on assets result can be compared to returns on other investments owned by the practice owner. For example, a 5% return on assets means the owner could make just as much money if he or she invested in a bank account paying 5% interest, as from investing in the practice. A 20% return on assets will compare favorably with many financial market investments.

Income statement ratios

Income statement ratios are calculated by dividing a particular revenue or expense amount by total gross revenue with the result expressed as a percentage. These ratios are then compared internally from year to year, and/or to industry standards. While comparison with industry standards is very useful for identifying areas that a practice is successful in versus those that may need further investigation, it is important to remember that every practice is unique and industry standards aren't always the "right" answer for every practice.

When comparing ratios to internal data, both trend comparison as well as comparison of data from one period to the same period in the prior year are useful tools. An example of trend comparison would be to review total revenues for each month of a year to see if they are increasing or decreasing and by how much. Comparing data from one period to the same period in the prior year adds additional information and eliminates some of the flawed results that can be seen in businesses with a cyclical nature if only trend comparison is used. For example, if revenue has been increasing each month but suddenly falls off in September, it may appear that something has gone wrong to cause this decline. However, comparison with prior years may show that this always happens in September and that even though September's revenue is less than August's revenue, both are still above the same months last year. Or when comparing revenue from the 1st to the 2nd to the 3rd quarter of the current year, it may appear that a practice is doing well because the revenue is steadily increasing. However, if the revenue is compared to the same quarters in the prior year, it may be noted that while the revenue is increasing, the total for each quarter is still less than that in the previous year.

Revenue

The revenue section of a typical income statement is usually composed of just a few lines; for example, Fees for Professional Services, Refunds, and Discounts with the net of these amounts being total revenue for the practice.

For more useful analysis, a detailed breakdown of revenue categories is needed so that the individual key revenue items can be reviewed. While this level of detail is not usually contained in a practice's income statement, it should be available from the practice's invoicing software.

Commonly used categories of revenue include: exam fees and office calls, vaccination revenue, outpatient procedures, laboratory income, hospital-ization income, radiology revenue, dietary product revenue, pharmacy income, surgery income, dentistry income, boarding revenue, grooming revenue, and ancillary product revenue.

When individual revenue center income is expressed as a percentage of total revenue, comparisons can easily be made between prior periods and to industry benchmarks available from the American Animal Hospital Association (Financial and Productivity Pulsepoints, AAHA Press 1998), Veterinary Economics, and the American Veterinary Medical Association, amongst others.

For example, laboratory income as a percentage of gross income per the American Animal Hospital Association (Financial and Productivity Pulsepoints, AAHA Press 1998) is as follows:

U.S. total (Mixed and small animal practices)	11.9%	Median
	11.9%	Average
Mixed practices	9.6%	Median
	9.8%	Average
Small animal practices	12.6%	Median
	12.5%	Average

From a financial viewpoint, it is generally acknowledged that diagnostic services have a higher profit margin than do some other income areas and a practice whose laboratory income is less than the figures shown above may want to take steps to increase the revenue in this area of their practice.

Areas in which the profit margins are generally lower in veterinary practices include boarding and grooming services, product sales and vaccinations.

Practices with a high concentration in these areas should consider the impact on profits.

Expenses

In order to maximize profit, it is important to review expenses and investigate any that appear to be out of line. Small business owners often focus most of their analysis effort on expenses rather than revenues because they are easier to understand and perhaps control. For example, if insurance costs have been rising, it is simple to call four agents and get a new quote for workers compensation insurance. If long distance calls are increasing in cost, price-shopping various plans may result in a cheaper alternative. However, the most effective way to increase profits is to focus on increasing revenues, not on shaving pennies off the postage expense. Expenses should be reviewed periodically to insure they have not gotten out of control, but most of the practice's efforts should be devoted to increasing revenue through client education, marketing, the offering of new services or other means.

The biggest expenses in most practices are those included in the Cost of Professional Services section of the income statement (drugs and medical supplies, laboratory costs, surgery costs, etc) as well as support staff, associate veterinarians, and facility rental costs. This information is generally available directly from the income statement. Efforts to control these costs will yield more benefit than controlling much smaller expense items. Expense ratios are calculated by dividing the dollar amount of the expense by the total gross revenue and then comparing this figure to prior results or industry benchmarks.

For example, drugs and medical supplies expense as a percentage of gross income per the American Animal Hospital Association (Financial and Productivity Pulsepoints, AAHA Press 1998) is as follows:

U.S. total (Mixed and small animal practices)	15.6%	Median
	15.9%	Average
Mixed practices	18.1%	Median
	18.5%	Average
Small animal practices	14.8%	Median
	15.2%	Average

A practice with drug and supplies costs significantly higher than those shown here may have problems with inventory theft, overstocking, or higher than normal costs for inventory items.

Profit margin

The profit margin is calculated as:

$$\frac{\text{Annual net profit}}{\text{Annual sales}}$$

Exceptionally well run practices will often have profit margins >20% of sales; however many practices do not come near this level. It is important that the net profit figure used in the calculation contain a fair salary for the owner's medical and management work, a fair market value facility rent number if the practice owner also owns the real estate and excludes any "perks" paid on behalf of the owner by the practice. The owner's salary should not include amounts that are really return on investment or the net profit figure will be understated. A practice's financial advisor can help with this calculation.

Profit Center Analysis

Analysis of profits by income center is important to know when planning the future expansion of a business and in allocating resources within the current environment. Profit center accounting is an extension of the basic financial information contained in the income statement that allows for improved management of a business.

A profit center is essentially a small business within a business. Within a veterinary practice, surgery is a profit center as is the pharmacy. Every aspect of a business can be divided into profit centers—the centers for a typical clinic might be as follows: office procedures (exams, vaccinations, and outpatient procedures), hospitalization (and related treatments and procedures), laboratory, surgery, boarding and grooming, pharmacy, food and over-the-counter products, radiology, etc. Income is tracked by profit center and expenses related to the center are allocated to it. It is then possible to analyze which segments of the operations are profitable and which are not. Armed with this information, a business owner can make better decisions.

For example, let's assume a practice owner has a clinic that realized a profit of $90,000 last year. Overall, this looks healthy. But could it be better? And which segments of the business are contributing most to the profits? In an effort to find out more about the business, the owner reviews the profit center information. He or she concludes that surgery and the pharmacy are doing very well, but the lab is only marginally profitable and boarding/grooming is losing money. What should be done about this? First of all, it is important to investigate a little further and determine why these areas are losing money. Was a new in-house blood chemistry machine purchased this year? Are the boarding fees $1.00 per day lower than that of competitors? Once the reasons behind the profits or loss are better understood, a manager can decide if a change is necessary. He or she may decide to raise the lab fees. Or perhaps the owner feels the market won't bear an increase in lab fees at this time, but is willing to accept decreased profitability because of the improved medical care and the future expectations of profitability once the new machine is paid off. Raising boarding fees is clearly indicated, but the practice owner may also decide that boarding is not an area to be expanded in the future. With profit center accounting, practice owners and managers have the information to make business decisions based on a solid understanding of the individual business's facts and circumstances and the related costs and benefits.

To truly realize the benefits of profit center accounting, a practice needs to be computerized. This would include practice software for tracking revenues and an accounting program for tracking expenses. While expenses are not difficult to track manually, tracking revenues without a computer is very time-consuming.

The first step in profit center analysis is to assign all medical procedures and drugs and supplies sales set up in the invoicing module of the clinic's practice management system to a profit center. For example, CBCs and fecals are assigned to the laboratory center, heartworm preventative sales are assigned to pharmacy, etc.

Direct expenses are generally easy to identify and are allocated at the time the bills are paid. For example, new x-ray film is charged to radiology. Oral antibiotics are charged to pharmacy.

At this point, it would be possible to analyze the profitability of income centers based strictly on direct costs. However, this is not recommended because two significant costs are not included in the analysis—doctor and support staff costs, and facility costs.

Facility expense (rent, utilities, janitorial, etc) should be allocated based on the square footage used by the profit center. For example, if the surgery suite represents 15% of the total revenue-generating square footage of the hospital, then 15% of all facility costs should be allocated to the surgery profit center. Support staff salaries and benefits should be allocated based on time studies. Earnings and benefits for salaried veterinarians can be allocated based on the percentage of income they generate in each area or on time studies. Administrative costs can be allocated based on a % of revenue generated in each area or included in a separate administrative category.

Some expenses and revenues are easy to allocate—they clearly belong in one category. Others are more complex and need to be divided. It is not important to exactly allocate every cotton ball to the center in which it was used. Instead, find a reasonable basis for dividing these costs and stick with it unless significant changes in operations occur. Minor variations won't affect the analysis.

This kind of analysis becomes more useful every month that it is used. Not only will an owner or manager have current period results, but trends will also become apparent. As one becomes more comfortable with the information produced, additional ways it can benefit decision-making will become apparent.

Time Value Of Money

While most adults understand the basic concept of interest—i.e. one earns it when putting money into a bank account and pays it when writing a check for student loan or car payments—understanding this concept in terms of financial decision making is often seen as confusing and complicated. So, while the time value of money is covered elsewhere in this book, it is worth reviewing here as well.

Intuitively, we know that having $100 today is better than having the same $100 in a year. First of all, we may have an immediate use for the money and if not, we can decide to invest it, knowing that it will be worth more in the future assuming it is put into a reasonably safe investment and not hidden under the mattress. Assuming the $100 is deposited in a bank account that pays 4% interest compounded annually, then the $100 will be worth $104 in one year. While $4 doesn't seem like much to worry about, the amounts grow quickly with bigger starting sums, higher interest rates and longer periods.

For example, if the $100 were deposited for 5 years at 4% compounded annually, it would grow to $122.

Mathematically, the formula illustrating this concept is:

$$P_n = P_0 (1 + i)^n$$ where P_n is the compound amount at the end of the period, P_0 is the principal amount at the beginning of the period, i is the interest rate and n is the number of periods.

This formula and the above calculation illustrate how to find the **future value** of a sum of money—i.e. what a current sum of money will be worth in the future given a certain interest rate and number of years.

Present value, intuitively, is the opposite of future value. It is the value today of a payment to be received in the future. Whereas, the future value of money invested today will be higher than the amount currently on hand, the present value of money to be received in the future will be less because it has not been invested during the time between now and the future.

These concepts are very important in financial decision making, particularly during times of high interest rates. Investing in an ultrasound may at first look profitable with calculations that exclude the time value of money, but after adding in this factor, it may be clear that the decision is not a prudent one. The time value of money will generally have a larger impact on decision making with higher interest rates, longer periods of investment or return, or if the initial profit margin is slim.

The above discussion illustrates the time value of money in its simplest form. There are, however, a number of issues that need to be discussed further because the choices made can impact the calculations greatly or the variations on the above can allow for more sophisticated analysis.

The choice of the interest rate used in the calculations is, of course, critical. In calculating future value, an assumed interest rate that is higher than that actually seen will result in less value in the future than was anticipated. For example, if an investor wants to accumulate $30,000 at the end of a ten-year period, how much will he or she have to invest now? If interest rates are expected to be 10% over the ten-year period, then the amount to invest now is $11,566 (i.e., $30,000/1.1^{10}$). But, let's say interest rates don't actually reach 10% on average for the 10-year period; instead they average 8%. The amount of money accumulated at the end of the 10-year period will only be $24, 970 (i.e., $11,566 x 1.08^{10}$) instead of the $30,000 desired. Interest rates can be very difficult to predict based on the volatility of financial markets and world economies and this uncertainty increases as the forecasted time period becomes longer.

Compounding is also an important concept to understand. The compounding period is essentially the point at which the interest calculations will be made and added to the value of the original investment. If $10,000 is invested today at 10% and is compounded annually, the future value of this amount at the end of one year will be $11,000. ($10,000 x 1.10^{1}$). If however, the investment is compounded daily, the future value will be greater than $11,000 because interest is being earned not only on the original investment of $10,000 but also on the previously earned interest.

The choice of periods can also be critical to a transaction analysis. Assume a veterinarian wishes to purchase an ultrasound machine and wants to estimate the profitability of such a transaction. Knowing how long that ultrasound will last and be usable to generate revenue is critical. A machine that can generate revenue for 7 years without significant upgrading and technological obsolescence will certainly be more profitable than one that will only last five years, all other factors being equal.

Annuity calculations can also be very useful in financial management, particularly in analyzing the expected return on investments in equipment. In the examples discussed above, one investment was made—i.e. $10,000 was deposited on the first day of the 10-year period and no additional amounts were added to it except for the interest earned.

An annuity is a series of payments invested or a series of payments expected as a return on an investment. For example, if a veterinarian invested in an ultrasound machine, he or she would anticipate receiving income from the fees charged to clients for ultrasound examinations for multiple years in the future. This series of returns is an annuity. Financial planners often advise investing regularly in a retirement account—for example, $200 per month is put into the fund. The series of these investments is an annuity. The amount of each payment or receipt in an annuity series is always the same and the payments or receipts are made at the same time interval. Compounding is done each time period and a distinction has to be made between annuities in which the payments are made at the beginning of the time period versus the end of the time period. Transactions involving a series of receipts or payments of varying amounts or at erratic time periods are calculated as a series of individual transactions rather than as an annuity.

In the same way that future value and present value calculations can be done using single investments, they can also be done using an annuity stream. This kind of analysis often more closely mirrors the expected cash inflows and outflows of a business transaction than a lump sum analysis.

Obviously, it would be very tedious to have to apply the mathematical formula illustrated above (especially with the more complicated compounding and annuity variations) to every project analyzed. Fortunately, there is a way to avoid this. Prior to the common usage of computers for financial analysis, tables were relied upon that could be used to determine the factor for a particular combination of circumstances (compounding, period of investment, interest rate, annuity, etc). With the advent of the computer age, even the simplest of spreadsheet programs often include easy-to-use formulas to calculate present value and future value under different circumstances. Illustrations of the use of these time-value-of-money concepts in decision making in a veterinary practice will be shown later in the chapter.

Breakeven Analysis

Breakeven analysis is a very useful tool for studying the relationships between revenues, fixed costs, and variable costs. It is particularly helpful in analyzing the consequences of starting or expanding a business or when acquiring significant pieces of new equipment.

The breakeven point is the level of sales that will just cover all costs, both fixed and variable. Variable costs are those that fluctuate directly with revenue. For example, variable costs in a veterinary practice would include anesthesia, drugs and supplies. If no patients are seen, none of these items are used and there is no associated cost.

Fixed costs are those that do not fluctuate with revenue over some range of this revenue. For example, the rent paid to lease the building a veterinary practice is located in is a fixed cost. Even if no clients come in the door and no revenue is generated by the practice, the business still has to pay rent. Very few fixed costs, however, are fixed forever over the life of the business. A 2-exam room veterinary hospital may spend $1,500/month in rent payments for the facility. This amount will be the same whether the practice generates $300,000 or $600,000 in revenue per year. There will come a point, however, at which the building is simply too small to accommodate any more clients or any more revenue growth. In order to continue growing the business, facility expansion will have to occur and this cost will increase. Rent is a fixed cost over a very wide range of revenue (in this case from $0 to perhaps $900,000) but at some point the cost will change. It is important to recognize that if there were no fixed costs, there would be no breakeven point. A practice would have no costs if it had no revenue.

Some costs that don't fluctuate directly with revenue but must be increased over shorter ranges of revenue than an item like rent are often called semi-variable costs—staff salaries would be an example in a veterinary clinic.

At the breakeven point:

Revenue = fixed costs plus variable costs

or

Revenue = total costs

The formula for calculating the quantity of items sold (or in a veterinary practice, the number of patient visits) at which the business breaks even is as follows:

$$\text{\# of patient visits} = \frac{\text{fixed costs}}{\text{average transaction charge less average variable costs per transaction}}$$

An example may help illustrate this concept more simply. Dr. Felsted wants to open a cat clinic. She has found a leasehold space that suits her needs and has prepared a budget for the first year of operation. She estimates that staff costs will run about $75,000 during the first year, administrative costs about $70,000, and rent $24,000. She estimates that drugs, supplies, laboratory and other direct patient care costs will run about 20% of fees. In her previous practice, Dr. Felsted had an ATC (average transaction charge) of about $120 and feels she will be able to match that in her new practice. Therefore, her variable costs are expected to be about $24 per transaction (20% of $120). Dr. Felsted does not have another source of income and feels she will need to take a salary of $40,000 the first year and will have debt payments of $13,933 to finance the $100,000 she has borrowed to start the practice. Therefore, her fixed costs are $222,933 for the year.

The # of patient visits necessary to break even is:

$$\frac{\text{Patient}}{\text{Visits}} = \frac{\text{Fixed costs (i.e., } \$75,000 + \$70,000 + \$24,000 + \$40,000 + \$13,933)}{\text{ATC (\$120) less average variable costs/transaction (\$120 \times 20\%)}}$$

$$= \frac{\$222,933}{96}$$

$$= 2,322$$

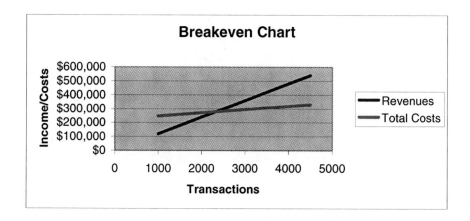

Dr. Felsted must see 2,322 patients (where the line for revenues intersects the line for total costs) during the first year to break even. Assuming she will be open 6 days a week during the year, will not take a vacation the first year, and will be closed for 6 holidays, this averages about 7 ½ patients a day. Dr. Felsted has a loyal following in the area and expects to draw many new clients from a newly built housing division and thus feels it is reasonable to expect she will be able to see, on average, at least this number of patients per day.

Breakeven analysis can also be used effectively for new equipment decisions. For example, let's assume the Felsted Cat Clinic has been in existence for 5 years and has been doing very well. Dr. Felsted decides to buy a new x-ray machine and wants to know how many radiographs she will have to take in order to pay off this machine. The machine costs $16,000 and the average fee charged to clients per series (2 views) is $60.00. Costs to the practice for each radiographic series are $32 and include veterinarian compensation related to provision of the service, staff time, supplies, and maintenance.

Number of   =   Fixed costs (i.e., $16,000)
Radiographs   Fee for radiographs (i.e., $60) less cost per
                       series ($32)

                  =   571

Dr. Felsted must take 571 radiographic series in order to pay for this machine and start making a profit. Since she takes about 5 series a week (260 per year) she feels this machine can be paid for in a reasonable amount of time—just over two years. It is important to note that this is a fairly simple example that excludes the time value of money. Further analysis tools for this purchase will be shown later.

While breakeven analysis is very useful in understanding the relationships between transaction volume, prices and costs, it does have some weaknesses. As with all analyses, reasonable estimates are essential. The linear assumptions made may not hold true in all cases; for example, as the volume of transactions increases, variable costs may increase or decrease on a per unit basis. The clientele or mix of services may change and the ATC generated by the practice may change over time.

Capital Asset Acquisition and Capital Budgeting

The term "capital budgeting" involves all of the financial planning and analysis tasks associated with buying capital assets. Capital assets are those with a life of greater than one year and expected returns over a period greater than one year. The one year cut-off is somewhat arbitrary but conforms with the concept of current and long-term assets and liabilities that is typically used in financial statement preparation.

The process of capital budgeting can be loosely divided into two sections—analyzing the acquisition of certain assets for profitability and, assuming that a transaction appears to be a sound one, determining if the cash flow necessary to finance the transaction will be available from the business or must be obtained elsewhere

.

There are many decisions associated with planning and implementing the purchase of assets of this kind including budget implications, payback period, net present value and other analyses, as well as financing alternatives. The decision to purchase some capital assets may be an easy one— for example, it may be clear that the practice needs a new anesthetic machine and even though this is a long term asset, its cost is not so great and its use so routine, that debate is not necessary.

The purchase of more expensive assets and those not previously used in the practice, however, requires more planning and forethought than does the purchase of equipment or supplies with a much shorter life. As with any asset, it is important to understand why the new equipment is necessary. The most common reasons are to improve patient care, lower operating costs (either direct costs or via increased staff efficiency), increase revenues or to replace a current piece of equipment that does one of the above. However, because the cost of certain capital assets is high, the positive results may not be seen immediately and other aspects of a practice may also be impacted by the purchase, the risk associated with their purchase is much greater. Clearly, a $500 piece of equipment that sits in the corner and gathers dust is not nearly as much of a problem as a $15,000 such item. For example, a veterinary practice may want to purchase an ultrasound unit costing $30,000. This clearly is much more expensive than an anesthesia machine and if this is the first such ultrasound to be owned by the practice, it may not be clear if there will be enough usage to justify the purchase. It is unlikely the payback on the machine will occur within the first year or two and other questions will also have to be addressed.

- What kinds of cases will benefit from an ultrasound exam?
- Are all of the doctors in the practice committed to using the machine?
- How will the doctors be trained in its usage?
- Will outside interpretation of the images need to be made during the early months of usage? How much will this support cost?
- Will additional support staff be needed if the ultrasound is used frequently?
- How will clients be educated as to the benefits of the new diagnostic tests?
- How will the machine be financed?
- Are there timing issues to consider in the acquisition?
- What fees will be charged for the exams?

There are a number of capital budgeting techniques that are extremely useful in analyzing the purchase of new equipment. These techniques can be used in contemplating the purchase of just one asset (for example, the ultrasound) or in comparing the benefits of two different assets (for example, an ultrasound versus a laser surgical unit.)

As with any analysis, good data is critical to good results. A number of variables will be used in these calculations such as the cost of the equipment, the additional annual costs associated with the asset (such as a service contract or supplies), the expected cost savings to be obtained from usage or the anticipated increase in revenues. If these items are not accurately estimated, the results of the acquisition analysis may be erroneous. For example, cost of equipment does not just include the sticker price. Other components of cost include tax, installation, training, and interest costs if the asset is financed.

The **payback period** is the number of years necessary to break even on the purchase of the asset (the breakeven analysis presented previously calculated the number of procedures that would have to be done to break even.) After this point, the practice will start to realize a profit on the acquisition assuming the figures used in the analysis are accurate and reality conforms to the assumptions made in the analysis.

The payback period is calculated as:

$$\frac{\text{Total purchase price}}{\text{Annual net income (i.e. revenue minus operating costs for a year)}}$$

Example:

The Felsted Cat Clinic is planning to purchase an x-ray machine at a total cost of $16,000. The average fee charged to clients per series is $60.00. On average the practice takes 5 radiographs per week or 260 per year at a cost to the practice of $32.00 each. Costs to the practice include veterinarian compensation related to provision of the service, staff time, supplies, and maintenance.

Payback period = $$\frac{\$16,000}{(\$60\text{-}32) \times 260}$$

=   2.20

In other words, it will take 2.20 years to pay for this machine and before any profits will be made by the clinic on this service.

The payback period is not the only tool that should be used in analyzing an asset purchase. Acquisitions with the shortest payback period may not be the ones that are ultimately the most profitable to the practice. It is also important to remember that the time value of money has not been factored into this calculation.

Net present value (NPV) analysis estimates the total cash outflows involved with the purchase of an asset compared to the total inflows. A positive outcome equals a profitable purchase. NPV analysis also incorporates the time value of money into the calculations.

The difference in value of an investment compared with and without the time value of money component depends on the interest rate used in the calculation. Differences get larger with higher interest rates and longer payback periods.

While this calculation gives more accurate information, it is also more difficult to do and many small business owners will enlist the aid of their accountant or financial advisor in performing this calculation.

Continuing the example used above, the NPV analysis for the first three years of the life of the x-ray machine is as follows. The first chart calculates the cash flow related to the purchase as well as the income expected each year less operating costs and an overhaul of the machine in year 3.

Year	Cash out	Cash in	Net flow
0	$16,000 (purchase)		($16,000)
1		$7280 (annual net income)	$7280
2		$7280	$7280
3	$500 (overhaul)	$7280	$6780

The next chart calculates the discounted cash flow using present value factors.

Year	Net cash flow	10% PV factor	Discounted net cash flow
0	($16,000)	1	($16,000)
1	$7280	.909	$6617
2	$7280	.826	$6013
3	$6780	.751	$5092
			$1722

After allowing for the time value of money, it is expected that use of the new x-ray machine will generate profits of $1,722 during the third year of its usage. If this analysis is done on a monthly basis instead of an annual basis, the payback period turns out to be 2.75 years instead of 2.2 years due to the time value of money.

This analysis could be performed over the full expected life of the equipment in order to estimate the total profitability. If this were done, any amounts expected to be realized from the sale of the equipment at the end of its life (salvage value) should be recognized as an inflow and any costs of disposal should be recognized as an outflow.

Tax effects and alternative financing can be included for even more precise analysis, but those calculations are beyond the scope of this chapter.

Internal rate of return (IRR) is another tool for analyzing the feasibility of asset acquisition. This calculation can be difficult to do without a spreadsheet program (such as Microsoft® Excel) or a financial calculator and, again, a practice owner may wish to enlist the aid of their accountant or financial advisor.

The IRR is the time-adjusted real rate earned on a proposed project. This rate is a "break-even" rate and represents the maximum rate of interest that can be paid for financing without having the investment become unprofitable. Thus this figure can be compared to the cost of the capital needed to finance the acquisition to determine if the project makes sense. If the asset has an IRR of 10% and it will only cost 6% to borrow the funds necessary to buy the equipment, then the project will be profitable.

Financing alternatives

Generally there are three ways to obtain an asset:

- Cash purchase
- Purchase using bank or other lender financing
- Lease

A cash purchase is attractive in that it is simple and leaves the practice unencumbered with debt. Additionally, no financing charges are incurred. Cash is, of course, not available for other purposes later on down the line and cannot be put into investments which may have a greater return than the interest rate charged for the financing. It is critical to recognize that owner financing has a cost just as does outside financing. That cost is the foregone investment income that could have been generated from the investment of that cash. Financing a purchase may also help a new entity build up a credit rating.

Bank or lender financing is useful for practices in need of equipment, but without the cash reserves to purchase it outright. Terms and interest rates at several institutions should be compared before making a decision as to which financial institution will be used. The practice will obviously incur costs related to the financing in the form of interest and a large amount of debt on the books may limit the practice from future borrowings or cause cash flow difficulties. A down payment is frequently required on the equipment.

Leases are perhaps the most complicated method of financing and the one least understood by small business owners. Leases can be attractive alternatives if a practice is low on cash because a down payment is not required and monthly payments may be lower than with purchase financing. Lease agreements may be less complicated and include fewer requirements than financing documents.

With a true lease, a business pays a specified amount per month for the use of a piece of equipment for a period of time. The lessee does not own the equipment and at the end of the lease term (or potentially before if desired), returns the equipment to the lease company and has no option to purchase it. This is called an operating lease. The leasing company estimates the value of the equipment at the time it is returned and adds an interest factor in determining the monthly lease payments. Both of these values can significantly impact the amount of the lease payments. The monthly payments are generally lower than with purchase financing because the equipment user is only paying for the decline in the value of the equipment to the point at which it is returned.

Some leases, however, are more accurately characterized as installment loans, but are called leases. These are capital leases and for financial statement and tax return purposes are treated as the purchase of equipment using a loan.

It is important to compare the costs of leasing equipment not only with those of outright purchase but also amongst the different kinds of leases. Again, it may be helpful to have an accountant involved with this analysis because the IRS has certain guidelines that determine whether a lease is an operating or capital lease and the tax and other calculations can be complicated. Some of the issues to consider include:

- Depreciation ramifications of each alternative—it is obviously to a business's benefit to get the biggest tax deductions possible as early as possible as seen with capital leases or outright purchase options
- Monthly cash requirements—operating leases usually have a lower monthly payment
- Interest rate—this may not be clear if you're just quoted terms of "$300/month for 36 months" and the interest rate may be much higher than market rates
- Purchase options at end of lease—this is one of the most important items in determining the type of lease
- Obsolescence of equipment—an operating lease may be more advantageous for equipment that becomes obsolete quickly or a practice will want to replace soon
- Sales tax—in a lease, sales tax is generally calculated on both the principle and interest portions of the lease payment whereas in an outright purchase, tax is paid only on the equipment value
- Early termination penalties/cancellation clauses
- Signing or documentation fees
- Personal property tax payments
- Responsibility for maintenance and insurance
- Cost of equipment at the beginning of the lease
- Value of equipment at the end of the lease
- Insurance requirements

Traditionally, leases have often been less attractive from a truly financial viewpoint, but bargains do exist—either very low interest rates or free supplies are included. Some more unusual leases also exist that may be attractive—for example, a practice leases a blood analyzer from a vendor and the payments are waived each month a certain amount of drugs and supplies are purchased. These are particularly complicated to analyze and account for, but can represent a good deal in certain circumstances. In making the decision to purchase or lease equipment, both the practice's financial position and the cost of each option must be reviewed.

If a precise determination needs to be made regarding purchase versus lease, it is necessary to compare the present value of after-tax cash flows for both, and select the one with the better disposition.

Investment Risk And Uncertainty

Risk and uncertainty are financial terms used to express the variability of the potential return on an investment. These concepts are important to all business owners, as very few actions have guaranteed reactions. For example, in a veterinary practice, there is risk and uncertainty associated with establishing or purchasing a practice, as with smaller decisions such as whether or not to remodel an exam room or purchase a piece of equipment.

The concept of risk includes both the **variability** of the return (i.e. whether the investment might earn 2%, 5% or 20%) as well as the likelihood or **probability** of each of these possible returns. Most investors already have some awareness of risk, with the knowledge that higher risk is often related to higher return (although the status of the stock market has not always adhered to that principle).

An example of the importance of risk analysis in veterinary decision-making is as follows. Suppose that Dr. Felsted were to buy a $10,000 5-year certificate of deposit from an insured institution at a guaranteed interest rate of 5% instead of purchasing equipment for the clinic. In this case, the return on the CD could be precisely calculated; there is no variability and no risk in this investment whereas there is always risk in purchasing a new piece of equipment and generating the fees necessary to make this a profitable venture.

On the other hand, the equipment might generate an even higher return in revenues than the 5% on the CD. All returns should be considered in terms of potential risk and the risk-averseness of the decision makers. Not all individuals look at risk in the same light; some practice owners are very comfortable with a higher level of risk that is potentially rewarded with higher returns whereas others would prefer a more conservative route.

Owners or practice managers may not want to invest the time in performing complex risk analysis. However, the concept is useful and can often be applied to other financial calculations. For example, in the section in this chapter on payback, Dr. Felsted determined how long it would take to pay off her x-ray machine. A simple chart that varies the number of radiographs the clinic might take in the course of a year, can show the *variability* or *risk* in the length of the payback period, and hence in the return on that investment.

Much more sophisticated risk analysis tools are available, but are beyond the scope of this chapter.

As discussed at the beginning of this chapter, strong financial analysis and control is essential for the well being and financial success of a small business. Tools such as those illustrated above are relatively simple to use and can provide powerful information to improve decision-making.

OPERATIONS MANAGEMENT

Lowell Ackerman DVM DACVD MBA MPA

Dr. Lowell Ackerman is a Diplomate of the American College of Veterinary Dermatology and in addition holds an MBA from the University of Phoenix and an MPA from Harvard University. He is involved in clinical practice as a clinical assistant professor at Tufts University School of Veterinary Medicine as well as helping to develop the business skills curriculum there. In addition, Dr. Ackerman is affiliated with Veterinary Healthcare Consultants, primarily dealing with practice administration and management issues. Dr. Ackerman is the author/co-author of 74 books to date and numerous book chapters and articles. He lectures extensively, on an international basis.

Total Quality Management (TQM)

No matter where you plan to work, or what you plan to do, today's businesses are strongly behind the process of total quality management (TQM) and you should be as well. Be aware, though, that TQM isn't just about the efficient production of widgets. The process is about value chain management and team building, and ultimately about customer satisfaction. The same rules apply when you use TQM for your career planning or business operation.

There are many different buzzwords and catch-phrases to describe what TQM does, but at the root of it all is a very simple paradigm often referred to as the PDCA cycle—Plan, Do, Check, Act. The concept is that you create a detailed Action Plan, implement that plan, check the outcomes against your original objectives and make appropriate revisions, and then act on those revisions utilizing the new game plan. But don't stop there. While implementing that plan, you will generate new outcomes to compare against your objectives, make more refinements and start the whole process over again. As your outcomes more closely parallel your goals, you might increase your objectives (even higher client satisfaction, client throughput, surgical efficiency, etc.) to continually refine and improve the process.

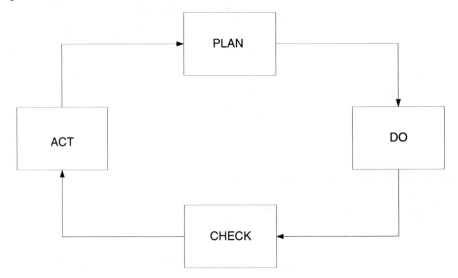

In responding to changes in the marketplace, there is still time to respond quickly and utilize the principles of TQM. This is accomplished by utilizing the three Ms of TQM: Map, Mobilize, and Measure (or monitor). We often do this intuitively, but TQM aims to standardize the process and force us to look at outcomes. More and more we are also doing this in the actual practice of medicine, using objective outcomes (evidence-based medicine) to refine medical processes. We are starting to do this with even age-old veterinary practices such as vaccination. Should we be vaccinating on an annual basis? Should a 5-pound Chihuahua be given the same dose of vaccine as a 150-pound Great Dane? Should a Doberman pinscher receive the same dose of parvovirus vaccine as a Labrador retriever? Only by continuing to ask questions do we allow the real evidence to direct our actions.

Learning Curve

Veterinary medicine is all about learning new tasks, and while the learning is very exciting, it also means that novices are bound to take more time doing procedures (of all sorts) than veterans of the trade. Whether it is doing a spay, mastering a new computer management program, or doing a laser procedure, it takes time to get up to speed on any new duty. But, how long should it take? If you know what's likely, you can plan for it.

The concept of learning curves was first introduced to the aircraft industry by T.P. Wright in 1936 but it is now routinely applied to most learning events. The notion is that repetition of a specific task allows us to improve our performance time the more times that we perform the same task. In general, our performance time tends to decrease by a fixed percentage as the number of procedures we do double.

For most medical and technical tasks, we can improve our performance by 5-20% per procedure as the numbers of procedures double, reflecting a learning rate of 80-95%.

For example, the first time that we do a specific procedure, it may take 50 minutes to perform. If we envision a learning rate of 85%, this means that there is a 15% improvement in performance time with each doubling of the number of procedures done. So, the second time we do the procedure, we can improve our performance by 7 ½ minutes (15% of 50 minutes), completing the task in 42-½ minutes. By the time we have done four procedures, our cumulative average time is down to just over 36 minutes (an improvement of 15% of 42.5 minutes). How are we doing by the time we reach 30 procedures?

When we assume that production time per procedure is reduced by a fixed percentage each time production is doubled, we can calculate likely improved times with a formula:

$$K_n = K_1 \times n^{\frac{\log r}{\log 2}}$$

where,

K_n = the required time for the nth procedure
K_1 = the required time for the first procedure
n = the procedure number of interest
r = the learning rate (improvement of 15% = learning rate of 0.85)

To calculate the improvement in time after doing 30 procedures, we just plug in the numbers as follows:

$$K_{40} = 50 \text{ minutes} \times 30^{\log 0.85/\log 2}$$
$$= 22.52 \text{ minutes}$$

Therefore, if a procedure took 50 minutes initially and there was a 15% improvement as the number of procedures doubled, after having completed 30 procedures, the time per procedure would require 22 ½ minutes.

Let's face it—you probably won't ever voluntarily calculate logarithms to predict your procedure times. It is therefore fortunate that you can do it relatively simply on a variety of web sites, such as www.jsc.nasa.gov/bu2/learn.html. Just plug in your learning rate and your initial time and it will calculate the new time for the procedure number that you specify.

To help further, below is a table depicting times to do procedures depending on different learning rates, from 80% to 95% for a procedure that requires 60 minutes to complete the first time.

Table10-1: Improvements in performing a procedure that originally required 60 minutes, assuming different learning rates

Procedure#	Learning rates (%)			
	80	85	90	95
1	60	60	60	60
2	48	51	54	57
5	35.74	41.14	46.98	53.26
10	28.59	34.97	42.28	50.60
15	25.09	31.80	39.75	49.10
20	22.87	29.72	38.05	48.07
25	21.29	28.21	36.78	47.28
30	20.07	27.03	35.78	46.65
40	18.30	25.27	34.25	45.67

Of course, it is not possible to improve times indefinitely, at least not at initial rates. For the most part, the initial learning rate only applies to the first 30 or so procedures. Both learning and improvement continue, but not at the same rate as they did initially. So, if the procedure had an initial learning rate of 80% for the first thirty times, the learning rate for the next thirty procedures may be at a rate of 95% instead, with only 5% improvement with doubling. After that, the improvement may be only 1% with doubling. For example, it may take a novice 60 minutes to do their first spay, and applying an 80% learning rate, they can get that time down to about 20 minutes by the 30th procedure. Thereafter, further improvements are miniscule in comparison, even after 1,000 spays. If the learning rate were 99%, then after the 1000th spay, surgical time would be down to about 18 minutes. That is, once a skill is "mastered", the learning rate is no longer applicable at the initial rate, and further refinements often have to do with re-engineering the process, and using TQM principles. For example, using staples rather than suture to close an incision may save additional time.

Constraints

Veterinary hospitals run like regular businesses, often on a 7-day-a-week schedule, but operations management notions are only in their infancy in the veterinary field. While pets are not a commodity like widgets, a veterinary hospital still needs to schedule and staff efficiently, take animals in, and then (hopefully) discharge them healthy once again.

Because most veterinary hospitals don't utilize well the principles that are already in force in human hospitals, there are great benefits to be had by beginning to implement some of these processes without delay. The utilization rate (the productive work time divided by the total work time available) tends to be relatively low in veterinary hospitals. We don't hear many veterinary hospital administrators talk about job flow time (the time of completion minus the time at which the job was first available to be worked on), makespan (the total amount of time required to complete a group of jobs), or the slack per remaining operations (the difference between the time remaining to complete a job and the total time remaining, including that of the operation being scheduled).

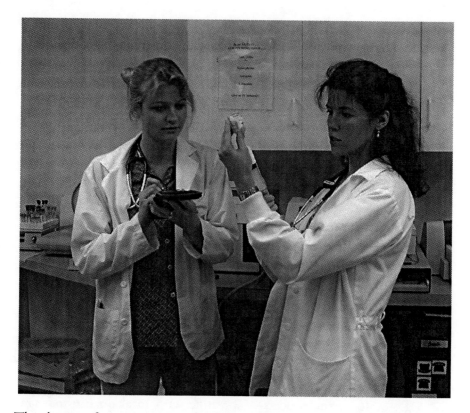

The theory of constraints, sometimes referred to as the drum-buffer-rope method, tries to address the problem of bottlenecks in an operation. This is especially troublesome in a veterinary hospital. Imagine an assembly-line situation in a hospital in which a dozen routine surgeries are scheduled in a morning. The trained technicians have allotted 20 minutes for each surgery and have coordinated their efforts regarding anesthesia, surgical assisting and patient recovery. All goes well until the receptionist interrupts the process for the doctor to start seeing some unscheduled drop-in appointments. A bottleneck is formed because the technicians cannot advance in their schedule without the doctor. There is no point in anesthetizing the animals on schedule without the doctor to do the surgery. Without the surgery, the technicians cannot assist, and there are no animals for recovery. The process grinds to a halt. Clearly some planning is needed. Here's what application of theory of constraints would address:

- Identify the system bottleneck—in this case it is the doctor, who screws up the schedule by seeing unscheduled appointments
- Exploit the bottleneck—Schedules need to be changed to maximize the throughput of the doctor. That likely means not accepting unscheduled appointments during surgery time.
- Subordinate other processes to the bottleneck—The technicians should be scheduled to support the schedule of the veterinarian and not produce more than s/he can handle. If the doctor really must see intermittent appointments, it is best for the technicians to assist in that procedure to hasten the doctor getting back on task.
- Elevate the bottleneck—After the above improvements have been implemented, if there is still a constraint to throughput, then management needs to consider changing the schedule (a longer work day), or bringing in more resources (hire another veterinarian).
- Re-evaluate the process—Continue with total quality management to address new concerns. If another doctor is hired, perhaps the next bottleneck will be a shortage of technicians, or receptionists!

It is not possible to cover even a small portion of the principles of operations management here, but this is the way that most businesses run, so other resources are plentiful. Just to whet your appetite, here is one solution that has plagued veterinary hospitals continually—how to staff a hospital effectively 7 days a week, but still give employees two consecutive days off each week. Let's see how this can be accomplished.

The first step is to identify the total number of staff needed for each day of the week. The following is an example:

Monday	Tuesday	Wednesday	Thursday	Friday	Saturday	Sunday
8	6	3	5	7	4	3

The maximum requirement is 8 employees, on Monday. We look for all the pairs of consecutive days that exclude the maximum daily requirements and select the pair that has the lowest total requirements for the two days. In this case, Saturday and Sunday have the lowest requirements (4+3=7). If there is a tie, you can use any fair method you like to arbitrarily decide.

- Assign the first employee the two days off (in this case Saturday and Sunday), meaning that they will be working Monday through Friday. For those days that now have a worker, subtract 1 from each of those days' requirement. In this case, nothing is subtracted from Saturday or Sunday because nobody is working those days yet. The chart will then look like this:

Monday	Tuesday	Wednesday	Thursday	Friday	Saturday	Sunday
7	5	2	4	6	4	3

- For assigning the next worker, the lowest 2-day requirement is now Wednesday-Thursday (2+4 =6). Assign those days off to an employee and subtract 1 from each of the working days (i.e., Monday, Tuesday, Friday, Saturday and Sunday). This will yield:

Monday	Tuesday	Wednesday	Thursday	Friday	Saturday	Sunday
6	4	2	4	5	3	2

- Now the lowest combination pair is once again Saturday-Sunday (3+2=5) so that 2-day combination is assigned to an employee, numbers are subtracted from working days, and the process continues.

Monday	Tuesday	Wednesday	Thursday	Friday	Saturday	Sunday
5	3	1	3	4	3	2

The lowest pair is now Tuesday-Wednesday (or Wednesday-Thursday). We assign an employee Tuesday-Wednesday off, subtract from working days, and continue

Monday	Tuesday	Wednesday	Thursday	Friday	Saturday	Sunday
4	3	1	2	3	2	1

- The lowest pair is Saturday-Sunday (2+1=3) or Wednesday-Thursday, so we assign an employee the weekend off, and continue the process.

Monday	Tuesday	Wednesday	Thursday	Friday	Saturday	Sunday
3	2	0	1	2	2	1

- The lowest pair is now Wednesday-Thursday, so we give those days off to an employee and continue

Monday	Tuesday	Wednesday	Thursday	Friday	Saturday	Sunday
2	1	0	1	1	1	0

- At this point, we can see that the balance can either be filled by one full-time employee (who doesn't get two consecutive days off,) and one part-time employee (to work on Mondays), or to utilize two part-time employees. One part-time employee might work Monday, Tuesday, and Thursday, while the other works Monday, Friday and Saturday, or they could split shifts amongst themselves. This also tells you that you need six full-time employees who will have two consecutive days off each week, and two part-time employees. Another option is to maintain the two employees as full-time rather than part-time so that there is "slack" and the ability to have staff on hand when business grows to meet demand. It just takes a little planning.

Employee#	Days Off
1	Saturday-Sunday
2	Wednesday-Thursday
3	Saturday-Sunday
4	Tuesday-Wednesday
5	Saturday-Sunday
6	Wednesday-Thursday
7	Part-time
8	Part-time

Activity-based Management

Activity-based Costing

Activity-based costing, probably not surprising, involves differentiating costs based on the activity to which they can be attributed. For instance, the cost of suture material can likely be attributed to surgery and the costs of maintenance on the x-ray machine can be directly attributed to radiology. Only by correctly understanding the cost basis of an activity can one be assured that it is profitably priced to the consumer, and that the activity accounts for its fair share of hospital expenses.

This branch of management accounting has its own vocabulary, and it is worth gaining familiarity with some of these terms, notably:

Cost object	Any activity for which costs are measured and assigned
Direct Tracing	Assigning a cost legitimately to a cost object
Driver Tracing	Using factors to assign costs to cost objects
Allocation	Somewhat arbitrarily assigning costs to an activity when there is no causal relationship between them.
Cost Behavior	The change in costs based on output; a function of fixed and variable costs.

The purpose of such an exercise is to look at all of the costs of a venture, in this case a veterinary practice, and then to share those costs equitably amongst all activities. For instance, if you set up a dental operatory and send out an advertising pamphlet to hospital clients, you can *directly trace* the costs of such advertising and mailing to dentistry; it shouldn't be coming out of the budget for dermatology, for example. When it comes to wages, one might use *driver tracing* to assign the costs of wages and benefits to the dentistry department, based on hours of operation and staffing needs. Allocation is used for indirect expenses. For example, one might *allocate* a proportion of utilities used in the hospital to dentistry, based on the floor space that dentistry occupies. Allocation is the most arbitrary way to assign costs, because it is not based on direct usage of resources. In the end, all hospital expenses need to be traced or allocated to profit centers, if those profit centers are expected to pay those costs in the course of doing business. The receptionist area, the hospital manager, the staff lounge and every other person, space or activity that does not generate revenue directly must be paid for by those services that do generate revenue.

Cost behavior is concerned with changes in costs based on volume of output. For example, if you have an in-house laboratory, how do costs change depending on utilization? To illustrate, let's take a simplistic look at 2 months of laboratory costs using appointments as a "driver". In one month, the practice saw 430 appointments and the costs associated with the in-house laboratory were $2,240. The next month, there were 475 appointments and the laboratory costs were $2,376. In the first month, the laboratory cost was $2,240/430 or $5.21 per appointment; in the second month, it was $2,376/475 or $5.00 per appointment. Part of the monthly laboratory expense is the fixed cost of having and maintaining the equipment, but a portion is also a variable expense, reflecting increased usage. One can determine the relative proportions of fixed and variable expenses with some basic mathematics. The first step is calculating the variable expense per appointment based on the change in costs between periods; the second step is plugging in the number calculated for variable expense, to determine fixed expense. The benefit of this exercise is that one can then create a linear equation to predict total costs based on client traffic.

Step 1: The variable expense is calculated by dividing the difference in costs (i.e., $2,376—$2,240) by the difference in appointment numbers (i.e., 475-430).

$$\text{Variable cost} = \frac{\$2,376 - \$2,240}{475 - 430} = \frac{\$136}{45} = \$3.02 \text{ per appointment}$$

Step 2: The fixed expense is then calculated by looking at the total expense for either period and subtracting out the number of appointments for that period multiplied by the variable expense.

$$
\begin{aligned}
\text{Fixed expense for month 2} &= \$2,376 - (475)(\$3.02) \\
&= \$2,376 - \$1434.50 \\
&= \$941.50
\end{aligned}
$$

Since the fixed expense will be the same each month regardless of client traffic, appointments can be used as a driver for anticipated laboratory expense following a linear formula. So, anticipated in-house laboratory expenses will be:

In-house laboratory expenses = $941.50 + $3.02 x, where x = number of appointments. This represents the formula for a straight line (i.e., y = b + mx). While the fixed cost is the same for each month, the unit cost, the cost per appointment, will continue to decrease the more appointments that are seen. This is just the effect of spreading the costs over more appointments. So, the more clients seen, the bigger the savings for the hospital. In no case, however, will the monthly laboratory charges be less than the fixed cost.

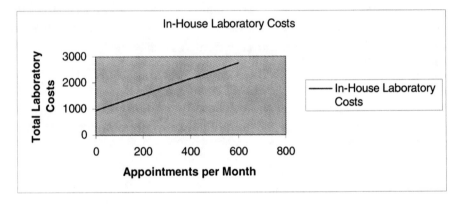

Figure 10-1. Laboratory costs as a function of Appointment Numbers

Value-added Analysis

Value-added analysis is an important concept in Total Quality Management (TQM). When veterinarians provide services or sell goods, they do so at an expense related to materials, labor and overhead. Interestingly enough, however, the value added is actually independent of the costs. Imagine considering a pharmaceutical dispensing machine, such as used in large hospitals and pharmacies. The price tag is $1.5 million, but the machine counts the drugs, puts them in a vial and labels them, with near perfect efficiency. Based on your current dispensing load, you estimate that this will add approximately $85 to each prescription. While such a gadget is useful, and certainly will save technician time, does it really deliver "value" to clients? The answer is that while clients might be impressed with this expensive piece of technology, they aren't likely to pay more for it because it really doesn't add to their utility (i.e., they just want the medication and don't really care if the technician counts the pills, or the machine). By adding functionality, convenience, aesthetics, branding and so forth, value is added that makes the final product or service more valuable to the consumer. The "added value" of a product or service is the value to the client after your intervention less the value before you were involved. Just as the credit card commercials suggest, some activities are "priceless" when compared to others that are a sum of their costs. It is this differential that allows veterinarians to earn a respectable livelihood by delivering true added value to clients—the good health and longevity of their pets.

The important point to keep in mind is that value to the customer is independent of cost. This is a fact, not wishful thinking. Therefore, in a value-added analysis, one assesses the processes used in client transactions to determine which provide true value and which don't. We divide these activities into three categories:

- Real value-adding activities (RVA) that are important to clients
- Medical value-adding activities (MVA) that don't add value for clients, but are necessary from a medical or hospital perspective
- Non value-adding activities (NVA) that neither add value from the perspective of the client nor the hospital

The goal of such an exercise is to see how much of the total cost is attributable to each category, and ideally to eliminate non-value-adding activities and minimize medical value-adding activities. Since clients will still pay the going rate for the end product, reducing such activities increases profits for the organization. In fact, removing some steps may actually increase value for the client.

For example, in evaluating the processes involved in something as routine as an ovariohysterectomy (spay), the clients value most the safe use of anesthesia, pain management, lack of trauma, and getting their pets back quickly. These are valued even more than the premise for having the surgery—making sure the pet doesn't produce offspring. From a medical perspective, there is value in safe anesthesia, having the surgery completed in a reasonable period of time, and discharging the patient, without incident, back to the client. In reviewing the processes, a practice could make some bold changes to highlight the real value-adding activities, minimize the medical value-adding activities, and hopefully eliminating the non value-adding activities. This is not only cost-cutting, but potentially profit enhancing as well. Pain management is definitely value adding and pre-emptive analgesic regimens should become part of every elective surgery.

Recovery is another value-adding activity that is ignored in most practices. While most hospitals allow anesthetized animals to recover on the floor or in a cage with a technician somewhere in the vicinity, most clients would gladly pay a premium to have a nurse hold their pet and comfort them continuously as they recovered from anesthesia. On the other hand, using sutures versus staples or selecting isoflurane versus sevoflurane is a medical value-adding activity that has only marginal value for clients; they expect veterinarians to select what would be medically appropriate for their pet. That is one of the reasons that adding pain management to elective surgeries has sometimes elicited unexpected comments from clients. Many find it troublesome that pain management would be optional and just expect that veterinarians already do everything in their power to alleviate suffering. Why would they not provide pain management for such procedures—surely not just for monetary reasons? Pain management should be included in every veterinary practice and most clients perceive it not only as real value-added, but clearly providing medical value as well.

As far as non value-adding activities, this sometimes involves questioning protocols and processes and challenging convention. For example, with today's anesthetic regimens, why are elective surgical patients kept overnight in the hospital? This is especially troubling in hospitals that do not have an attendant supervising the animals during the night. In this scenario, would it not be better to discharge the pet to the care of the owners, with instructions to monitor closely overnight and go to the emergency clinic if there were any problems? Clients may even pay a premium for such a "day surgery", would invariably more closely monitor their pets than would be the situation in an unstaffed hospital, and this is turn would reduce costs for the practice.

Scheduling

Makespan

Makespan is the total amount of time required to complete a group of jobs. For example, in a veterinary practice, one may look at the makespan of surgical procedures, or of in-hospital patient care, or even of client appointments. When these grouped activities are completed over a span of time, makespan is calculated as follows:

$$\text{Makespan} = \text{Time of completion of last job} - \text{Starting time of first job}$$

Obviously, decreasing makespan is an important concept in operations management, because it ultimately determines how many jobs (patients) can be completed in a day and how revenue can be maximized.

Whereas most veterinarians do not necessarily schedule patient activities to minimize makespan, most use at least some of the principles on a regular basis. When patients are prioritized based on earliest due date (EDD), the patient that has to go home first gets scheduled next. First come, first served (FCFS) implies that the patient first in the door gets taken care of first and patients are queued accordingly thereafter. Jobs may also be scheduled according to shortest processing time (SPT). For example, between a dog that needed a nail trim and one that needed to be catheterized (but not as an emergency), the nail trim would come first so that it could be completed and discharged.

Veterinarians and technical nursing staff act inefficiently in many busy practices, because for hospitalized patients, the veterinarian often needs to perform evaluations and write up medical records before the technicians can start doing treatments. Either the technicians follow the veterinarian around trying to get instructions at the time of examination, which slows down the veterinarian, or the technicians wait for the doctors to finish their evaluations before getting started, which slows down the technicians. In this regard, hospitals have a lot that could be learned from workshops that specialize in optimizing makespan.

Johnson's Rule minimizes makespan in scheduling a group of jobs involving two groups or workstations. This maximizes utilization because the first workstation (veterinarian) is allowed to proceed continuously until it processes its last job, and this minimizes the idle time of the second workstation (the technicians). Let's see how the rule would apply for in-hospital patient care, in which the doctor first needs to evaluate each patient, determine the next intervention (laboratory work, radiography, treatments, etc.), write up directions in the medical record and allow the technicians to then start working on the intervention. The doctor or head technician may estimate the time requirements for each patient based on morning rounds or on presenting complaint (e.g., diarrhea, acute abdomen, cat not urinating properly, etc.).

Step 1: Create a table of the patients to be seen for in-hospital care and a rough estimate of how much time will likely be required by doctor and technical staff.

Step 2: Find the shortest time requirement among the jobs not yet scheduled. In case of tie, select one arbitrarily.

Step 3: If the shortest processing time is for the doctor, schedule the job at the earliest available time. If the shortest processing time is for the technicians, schedule the job as late as possible. Remove that job from the list of remaining procedures.

Step 4: Repeat steps 1 and 2 until all jobs have been scheduled. This causes patients requiring the shortest doctor time to be scheduled first and those requiring the shortest technician time to be scheduled last.

For example, in our fictional one-doctor small animal hospital, in-hospital treatments are typically done between 8AM and 10AM, at which time appointments start. It is important to minimize makespan so that the doctor does not start appointments late and cause the entire day to fall behind schedule. Elective surgeries are only performed on Tuesdays and Thursdays, and this happens to be a non-surgical day. Here are the estimates for the doctor and technical staff scheduling regarding the 5 in-hospital patients. The assumption is that all patients need to be seen by the doctor first, and the technical staff can only perform interventions once the patient has completed the doctor portion of the evaluation. Those requiring the least doctor time are scheduled first; those requiring the least technician time are scheduled last.

Patient	Doctor (minutes)	Technical Staff (minutes)
P1	12	18
P2	5	9
P3	8	13
P4	14	16
P5	10	7

Establishing the Job Sequence

According to Johnson's Rule, we first look for the shortest processing time. In this case, it is Patient #2, requiring 5 minutes of doctor time. Therefore, patient 2 is scheduled first.

P2				

The next shortest time is Patient#5, requiring 7 minutes of technician time. It is scheduled in the last available time slot.

P2				P5

The next shortest time is Patient #3, requiring 8 minutes of doctor time. So, Patient#3 is scheduled in the next available time slot.

P2	P3			P5

The next shortest time (of the patients yet unscheduled) is Patient#1, requiring 12 minutes of doctor time. It is scheduled accordingly in the 3rd time slot.

P2	P3	P1		P5

This leaves Patient#4 to be placed in the last remaining time slot.

P2	P3	P1	P4	P5

We know that this combination produces the optimal makespan, but we can use another tool, a Gantt chart, to map out our schedule to see how the morning will progress.

Workstation	Patient								
Doctor	P2 (5)	P3 (8)	P1 (12)	P4 (14)		P5 (10)	Available for other work, review lab data, radiographs, etc.		
Technicians		P2 (9)	P3 (13)		P1 (18)		P4 (16)	P5 (10)	
Time	0	10	20	30	40	50	60	70	80

No other sequence of jobs will produce a lower makespan, the schedule minimizes the idle time of the technicians (only the first 5 minutes in this case), and this gives the fastest time to compete all jobs. Note also that the schedule recognizes that the technicians can't start working with a patient until it has seen the doctor.

Inventory Management

Product sales currently provide about 25% of revenues for veterinary hospitals, so inventory management is critical to ensuring profit. The goal is obviously to "turn" inventory quickly, preferably so that money is recouped in revenues before the bill for the products needs to be paid. As distribution channels for inventory items improve, often utilizing some form of business-to-business (b2b) connection, Just in Time (JIT) inventory is accessible to more and more veterinarians.

To calculate inventory turns, and this is something that should be done in any business that depends on retail sales, it is necessary to periodically count inventory available for sale. The average inventory is then the beginning inventory plus the ending inventory for a period, divided by two. Inventory "turns" can then be calculated by dividing the total purchases for that period by the average inventory. Dividing 365 days per year by the number of turns gives you shelf life. A business that turns products 8-10 times a year has product that averages 35-45 days on the shelf. If your practice only has four turns a year, there is 3 months worth of inventory on your shelves (365 days/4 turns = 91 days). That's not a very efficient use of your money! Aim to turn pharmaceutical inventory 12 times a year, for a shelf life of 30 days (365/12), and plan on twice that rate for pet foods and point-of-purchase sales.

It's good to have frequent turnover, but very high turnover rates often have consequently higher ordering costs and may run the risk of creating shortages. After all, even with a dedicated inventory team, you don't want to be in surgery and find out you don't have suture material because the 2-day stock that was on hand got depleted when a delivery truck failed to make its appointed rounds.

Making inventory profitable takes more than Just in Time delivery and ensuring adequate turns. Remember Pareto's Law that 20% of inventory will account for 80% of revenues. This is important because free space is often in short supply in veterinary hospitals, so one should concentrate on products sold often and profitably. More often than not, it is more cost effective to write prescriptions for products that are expensive or not routinely dispensed.

Holding costs are assumed to be directly proportional to average inventory, at least in this simplistic model. They are thus mathematically represented as the holding cost per unit, H, multiplied by the average inventory, Q/2 (i.e., HQ/2). Ordering costs are represented by the fixed ordering cost per order, multiplied by the number of orders per period. For the sake of simplicity, holding costs are considered to be variable, and ordering costs fixed, although a combination is actually at work for both.

There are a number of simple ways of curbing inventory costs. Companies that bill for products have a billing cutoff for each statement period. You might notice that your credit card statement always reflects sales through the 12th of each month, for example. Making your order after the billing cutoff date by even one day pushes the purchase into the next statement period, giving more time for products to be sold before payment is due.

When to place inventory orders has to do with how long it takes to get a delivery, how fast the inventory is being used, and the safety stock level, the cushion against running out of product. Many practice management software packages have automated this process. The goal is to balance safety stock so that the holding costs are minimized by keeping counts down, but not too low as to risk stock-outs.

The order quantity at which total holding costs and total order placements costs are at the minimum is called the Economic Order Quantity (EOQ). It can be used to calculate optimal order quantities considering unit costs, ordering costs, and holding costs, and discounts that might be offered by distributors.

$$EOQ = \sqrt{\frac{2DO}{H}}$$

Where, D = Annual Demand
O = Order Placement Costs, per order
H = Annual Holding Cost (per unit)

Here's an example. You want to minimize inventory costs on heartworm prevention medications. Last year you sold 1,067 packages and you anticipate doing about the same this year; each package costs $25 with holding costs of 20% ($5.00). The cost of placing and receiving the order is 15% per unit ($3.75). The Economic Order Quantity (EOC) is:

$$EOC = \sqrt{\frac{(2)(1,067)($3.75)}{$5.00}}$$

$$= \sqrt{1600}$$
$$= 40 \text{ packages}$$

You should thus be ordering 40 packages at a time to minimize inventory costs. You can also determine your inventory cycle given this information and your average daily demand (i.e., 1,067 / 365 days per year, or 2.92). The optimal length of an inventory cycle is the economic order quantity (40) divided by the average daily demand (2.92) to yield 13.7 days. You should thus be placing orders every 14 days or so. Knowing your annual demand and your EOQ, you can also determine how many orders you will be making in a year.

Number of orders = $\dfrac{\text{Demand}}{\text{EOC}}$ = $\dfrac{1,067}{40}$ = 27 orders per year

Keep in mind that placing many small orders a year keeps inventory low and holding costs reasonable, but that it also results in higher order placement costs. Increasing order size reduces order placement costs, but holding costs increase. The economic order quantity reflects the trade-off between both costs, offering the best combination. The reorder point can be easily calculated by multiplying the average daily demand for a product by the lead time required to ensure delivery of the product (i.e., the time between order placement and receipt of shipment).

Recommended Reading:

Anderson, B: Business Process Improvement Toolbox. ASQ Quality Press, Milwaukee, 1999, 233pp.

Harvard Business Review: Measuring Corporate Performance. Harvard Business School Press, Boston, 1998, 229pp.

Heinke, ML; McCarthy, JB: Practice made Perfect. A Guide to Veterinary Practice Management. AAHA Press, Lakewood Colorado, 2001, 459pp.

Heller, R (Ed). Manager's Handbook. DK, London, 2002. 256pp.

ABOUT THE AUTHORS

Lowell Ackerman DVM DACVD MBA MPA

Dr. Lowell Ackerman is a Diplomate of the American College of Veterinary Dermatology and in addition holds an MBA from the University of Phoenix and an MPA from Harvard University. He is involved in clinical practice as a clinical assistant professor at Tufts University School of Veterinary Medicine as well as helping to develop the business skills curriculum there. In addition, Dr. Ackerman is affiliated with Veterinary Healthcare Consultants, primarily dealing with practice administration and management issues. Dr. Ackerman is the author/co-author of 74 books to date and numerous book chapters and articles. He lectures extensively, on an international basis.

Karen Felsted CPA MS DVM CVPM

Dr. Felsted graduated from the University of Texas at Austin with a degree in marketing. She spent 12 years in accounting and business management, six of it with the "Big-8" accounting firm of Arthur Young (now Ernst & Young.) During this time, she also obtained an MS degree in Management and Administrative Science (concentration: accounting) from the University of Texas at Dallas.

After graduating from the Texas A&M University College of Veterinary Medicine, Dr. Felsted began her career as a veterinary practitioner in both small animal and emergency medicine while maintaining her existing veterinary accounting and consulting practice. In 1999 she opened and became Manager-in-Charge of the Dallas office of Owen E. McCafferty, CPA, Inc., a national public accounting firm specializing in tax, accounting and practice management services for veterinarians. During this time she received her Certified Veterinary Practice Manager certificate. In 2001, she joined Brakke Consulting, Inc., where she continues to offer practice management consulting services to veterinarians. She also runs her own accounting firm specializing in financial services for veterinarians.

Dr. Felsted has been published in numerous national and international veterinary journals including Veterinary Economics and Texas Veterinarian. She has spoken at many local, national and international veterinary meetings.

Kurt A. Oster, MS, SPHR

Kurt A. Oster, MS, SPHR has worked as a Hospital Administrator in a variety of practice formats and is currently a practice management consultant with Veterinary Healthcare Consultants, LLC of Haverhill, Massachusetts. Mr. Oster consults regularly with veterinary practices on human resources, operations, demographics and financial issues.

Sarah Taylor DVM MBA

Dr. Sarah Taylor is a 1997 graduate of the Ontario Veterinary College and earned her Master of Business Administration in 2001 from Bryant College. She is currently employed as a Professional Services veterinarian with Novartis Animal Health, US, Inc.

Amy K. Thieling, CPA

Amy Thieling received her accounting degree from Indiana University and is currently the manager of the Veterinary Practice Division of Thieling Co, CPA. Thieling Co., CPA has worked with veterinarians for approximately 30 years and now specializes in providing accounting, tax, management, and financial advice to the veterinary profession. Ms Thieling is a graduate of

AAHA/Purdue University Veterinary Management Institute, and is a member of American Animal Hospital Association, Veterinary Hospital Managers' Association, American Institute of Certified Public Accountants, Association of Certified Fraud Examiners, Indiana CPA Society, and the Indiana CPA Society Young Professionals development team.

Appendix

Writing the Business Plan

Sarah Taylor DVM MBA

Dr. Sarah Taylor is a 1997 graduate of the Ontario Veterinary College and earned her Master of Business Administration in 2001 from Bryant College. She is currently employed as a Professional Services veterinarian with Novartis Animal Health, US, Inc.

Almost every veterinarian, at some point in his/her career, entertains the notion of owning and running their own practice. Unfortunately, this notion on its own will not be enough to start a veterinary clinic from scratch. Thus, it will be necessary to experience both the joy and frustration of preparing a business plan.

Creating a business plan is an excellent exercise because it forces one to research, evaluate and define exactly what their business will be. For any business plan to achieve the desirable results, one must pay close attention to the audience reading the plan. For a veterinary clinic start-up venture, the usual source of financing will be through a commercial bank, not a venture capitalist group or individual investor(s). If the latter two parties were to be considered potential investors then the business plan would have to be tailored accordingly. For example, a venture capitalist likely will have such concerns as what will be the exit strategy, what will be the return on the investment and when will this be realized, and what are the options for going public? These issues differ from the usual questions that the loan officer of the bank would want addressed like how soon will the clinic be profitable, how long will the loan be outstanding and what kinds of collateral are in place to repay the loan should the venture fail?

This appendix's objective is to describe the basic format and content of the business plan. The vast array of variations of any individual business plan as it is tailored to different investors will not be covered.

The Plan

It is important that the business plan be clearly written and relatively short (40 pages has been suggested as appropriate for most ventures; however, even half of that may be sufficient for a veterinary clinic). It is also imperative to have supporting evidence for every major point discussed—this requires research and explains why the plan can take months to properly prepare. The major components of the business plan will describe what your practice will be, outline your goals and the planned steps to achieve them and propose projected financial results. The plan should include the following sections: Executive Summary, Description of the Practice, The Service Product, The Market Analysis and Competition, Marketing Plan, Operations, Financials and the Appendix. The concept of the Value Proposition of the venture was discussed in the Planning chapter.

The Executive Summary

The first and most critical pages of the plan will be the executive summary. This section will provide the "first impression" for the potential investor or financier of the veterinary hospital venture. It is desirable to limit the executive summary to one to two pages but in those pages, one must highlight clearly and succinctly the major points of the business. The following points should be included:

- The practice's proposed management
- The practice's mission statement and description of the products and services to be provided and their benefits
- The veterinary market and competition
- Summary of financial prospects—sales objectives, growth projections, revenue and profit goals. Ensure that the proposed statistics are specific, realistic and measurable.
- The amount of money needed and how it will be used.

The Description of the Practice

In this segment one needs to outline what legal entity the practice will be (i.e. sole proprietorship, partnership, limited liability company, or corporation). There are certain advantages and drawbacks with respect to taxation and liability with each entity and it is best to consult with an accountant and lawyer to make the most appropriate decision.

This segment should also fully describe the practice's objectives, strategies, strengths and potential weaknesses, and background data on you as the veterinarian and manager or the management team, if appropriate. This helps the potential investor get a sense of history behind the start-up and shows that you have given some thought to the strategy of running a veterinary hospital as well as dealing with any possible challenges.

Although it may seem obvious, it is imperative to list the products and services you will offer and the geographic area you will serve. It is prudent to include a proposed price list and an analysis of competing hospitals' prices. Also include what types of items are needed to start the practice and their costs.

Much of this information will be presented in other sections of the business plan in different formats but needs to be fully outlined in the Practice Description. Now that you have described what your practice will be and how you will get there, the next step is to provide more detail on what the service product will be.

The Service Product

This section provides the details of the services and products you will provide and what needs they fulfill for your clientele. It is especially beneficial to show the differentiation between what you will offer versus competing hospitals in the same geographic area. For example, if you have a special interest or expertise in a certain area of medicine or surgery, this should be identified and a plan elaborated on how this skill or expertise will provide a competitive advantage.

The Market Analysis

Thorough research of the veterinary market in general and within the specific proposed geographic location is essential. The bank or other investor will want to know that you have studied the market and understand it so that you are as prepared as possible to successfully serve the market. This research will include a demographic analysis, a proposed client base, growth potential (see marketing chapter) and data on the competing hospitals in the area. It may be advisable to have a separate Competition section to list the other veterinary hospitals' names, types of practice and services rendered. Information on the neighboring clinics will assist you in establishing your own practice niche and identify potential challenges and opportunities for you as a practice owner. Much of this data can be obtained from the U.S. Census Bureau (www.census.gov) or from the state's department of economic development.

The Marketing Plan

In the marketing plan, re-iterate the factors influencing the market as identified in your market analysis and how you will deal with these factors in marketing your practice. Again, you want to list your products and services, identify differentiating features and specifically outline how you intend to reach your target clients and increase your penetration or prevalence in the market over time.

Please refer to the marketing chapter for further details but briefly, the marketing plan needs to address the following key questions:

- Who are my clients?
- Where are they located?
- What services do they want?
- How will I reach them?

One should give as much detail as possible with reference to advertising and promotional campaigns. This will benefit you in the long term and assist potential investors in their evaluation of your practice start-up.

Operations

This section outlines all the resources—human and physical—that will be needed to operate the hospital. It needs to include an equipment/inventory list, financing costs, and a description of the space required. Also include whether you have decided to lease or buy any of the items listed and the details of the various leases' terms, leasehold improvement cost estimates (the cost to bring the facility/equipment into full operation status). Describe the human labor needs and provide an organizational chart for your hospital. Operational analysis also needs to consider outside suppliers and vendors—provide names of those companies who will be supplying your equipment and inventory of products and all available data on their business terms. Basically, the financier needs to know what you need to start up the clinic to become operational, and the associated costs.

Financials

The financials will cover the realistic financial projections for the next three to five years. A disclaimer note should be included at the beginning of this section that states that the financial figures are based on estimates and future returns are not guaranteed. Once stated, it will be necessary to have a net worth statement or some form of documentation showing assets to be used as collateral in order to minimize the risk for the investor.

Completing an itemized income statement will help you estimate service and product revenue, and the various operating and administrative expenses. From this document, cash flow projections can be elucidated. Specifically, the first two years of pro forma cash flow statements need to be separated out on a month-by-month basis, then generated for each year of the remaining one to three years. The more complete the data on projected expenses the better able you and financiers can predict cash flow needs. Thus, try to estimate, based on industry standards wherever available, expected revenue and expenses. A potential though not exhaustive statement should include estimates of revenue from products and services, cost of transactions, office/medical supplies and equipment costs, administrative and staff salaries, payroll costs, occupancy costs, utilities, telephone, licensing fees, marketing and advertising expenses and accounting and legal fees. Again, be detailed in your cost estimates whenever possible. For example, provide number of veterinary nurses (technicians), assistants, receptionists and animal caretakers required, together with their hourly wages and benefits.

As mentioned previously, the focus of the financier or investor in evaluating the financials will be to ensure a reasonable assumption that you will be profitable and able to repay the loan or provide an adequate return on their investment.

Appendix

For most veterinary practitioners, the appendix will consist of their individual résumés. However, if you are starting a veterinary clinic with multiple doctors, then each member of the management team should include a résumé.

Additionally, certificates of qualification, testimonial letters from clients, promotional clinic pieces or letters from suppliers may be included in the appendix.

After Completing the Business Plan

Once completed, it is highly advisable to have your business plan reviewed by a legal advisor, an accountant, and investors or bankers whom you will not be targeting for financing assistance.

Recommended Reading

Glassman, GI. Your business plan: A start-up must. Veterinary Economics 2002;43(7):42.

Schutte, JE. Preparing to start from scratch. Veterinary Economics 2002;43(7):36-40.

Stevenson, HH, Roberts, MJ, Grousbeck, HI, Bhide, AV. New Business Ventures and The Entrepreneur, 5th edition. Irwin, McGraw-Hill. New York, NY. 1999. 678 pp.

www.bizplanit.com

www.sba.gov/starting/indexbusplans.html

www.web.mit.edu

ABOUT THE AUTHOR

Dr. Lowell Ackerman is a board-certified veterinary dermatologist, an award-winning author, an international lecturer, and a consultant in veterinary practice management. He is a graduate of the Ontario Veterinary College and a Diplomate of the American College of Veterinary Dermatology. In addition to his veterinary training, he also has an MBA from the University of Phoenix and an MPA from Harvard University. Dr. Ackerman splits his time between clinical practice and consulting. He is a clinical assistant professor in the dermatology service of the Tufts University School of Veterinary Medicine and has also been involved in the development of a business skills curriculum there. In addition to veterinary specialty practice, Dr. Ackerman is a management consultant with Veterinary Healthcare Consultants, dealing specifically with issues such as veterinary fee structures, staff education, promotion, marketing, governance, and the development of in-hospital profit centers.

Dr. Ackerman is the author of 74 books and over 150 book chapters and journal articles. He lectures extensively, on an international basis. Dr. Ackerman is a member of the American Animal Hospital Association, the American Veterinary Medical Association, the American Society of Journalists and Authors, and the Association of Veterinary Communicators.

Some other books by Dr. Ackerman include:

The Contented Canine: Pet Parenting for Dog Owners. ASJA Press, 2001

The Genetic Connection: A Guide to Health Problems in Purebred Dogs. AAHA Press, 1999

Canine Nutrition: What every owner, breeder, and trainer should know. Alpine, 1999

Cat Health Encyclopedia. TFH Publications, 1999

Canine & Feline Dermatology. VLS, 1998 (with GH Nesbitt)

Handbook of Behavior Problems of the dog and cat. Butterworth-Heinemann, 1997 (with G. Landsberg & W. Hunthausen)

The Biology, Husbandry & Health Care of Reptiles (3-volume series). TFH Publications, 1997.

Onwner's Guide to Cat Health. TFH Publications, 1996.

Owner's Guide to Dog Health. TFH Publications, 1995.

Guide to Skin and Haircoat Problems in Dogs. Alpine, 1994

INDEX

0-595-25087-4

Printed in the United States
95463LV00006B/94/A